FIFTY GREAT
BUFFET
PARTIES

Other Books by the Author

SERVE IT COLD!
A Book of Delicious Cold Dishes (with June Crosby)

I LOVE TO COOK BOOK

Ruth Conrad Bateman

FIFTY GREAT BUFFET PARTIES

Doubleday & Company, Inc., Garden City, New York   1974

Library of Congress Cataloging in Publication Data

Bateman, Ruth Conrad, 1926–
  Fifty great buffet parties.

  1. Entertaining. I. Title.
TX731.B36   641.5'68
ISBN: 0-385-07785-8
Library of Congress Catalog Card Number 73–81122

To George, whose male viewpoint brings valued breadth to my world of women and recipes, and to Tu Su, our Siamese, who's always a willing taster.

Acknowledgments and Credits

I wish to thank many friends in the food and restaurant industries who have been helpful with suggestions, ideas, and recipes, particularly those who provided the beautiful color photographs. Special thanks also to *Woman's Day* and *House & Garden* for permission to use several recipes I previously developed for these publications. To Elena Quinn, who has always typed my manuscripts and dropped her own book this time to type mine, a big, big thank you. Thanks also to Kay Bloss for her invaluable help with editing, retyping, and proofreading, and to my young niece Linda Yerby for typing help and youthful observations.

Color Plate No. 1—Weekend Brunch—Courtesy of Sterno, Inc.

Color Plate No. 2—Luncheon for a V.I.P.—Courtesy of Pacific Kitchen for Alaska King Crab, North Pacific Halibut, Washington-Oregon Raspberries, Idaho-Oregon Sweet Spanish Onions, Pacific Coast Canned Pears.

Color Plate No. 3—Poolside Buffet—Courtesy of Heublein, Inc., for A 1 Steak Sauce, Grey Poupon Dijon Mustard, Regina Wine Vinegars, and Inglenook California Wines.

Color Plate No. 4—New Year's Eve Champagne Supper—Courtesy Moët Champagnes. Photo by George de Gennaro.

I am deeply indebted to my always helpful friend Philip S. Brown, food writer and wine connoisseur, for his practical and useful wine selections for these menus.

Ruth Conrad Bateman

Contents

IV DINNERS

V LATE SUPPERS

VI COCKTAIL PARTIES

VII DESSERT AND COFFEE PARTIES

VIII RECIPE REPERTORY

Items indicated by an asterisk * may be located by consulting the Index.

Wine selections by food writer and wine expert Philip S. Brown.

FIFTY GREAT BUFFET PARTIES

Introduction

Why a book about buffets? Because a buffet is the friendly, relaxed way our involved, do-it-yourself generation can entertain a goodly number of friends without too much strain. In the last decade, our tastes and interests in foods and cultures around the world have expanded greatly. On the other hand, the dining space in our homes has shrunk. The dining room, in fact, has become a multipurpose room used every hour of the day—for hobbies, television, various family activities.

Most of my friends who entertain frequently say they'd rather work like fiends for several days before a party and then serve it buffet. Once the food is on the buffet, they feel they can relax and visit with their guests. I feel the same way. Even when I can get help with extra cooking and serving, the soufflé often gets overcooked, the hollandaise curdles, or the salad is drenched with too much dressing while I'm playing hostess in the living room. I've found it simpler to plan every detail carefully and do only what I can cook and serve myself. Big receptions or cocktail parties might be the exception. I prepare everything possible several days in advance—frozen desserts, breads, dressings, sauces—keep last-minute preparations and details to a minimum. Then I arrange the food as beautifully as I can on a buffet or table. And let my guests help themselves. It's fun for everyone.

If you have second thoughts about how well a man enjoys buffets, you can forget it if you remember one thing. Make sure you provide a place where he can sit and enjoy his good food in comfort. Put up card tables all over the house or in the patio or back yard in summer. Or rent tables. And decorate them gaily with bright covers and flowers or appropriate candles and such to fit in with the buffet table. For cocktail parties, teas, and receptions tables are not necessary, of course. Food for these should be the easy pickup variety with no silver necessary.

This book is about buffets. All kinds, at all hours of the day with foods from all over the world. However, it's not loaded with soupy casseroles, sweet molded salads, and dreary platters of cold meats. Instead there are numerous easy-to-serve one-pot dishes inspired in most cases by the thrifty folk food of Europe and our own country. Savory pot-au-feu, a boiled beef and vegetable dinner, and an English steak and kidney pie are good examples. For a hungry crowd I've suggested such dishes as chile con carne, the superb French cassoulet and pastitsio, a Greek macaroni pie.

There are numerous articles in magazines and books on how to arrange plates, silver, napkins, etc., for a buffet meal, so I won't go into detail about that now. I make appropriate comments about such following each menu, however, and in most cases suggest that silver, glasses, napkins, butter, and so on be put on small tables where guests can eat in comfort. Though I've planned and entertained with buffet meals for years, I never ask our guests to haul a plate of food, a wineglass, napkins, and silver around the house in search of a spot to light. It simply is not thoughtful.

Several other points I feel are important in a buffet meal. Too many saucy foods on one plate are messy to look at and confuse the diner's senses. If the main dish is a stew or creamed dish, serve plain rice, baked grits or barley, or crisp potatoes with it. Though a fresh leafy salad is my favorite, I seldom serve it for a buffet unless the group is small and I can provide salad plates. Greens wilt too quickly, they're bulky on a buffet plate, and the dressing usually runs into the hot dish or vegetable. Instead, I plan cooked marinated vegetables such as asparagus, green beans, artichoke hearts, and the like. Or a more compact salad like potato or rice. These can all be done ahead and they're wiltproof. For something raw to munch on I serve sliced tomatoes, crisp onions, cucumbers, celery, hearts of fennel, or simply crisp leaves of romaine or watercress.

In organizing these buffets, I've planned several dishes to be done a day or several days ahead. If the menu has a number of dishes baked in the oven, I plan some to be cooked ahead and reheated. Or I have selected foods that can be cooked together at the same oven temperature. And, you'll find, there are few last-minute, top-stove dishes to take your time and attention away from your guests. Takes a bit of thinking through, but then, that's the whole idea of this book—plan and make ahead and serve it buffet.

When we think of a buffet, we usually think of a big, big party. And it does offer a pretty way to feed a crowd in limited space. But you can have a festive buffet for four—maybe 2 or 3 salads, or a selection of fillings for crêpes or omelets. By serving buffet, I simply mean that you spread your food, big meal or small, on the buffet or dining table, the kitchen counter or coffee table, or a bench by the pool and let your guests help themselves. It's a friendly, chatty kind of entertaining.

At home our dining room is small, so even our holiday dinners are served buffet if they get beyond eight guests. Everyone, especially the youngsters, loves them. At Christmas, a table is set up in the living room in front of one sofa complete with beautiful cloth, gay red satin ribbons, crystal candlesticks, bright berries, the works. It makes an effective living-room decoration and provides a good spot for grownups to set down a drink, for a bowl of crisp almonds or whatever light snacks we have before dinner. Later, our glass patio table is brought in and placed in front of the fireplace. Its cloth and decorations are ready on a tray nearby, in the den, along with silver, napkins, and glasses for each table. The youngsters usually put these on the table while I add relishes and dishes to the handsome buffet set up on our dining-room table. My husband carves the turkey or roast beef with much less strain than when everyone is seated and waiting. I usually help guests with potatoes, vegetables, gravy, and such—all kept warm on hot trays—and they help themselves to relishes and the extras. This is one example of the kind of buffet planned for this book.

This is not a natural foods cookbook. But it's full of natural, good fresh foods. That's the way I cook, usually from scratch. I like to use fresh foods when possible and put my own seasonings into them rather than pay the extra price for preseasoned combinations often with added preservatives. There are a number of good convenience foods on the market and I use and enjoy those that are. Many, however, are so doctored up with artificial seasonings and preservatives I often wonder if our youngsters will completely forget what honest, simple, good fresh food tastes like. Fortunately, many young people today are interested in fresh foods, in making homemade breads and such. There's plenty of ammunition for them in this book. And pleasing ways to serve them in a happy, relaxed setting.

Ruth Bateman

I   Brunches and Breakfasts

Brunch is an ugly word and I wish I knew a better one to describe this happy combination of breakfast and lunch. More and more this midday meal, which may start anytime from eleven to two and sometimes lasts all afternoon, is becoming a popular way to entertain. It's a wonderful choice for weekends. A brunch seems more festive than a breakfast, yet we usually find on the menu foods we welcome for our first meal such as bacon, eggs, hot breads, and the like. And somehow, a brunch has a more relaxed mood than a luncheon, not so bound by the traditions we often associate with luncheons. Yet, many of our favorite luncheon foods are served—crêpes, quiches, gratins of all sorts, light fish dishes, and even vegetables and salads.

It's one of my favorite ways to entertain. The drinks we serve are lighter and more fruity than those for dinner. Usually they're much less expensive, since punches and wine bowls are welcome, but not so suitable for the evening meal. Brunch foods are less expensive too and simpler to prepare. Eggs and cheese can be put together in many charming dishes with little expense and not a great deal of effort. Even the meats we serve for brunch—sausages, ham, chicken livers, kidney, and such—don't bite into the budget quite like the steaks or roasts we often plan for dinner.

CELEBRATION BRUNCH FOR TWELVE

CHAMPAGNE AND ORANGE JUICE
MELON WEDGES
BRAISED HAM, MADEIRA   EGGS MORNAY, TARECO
SALAD OF PETITS POIS
BRIOCHE*   CROISSANTS
COFFEE
COEUR À LA CRÈME

This could be an announcement party, an anniversary celebration, or an Easter brunch. It's appropriate for any season of the year, but I have in mind spring or summer when melons, strawberries, and fresh peas are abundant. Vodka Screwdrivers can be served in place of the champagne, but champagne is more festive. If you serve champagne, you might like to braise the ham in champagne rather than the Madeira or port suggested in the recipe. Cool melon—cantaloupe, Spanish or pale green honeydew—makes a beautiful and simple first course. Present it on a deep tray lined with green leaves interspersed with crushed ice. Provide small plates for it and have nearby a decanter of port wine and wedges of fresh lime or lemon. Guests may accent the melon as they choose. Carve enough of the warm but not hot ham for each guest to have several paper thin slices. Arrange it on a warm platter with the rest of the ham. After the egg dish is glazed briefly under the broiler, set it on a warming tray near the ham and warm plates. For this occasion, I suggest separate salad plates. Arrange the buffet table with fresh flowers—tulips in pots, or bright jonquils with asparagus fern would be stunning. Or fresh-looking white daisies, which are available at reasonable prices practically the year round. Repeat the decorations in smaller tables with colorful linen, silver, and glassware. The snowy dessert with its wreath of fruit can be served from a table in the living room with more coffee and brioches.

Do Ahead: Brioche dough may be made a week or so ahead and frozen (see recipe for specifics). Or it can be made several days ahead, refrigerated, then shaped and baked the day before or the morning of the party. Croissants are more difficult and time consuming, so I have not included a recipe for them. Buy them at a good bakery or use the excellent frozen croissants. Braise ham the day before and warm it for serving or bake it early in the morning so the oven will be free later for the brioches and egg dish. The mushroom base for the eggs can be made the day before, tightly covered, and refrigerated. However, make the Mornay sauce, poach the eggs, and assemble the dish for a quick reheating later the morning of the party. Make the *coeur à la crème* and allow it to drain overnight in the refrigerator. Cook vegetables for the salad, make dressing, and marinate overnight.

CHAMPAGNE AND ORANGE JUICE

A splendid and beautiful combination for a brunch. Chill champagne *sec* and oranges, then squeeze orange juice. Arrange on a self-service bar or a serving table where the host can serve: chilled champagne in an ice bucket or several bottles in punch bowl, a pitcher of chilled orange juice and tall, narrow tulip-shaped champagne glasses. Pour orange juice into glasses then add champagne, usually half of each.

BRAISED HAM, MADEIRA

The traditional French way with ham—braised slowly in wine over a bed of aromatic herbs and vegetables. Makes good ham wonderful and greatly improves some of our rather flavorless, highly processed hams.

8- to 12-pound precooked or processed ham (or half ham)	1 bay leaf, broken
Freshly ground black pepper	½ teaspoon thyme
2 tablespoons butter or margarine	6 whole cloves
4 carrots, scraped, finely chopped	2 cups Madeira wine (or port or cream sherry)
1 large onion, finely chopped	2 cups beef stock or bouillon
Handful celery leaves, chopped	Orange Mustard Glaze (below)
2 or 3 sprigs parsley, chopped	Wine Sauce for Ham (below)

Cut skin and all but a very thin layer of fat from ham. Sprinkle ham well with coarsely ground pepper. Melt butter in frying pan and add carrots, onion, and celery leaves. Cook slowly until soft. Add herbs and spices and transfer to a roasting pan large enough to hold ham. Place ham on top, fattest side up. Pour wine and stock into frying pan, heat to boiling, and pour over ham. Cover tightly with foil or a lid and braise slowly in 325° F. oven for about 2 hours. Lift lid or foil and baste ham with liquid occasionally. If you plan to glaze ham, remove from oven after 1¾ hours. Drain off sauce and vegetables and save them for a sauce. Spread ham with glaze and bake uncovered at 400° F. for about 30 minutes. Cool and cut into thin slices.

ORANGE MUSTARD GLAZE

Combine 1 teaspoon dry mustard with a tablespoon of the wine liquid and
¼ cup orange marmalade. Sprinkle ham lightly with ground cloves and
spread with glaze.

WINE SAUCE FOR HAM

If you serve the ham warm and wish a sauce (you don't need it with
this menu), this is delicious.

Strain wine braising liquid into saucepan, saving a tablespoon or two
of the vegetables. Skim all fat from liquid. Boil liquid over moderate
heat until reduced to about 2 cups. If desired, press 1 to 2 tablespoons
of the vegetables through a fine sieve and add to sauce. Make a *beurre
manié* by blending to a paste 1 tablespoon butter and 1 tablespoon flour.
Off heat, beat this into the hot liquid with wire whisk. Return to heat and
stir for a minute or two longer. Season with salt and pepper if needed.
Makes a flavorful, light, nonsweet sauce.

EGGS MORNAY, TARECO

Similar to eggs Florentine, except here the poached eggs are set on a
bed of mushrooms before the sauce is added. It has evolved from several
egg dishes I make for brunch parties.

2 pounds fresh mushrooms	*Salt and freshly milled pepper*
6 tablespoons butter or	*12 Poached Eggs (below)*
margarine	*2 cups Mornay Sauce**
½ cup minced shallots	*Grated Gruyère cheese*
1 cup heavy cream	

Wipe mushrooms with damp paper towels and cut off stems. Chop stems
very finely with about ¼ of the caps. Heat half the butter in a large
heavy skillet or chicken fryer and add chopped mushrooms and shallots.
Cook over low heat, stirring now and then, for about 10 minutes.
Slice mushroom caps. Add rest of butter and the caps to pan. Stir
over rather brisk heat for 2 or 3 minutes. Lower heat and add
cream. Cook over very low heat until mushrooms are a rich glossy
brown and most of mushroom liquid and cream have been absorbed.
Season lightly with salt and pepper. Spread evenly in shallow baking

dish large enough to hold 12 poached eggs. Arrange drained poached eggs on mushrooms, spoon Mornay sauce over the top to coat eggs well and mushrooms rather scantily. Sprinkle with cheese, using ⅓ to ½ cup. Heat in 450° F. oven until warm, 5 to 10 minutes. Run under broiler until sauce bubbles and is glazed with flecks of brown.

POACHED EGGS

Heat to boiling in large deep skillet enough water to cover eggs; add 1 tablespoon mild vinegar. Break each egg into small dish and slide carefully into boiling water. Quickly spoon hot water over egg to film yolk. Do only about 4 eggs at a time. Simmer for 3 to 4 minutes—just until egg holds its shape, the white is coagulated, and yolk is soft. Carefully lift egg out with slotted spoon, rest spoon briefly on a folded paper towel to drain, then serve egg as directed in specific recipe—on toast, spinach, mushrooms, in baked potato, etc. *To poach ahead*—Lift poached egg with slotted spoon from hot water into a pan of cold water. Set aside until ready to use. Reheat for a few seconds in hot water, or use as suggested in specific recipe.

SALAD OF PETITS POIS

Since fresh sweet peas and tiny carrots aren't always available, I've specified the petite-size frozen peas and frozen carrots no bigger than your little finger.

Clear chicken broth (about 3
*   cups)*
Salt
1 bay leaf
1 package (1 pound) frozen whole
*   baby carrots*
2 cups diagonal slices green celery
*   (½-inch pieces)*
Pinch of sugar
3 packages (10 ounces each)
*   frozen petite-size frozen peas*
6 tablespoons white wine
*   tarragon vinegar*

1 tablespoon chopped fresh
*   tarragon (or 1 teaspoon dried*
*   leaves)*
1 tablespoon finely chopped fresh
*   mint leaves*
¼ teaspoon dried thyme leaves
¾ cup salad oil
Salt and pepper
Bibb lettuce
Cherry tomatoes
¼ cup sour cream
¼ cup mayonnaise

Put 3 cups chicken broth, a little salt, and bay leaf in deep saucepan. Heat to boiling and add carrots and celery. Simmer gently until crisp-tender *only*, 8 to 10 minutes. With slotted spoon, carefully lift vegetables from broth into a bowl. Add pinch of sugar and more broth if needed to make 2 cups. Heat to boiling and add peas. Simmer gently for 1 to 2 minutes *only* after broth boils again. Lift peas with slotted spoon into bowl with carrots. Combine in glass jar vinegar, herbs, salad oil, and ¼ cup of the strained broth (save rest of broth for later). Shake until well blended. Pour about half of it over vegetables. Turn and stir gently with fork until they are coated and shiny. Season lightly with salt and pepper to taste. Cover and chill. To serve, line shallow glass salad bowl with lettuce leaves and heap drained salad in the center. Circle with halved tomatoes. Drizzle salad with a little of the dressing if necessary. Combine rest of dressing and any dressing drained from vegetables with sour cream and mayonnaise. Add a spoonful or two of the broth to make a light, creamy dressing. Serve in separate bowl with salad.

COEUR À LA CRÈME

Traditionally, this nonsweet French dessert is chilled in a heart-shaped basket so the whey can drain from the voluptuous cream. Any small wicker basket or mold that allows for drainage can be used—but it wouldn't be a coeur, of course. Heart-shaped baskets and perforated porcelain molds can usually be found in stores that carry quality housewares. Strawberries are the traditional garnish. I add juicy orange sections and marinate both in Grand Marnier.

Drain a pound of small curd (farmer-style) cottage cheese and force through a sieve. Put in large bowl of electric mixer with a pinch of salt, 1 tablespoon powdered sugar and start beating. Gradually beat in 1 pound softened cream cheese and 1 pint heavy cream. Beat until mixture is smooth. Line a large heart-shaped wicker basket or mold with wet cheesecloth. Smooth it out evenly. Press cheese mixture evenly into mold. Set on a rack over a pan or plate so liquid can drain. Chill overnight. An hour before serving, wash and hull a basket of strawberries. Place in bowl. Holding them over the bowl, peel 3 large navel oranges round and round to remove all the peel and white membrane. Section oranges and drop sections into bowl. Sprinkle fruit lightly with powdered sugar and about ¼ cup Grand Marnier. Cover and chill. Unmold coeur onto pretty plate and decorate with a wreath of strawberries and orange sections. Serve rest of fruit in bowl alongside. Cut coeur into wedges with cake server. Serve on dessert plates and spoon some of the fruit and sauce over each serving.

MIDDAY FISH FRY

ICED CLAM-TOMATO JUICE OR SCREWDRIVERS
GOLDEN FRIED TROUT
SKILLET SWEET CORN   FRESH ASPARAGUS
SLICED TOMATOES, NEW RADISHES, AND SCALLIONS
CRACKLING BREAD   BUTTER
COFFEE
STAR-OF-THE SEA STRAWBERRIES

An all-American midday feast for eight good friends. I promised to forgo most last-minute cooking. But for their best flavor, the corn and the asparagus as well as the trout should be cooked just before you're ready to eat. Fortunately they take only about 15 minutes, and I think you'll say it's all worth the scramble. Drink a Muscadet or California Chenin Blanc.

Do Ahead: Have everything prepared so that things move along smoothly once you've started the cooking. Make the cracklings anytime ahead. Clean and prepare the salad materials and the asparagus. Cover with plastic wrap and chill. Measure the ingredients for crackling bread and have trout dipped and ready to fry. Prepare corn and strawberries the last thing. Just before your guests arrive, put the bread in the oven. It will be cooked by the time you've greeted all your guests and settled them with a cool drink. Raise the oven temperature to 550° F. for the easy oven-fry trout (or have ready your biggest heavy skillet for the pan-fried trout). The corn and asparagus will cook while the trout is browning. Have plenty of coffee along with the meal and more to drink with the luscious strawberries and cream. Set the buffet outdoors on a gay gingham cloth if the weather is nice. We put all the food on one end of a picnic table and let guests help themselves before being seated. Otherwise, we line the food up on our kitchen counter where guests help themselves before sitting down at the dining-room table.

GOLDEN FRIED TROUT

Cook in a heavy skillet or in the oven, whichever suits your situation best. Either way the fish can be dipped and crumbed or floured ahead of time.

Oven-Fry Trout: Heat oven to 550° F. Generously butter an oblong glass baking dish large enough to hold fish in a single layer. You'll need 2 dishes for 8 good-sized trout. Spread a mound of very fine, dry bread crumbs in a shallow pan or tray. Alongside, pour milk into a shallow dish large enough to dip fish. Season with plenty of salt and a little freshly ground pepper. Dip each fish in milk, then crumbs to coat evenly. Place in dish and pour melted butter over them to moisten crumbs. Bake until crisp golden brown and tender when gently pierced with a fork. Takes 12 to 15 minutes. Remove to warm platter and garnish with juicy lemon wedges.

Pan-Fry Trout: Heat about ½ inch butter with a little oil in a large, heavy skillet. Dip whole trout in salted milk, then in mixture of flour and corn meal. Fry in bubbly hot butter until crisp and golden on each side, just a few minutes. Serve hot with lemon wedges.

CRACKLING BREAD

An American original. In the South, fresh side pork is used for the cracklings, while New Englanders usually make them from salt pork.

5 tablespoons butter or margarine
1 cup all-purpose flour
2½ teaspoons baking powder
½ teaspoon baking soda
2 teaspoons salt (a little less if
  salt pork cracklings used)

2 teaspoons sugar (optional)
1¾ cups yellow corn meal
4 eggs, well beaten
2 cups buttermilk
¾ cup Pork Cracklings (below)

Heat oven to 400° F. Divide butter and melt in the oven in 2 (9-inch) black skillets or round (8½-inch) pyrex dishes. Sift flour with baking powder, soda, salt, and sugar. Resift with corn meal (if very coarse, water-ground corn meal is used, simply stir it into the flour mixture). Beat eggs and stir in buttermilk. Beat into dry mixture until well blended. Turn melted butter around in pans to grease them well, then pour rest into batter. Stir in cracklings. Pour into pans and bake for about 20 minutes or until golden brown. Cut in wedges and serve warm from pans.

PORK CRACKLINGS

Cut fresh side pork or salt pork in ¼-inch cubes. Cook in heavy pan over low heat until fat has cooked out and cubes are crisp. Stir frequently and drain off fat as it accumulates. Drain on paper towels. One half pound pork makes ¾ to 1 cup cracklings.

SKILLET SWEET CORN

Husk 12 ears fresh sweet corn and remove silks. Cut kernels from cob with long sharp knife, then with back of knife scrape all the milky substance from the cob into corn. Heat 6 tablespoons butter or margarine in heavy skillet or sauté pan until bubbly. Add corn and all the milky substance. Cook gently, stirring lightly, for 3 to 4 minutes. Add ½ cup cream, a generous grinding of pepper, and a pinch of sugar. Cook and stir over very low heat for 2 to 3 minutes longer, until corn is cooked through. I never salt corn—it tastes fresher and sweeter without it. Those who wish add salt at the table.

FRESH ASPARAGUS

Cook asparagus your favorite way. This is mine—cooked in an open, wide pan in plenty of bubbling water.

Break off tough ends of 3 to 4 pounds asparagus and trim off the ears or tight scales that hold sand. Wash spears thoroughly and place in a wide kettle with enough boiling salted water to cover them. A deep skillet is fine. After water boils again, cook asparagus at a brisk bubble until it is just crisp-tender, 8 to 12 minutes. Drain and put into a warm shallow bowl. Dress with a little melted butter—very little, just enough to make it shiny, so you can taste the asparagus itself. Or drizzle a few spoonfuls of Sauce Vinaigrette (Classic French Dressing*) on top.

STAR-OF-THE-SEA STRAWBERRIES

Other fruits such as fresh pineapple are often served with a luscious liqueur-laced dipping cream at the Star of the Sea Restaurant in San Diego. The most spectacular, I think, uses the almost fist-sized strawberries mounded on ice with the sauce served separately in a silver compote. The restaurant flavors the cream with orange curaçao as well as Grand Marnier and dark rum. I've worked out a simpler combination for our midday brunch.

Wash and dry 3 baskets large strawberries. Leave stems on and chill. Whip a cup of heavy cream and fold it into a cup of dairy sour cream. Blend 4 tablespoons brown sugar with ¼ cup Grand Marnier and 2 tablespoons dark Jamaica rum. Carefully fold into cream at serving time. Heap berries in pretty glass bowl. Spoon sauce into smaller bowl. Provide small dishes for guests to serve themselves berries and cream for dipping. The sauce becomes rather runny toward the last, so dessert spoons are needed also.

ENGLISH COUNTRY BREAKFAST
(Planned for Twelve)

BRANDY COFFEE PUNCH

GRATIN OF FINNAN HADDIE   BROILED TOMATOES

POTATO PUFFS   HOMEMADE SAUSAGE

SCRAMBLED EGGS, ESCOFFIER

TOASTED ENGLISH MUFFINS   LEMON SAFFRON BUNS

MARMALADES   BUTTER   STRAWBERRY PRESERVES

COFFEE*   HOT TEA*

HOT FRUIT COMPOTE

An English country breakfast is a splendid feast and a grand way to entertain hungry friends on a leisurely weekend. A great variety of foods in generous amounts is traditional. Fish in some form, perhaps finnan haddie or codfish, is on the menu most always, along with England's beloved bangers or sausage with potatoes and eggs or a magnificent cut of ham, English muffins and marmalades, and some kind of yeast rolls or buns. In my husband's family, saffron buns are traditional. So I make them for such occasions. However, George's Cornish grandmother called her rolls saffron cake, and the light yeast batter she used was really more like the rich *Gugelhupf* coffeecake than the more typical English bun.

For this menu I've suggested homemade sausage seasoned in the Kentish style with fresh sage and nutmeg. You can use prepared sausage, if you prefer, or a fine baked ham. Sausages are not difficult to make, however. With sausage, an Englishman must have potatoes, preferably mashed.

The do-ahead potato puffs are velvet-textured duchess potatoes heated under the broiler for a few minutes at mealtime. The creamy scrambled eggs are kept warm and soft in a chafing dish. Serve the spicy hot fruit compote in a chafing dish too (borrow one from your neighbor for this party) to be enjoyed with more saffron buns. Buy some good yeast rolls if you don't want to make the buns—but they really are special and can be made ahead. Arrange everything on a sideboard or buffet, if you have one, to look like a genuine English country breakfast. Have plenty of huge white napkins and warm plates handy. And serve a pot of freshly made tea along with the coffee.

Do Ahead: Make the sausages 2 or 3 days ahead so the flavors can ripen. Bake yeast buns the day before (make dough a day before that) and reheat in the foil wrap for 10 to 15 minutes. Or refrigerate dough overnight and bake rolls first thing in the morning (refrigerated dough requires about 2 hours to rise, so plan accordingly). Poach finnan haddie day before, make béchamel sauce for it and assemble the dish to be reheated for 20 minutes at mealtime. Prepare the duchess potatoes and shape on buttered baking sheet to be glazed briefly under the broiler. Prepare tomatoes and set on baking sheet to be broiled just before you glaze the potatoes. Make the fruit compote and let it heat while rest of food is being eaten. Brown sausages last and prepare everything for scrambled eggs. Let sausages finish cooking in oven. Because of the volume, start eggs in a large heavy skillet; when they are warm through, transfer to chafing dish to complete.

BRANDY COFFEE PUNCH

For 12 servings, dissolve 3 tablespoons instant coffee and ¼ cup sugar in ½ cup boiling water. Cool and combine with 1 quart milk, 1 cup heavy cream, 1 cup brandy, and 2 tablespoons dark Jamaica rum. Pour into blender container (in 2 batches if necessary). Blend at high speed for 15 seconds. Pour into punch cups and sprinkle lightly with nutmeg.

GRATIN OF FINNAN HADDIE

3-pound slice of finnan haddie	*4 cups Sauce Béchamel**
6 to 8 green onions, finely	*Cayenne pepper*
chopped	*1 cup medium-fine dry bread*
1 cup sliced mushrooms	*crumbs (rice grain size)*
3 tablespoons butter or margarine	*2 tablespoons minced parsley*

Rinse fish with cold water. Place in large skillet and cover with cold water. Heat to simmering and simmer gently until it flakes when pierced with fork, about 15 minutes. Drain fish, separate into large flakes—don't mince it—and put into a shallow buttered dish. Sauté onions and mushrooms until soft in 2 tablespoons of melted butter. Make béchamel sauce, using 4 times the amounts given in the basic recipe. Add sautéed vegetables to the butter and flour roux before adding the milk. Season

as directed, adding a few grains of cayenne pepper. Pour sauce over
fish and jiggle pan so some of sauce can run through to bottom of dish.
Cover with foil placed directly over sauce. Refrigerate overnight. To
serve, remove from refrigerator. Toss crumbs in 1 tablespoon frothy hot
butter over low heat until lightly browned. Add parsley and sprinkle
over fish. Heat uncovered in 350° F. oven until bubbly hot and browned,
about 20 minutes.

HOMEMADE SAUSAGE

Seasoning fresh breakfast sausage is a matter of personal taste. These
are seasoned with fresh sage leaves (when available) and freshly grated
whole nutmeg. My recipe uses less fat than the original Kentish sausage.
Too little fat, however, will give you a dry, rather tough sausage. Season
the sausage at first, using my guidelines. Fry a tiny patty and taste it.
Then add more seasonings, if desired, and make a record of it for next
time.

Put through medium blade of meat chopper, 2½ pounds lean, fresh
pork leg or shoulder and 1 pound fresh pork fat. Mix and season well
with 1 tablespoon salt, about 1 tablespoon freshly ground pepper, 1
tablespoon finely chopped fresh sage leaves (or 1½ teaspoons dried
sage leaves), ½ teaspoon thyme and half of a whole nutmeg, grated
(or at least 1 teaspoon ground nutmeg). Mix well. This is not a highly
seasoned sausage. Add more seasonings after you've fried a patty and
tasted it. (There's a difference between subtle flavor and bland, or in-
sipid. These should be richly flavored but in a subtle way.) Refrigerate in
covered dish for a couple of days. Shape into patties, about 5 to a pound.
Brown lightly in heavy skillet. Drain, transfer to heavy pan. Cover with
foil and finish cooking in 350° F. oven for 10 to 15 minutes. Or cook and
serve them in an electric skillet.

POTATO PUFFS

Elegant and rich duchess potatoes you make ahead.

*8 to 10 medium potatoes (3
    pounds)*
Salt
¼ cup butter or margarine
½ cup light cream or milk
Freshly ground pepper

Pinch of nutmeg
2 whole eggs
2 egg yolks
*Beaten egg or grated Cheddar
    cheese*

Peel and halve or quarter potatoes to uniform size. Cook in boiling salted water until tender but not mushy. Drain and return pan to low heat. Shake gently to dry potatoes completely. Mash or put through ricer or food mill (it's amazing how delicious potatoes taste when riced). Return to low heat. With wooden spoon work in butter and cream and whip until very light and fluffy. Season with a little more salt and pepper to taste and a flick of nutmeg. Remove from heat. Beat eggs and yolks together, beat into potatoes. For later use, transfer potatoes to bowl, brush top with melted butter, and cover surface directly with foil. Set aside, or refrigerate if done several hours ahead. Shape in muffin-size puffs on buttered cooky sheet. Brush with beaten egg or sprinkle with a little grated Cheddar cheese or Parmesan. Brown lightly in very hot oven (500° F.) or run under the broiler for a few seconds until hot and glazed with brown.

BROILED TOMATOES

Cut 6 unpeeled tomatoes in halves crosswise. Hold upside down and squeeze lightly to press out seeds. Set on greased baking pan. Combine ½ cup cracker crumbs or fine dry bread crumbs, ¼ cup grated Parmesan cheese, 1 tablespoon each minced chives and parsley with ¼ cup melted butter. Sprinkle tomatoes with salt and pepper. Top with crumbs. Broil for 5 to 6 minutes, until hot and lightly browned. Do not overcook —they become softer after they're removed from heat.

SCRAMBLED EGGS, ESCOFFIER

Escoffier was French, of course, not English. But he devised this way of keeping scrambled eggs soft for a buffet when he presided over the kitchens of London's great Hotel Savoy.

18 eggs
1½ cups heavy cream, divided
Salt and freshly ground pepper
1 tablespoon chopped parsley
1 tablespoon chopped chives

1 teaspoon chopped fresh
tarragon (or 1 teaspoon dried
leaf tarragon)
1 cup butter or margarine,
divided

Beat eggs lightly with half the cream and season with salt, pepper, and herbs. Heat 1 to 2 cups water to boiling and pour into water pan or *bain-marie* of chafing dish. Light Sterno or alcohol burner under chafing dish. Melt half the butter in large heavy skillet over low heat. Pour in eggs and stir with wooden spoon for a few minutes, until eggs are warmed and beginning to cook. Turn into warm, buttered top pan or blazer of chafing dish. Set over hot water. Cook, stirring occasionally with wooden spoon in long even strokes, until eggs are lightly cooked but still soft and moist. Cut rest of butter into small pieces. Stir balance of cream and butter into eggs. Keep warm over hot, not *boiling,* water.

LEMON SAFFRON BUNS

This is a soft, rather sticky dough and makes delicious light rolls, not the typical more bready saffron bun. It's easier to knead in the bowl, keeping the flour to a minimum. Saffron is a favorite English seasoning for cakes and breads. Use cinnamon or another spice if you don't care for the flavor.

1½ cups milk
1 to 3 teaspoons chopped
* Spanish saffron threads (or ½*
* to 1 teaspoon powdered*
* saffron)*
2 packages or cakes yeast
⅓ cup lukewarm water (see
* yeast label)*
¾ cup sugar, divided
1½ teaspoons salt

½ cup butter or margarine
5½ to 6 cups (approximately)
* all-purpose flour*
2 eggs, beaten
½ cup dried currants
½ cup chopped, mixed glacé
* fruits*
1 egg white, lightly beaten
Grated peel of 1 lemon

Scald milk and pour ¼ cup of it over saffron threads in small cup. Cool, stirring now and then. Sprinkle or crumble yeast into warm water and let stand for at least 5 minutes. To rest of hot milk, add ½ cup sugar, salt, and butter and stir until it is blended. Pour milk mixture into a large warm bowl. With wooden spoon, beat in 2 cups flour. Add softened yeast, saffron infusion or dry saffron and eggs. Beat well. Beat in 3 cups flour, the currants, and glacé fruits. This will be a soft dough. Knead in the bowl—by lifting dough and slapping it back down onto itself, working in up to 1 cup flour. Use as little flour as possible. Or, sprinkle a canvas pastry cloth with part of the flour. Dump dough into the middle and knead by lifting corners of cloth and folding dough back over itself. Turn dough by lifting cloth, sprinkle with more flour, fold over itself and continue this until dough is smooth and springy. It will still be soft and maybe sticky. Place dough in greased bowl, turn to coat surfaces evenly with fat. Cover with foil and folded towel. Refrigerate overnight and shape later (cold dough is easier to shape; see note below). Or, let rise in warm place until doubled in bulk, 1 to 1½ hours. Punch dough down with fist, knead in bowl a few turns until smooth-looking.

Generously grease muffin tins with melted butter (3½ dozen of the 2½-inch size, 4 dozen of the small 2-inch size). With oiled fingers pinch off blobs of dough about the size of golf balls, shape as neatly as possible and turn in muffin tins to coat surfaces evenly with fat.

Cover with towel and let rise until doubled in size, about 1 hour. Brush with lightly beaten egg white. Grate lemon peel over the remaining ¼ cup sugar. Mix and sprinkle over rolls. Bake in hot oven (400° F.) until richly browned, 15 to 20 minutes. If baked day before, cool and wrap in foil. Reheat at 350° F. for 10 to 15 minutes.

To Bake Refrigerated Dough: Remove from refrigerator, shape into rolls or buns. Place in greased muffin tins. Cover and let rise until doubled in size, about 2 hours. Bake as above.

HOT FRUIT COMPOTE

Change fruits and seasonings in the syrup to suit your own taste and the season. Use canned, fresh, or frozen, whichever is best at the moment, keeping a contrast of colors, flavors, and shapes.

1 can (1 pound, 14 ounces) whole apricots
2 pounds fresh or frozen sweet cherries
1 can (1 pound, 13 ounces) cling peach halves
1½ cups port wine

¾ cup honey
2 cinnamon sticks, broken in pieces
½ teaspoon anise seeds
Grated peel of 1 lemon
2 large navel oranges

Drain apricots and set aside ¾ cup of the syrup. Defrost frozen cherries enough to separate, if used, and add syrup to apricot syrup. Drain peaches and cut each half in two. Place fruits in blazer pan of chafing dish. Combine in small saucepan the apricot and cherry syrup, port, honey, cinnamon, anise, and lemon peel. Grate peel from 1 orange, add to syrup. Heat to boiling, then simmer gently 5 minutes. Peel oranges, removing all white membrane. Cut into halves lengthwise and slice. Add to fruits in blazer pan and pour in spicy syrup. Heat for 10 to 20 minutes with the blazer placed directly over the chafing dish heat. Then set in the hot water jacket to keep warm. Set small sauce dishes on tray nearby so guests may serve themselves. Make compote in a large saucepan or electric skillet if you don't have a chafing dish.

OLD SOUTH BRUNCH FOR SIXTEEN

GIN FIZZES OR FROZEN DAIQUIRIS
COUNTRY HAM   OVEN-FRIED DRUMSTICKS
CURRIED WHOLE EGGS
ZEPHYR HOT BISCUITS   JAMS AND MARMALADES
GRITS PARMESAN
AMBROSIA, GRAND MARNIER   POUNDCAKE*
COFFEE

This is a happy menu for sixteen guests. Any one of the popular gin fizzes makes a festive eye opener. However, if making fizzes for a crowd doesn't seem wise, serve daiquiris made in a blender with frozen daiquiri mix.

Do Ahead: Soak country ham overnight and cook the day before serving, so it can be sliced wafer thin. Eggs may be cooked ahead and also the grits to be chilled and sliced for a quick trip to the oven. Peel and chill oranges the day before but assemble the ambrosia early next day. An hour or so before brunch time, oven-fry drumsticks so the oven will be free later for hot biscuits and baked grits.

COUNTRY HAM

The heavily cured and smoked, uncooked hams of Virginia (which includes the unique Smithfield variety), Kentucky, Tennessee, and Georgia are each a little different. They may be ordered by mail or through gourmet sections in food stores. And in some areas, ready-cooked country hams can be purchased. Directions for cooking usually come with these hams, but the directions here apply generally to all of them. If country style ham is not available, bake a quality precooked ham by the recipe for Braised Ham, Madeira.*

Scrub ham, then soak in water to cover 12 to 18 hours. Drain and heat to simmering in fresh water. Some cooks like to add whole cloves and herbs or wine to the cooking liquid; some add a cup each vinegar and sugar. But country hams are already very flavorful, so don't overdo it. Simmer ham for about 20 minutes per pound (do not allow it to boil), then cool in the liquor. Cut off the rind and glaze the ham lightly, if you wish, but it's not necessary with this type of ham. To glaze, sprinkle with a little ground cloves and spread lightly with honey, apricot jam, or a little brown sugar. Bake at 400° F. for 30 minutes. Serve cold in dainty, waferlike slices so thin you can practically see through them.

CURRIED WHOLE EGGS

1½ dozen eggs
6 cups Sauce Béchamel* (white sauce)
⅓ cup chopped shallots
1 tablespoon curry powder

1 teaspoon dry mustard
½ cup plumped currants
2 tablespoons minced parsley
¼ cup chopped toasted almonds

In deep kettle, cover eggs with cold water, set lid on loosely and heat water to boiling. Cover tightly and turn off heat. After 15 minutes, drain and run cold water over eggs, cracking shells lightly all over (they'll peel beautifully next day). Chill in plastic bag. When making béchamel sauce, cook shallots (or chopped green onions) in the butter before stirring in flour. Add curry powder and mustard with flour. Stir plumped currants and peeled eggs into sauce. Heat gently. Spoon eggs into deepish platter or shallow bowl, then cover with sauce. Top with parsley and almonds. Makes 16 servings.

OVEN-FRIED DRUMSTICKS

Use thighs also if you like and allow one piece for each guest. Rub chicken with freshly cut lemon and season well with salt and freshly ground black pepper. Dip in flour seasoned with a little sweet paprika and shake off all excess flour. For 16 pieces chicken, melt ⅓ cup butter or margarine in large shallow glass baking dish. Roll floured chicken in butter to coat evenly. Bake in 375° F. oven until crisp and tender, about 45 minutes. Drain on paper towels and keep warm. Attach a paper frill panty on each piece and place chicken upright in a shallow serving bowl.

ZEPHYR HOT BISCUITS

These are fabulously light and can be mixed ahead, chilled, and baked at
the last minute.

2 cups sifted all-purpose flour	*6 tablespoons shortening*
1 teaspoon sugar	*2 tablespoons butter*
½ teaspoon salt	*1 egg, beaten*
4 teaspoons baking powder	*⅔ cup milk*

Resift flour with sugar, salt, and baking powder into a mixing bowl. Work
in shortening and butter, squeezing it between your fingertips into crum-
bles and flakes. Combine egg and milk and add to flour. Stir with a fork
until the dough follows around bowl. Turn it out onto a floured board
or pastry cloth and knead lightly about 10 to 15 strokes. Roll dough ¾
inch thick and cut into 2-inch biscuits. Place on ungreased cooky sheet—
or, in the Southern style, first turn each lightly in melted butter. Biscuits
may be chilled up to 3 hours. Bake at 450° F. for 10 to 15 minutes, or
until crisply gold. Makes 2 dozen. (You'll need 2 recipes for this party.)

GRITS PARMESAN

Cook 2½ cups packaged hominy grits by label directions in 2½ quarts
boiling water with 2½ teaspoons salt. Pour into shallow square pan and
chill overnight. Before serving time, cut into 2-inch squares ½ inch
thick. Arrange squares slightly overlapping each other one layer deep in
shallow greased baking dish. Melt ¾ cup butter and pour evenly over
grits. Sprinkle lightly with freshly grated Parmesan cheese (about ½ cup
should be ample). Bake in hot oven (450° F.) for 20 to 30 minutes.
Baste with the pan butter, then run under broiler for a few minutes to
glaze with brown.

AMBROSIA, GRAND MARNIER

Peel 6 to 8 large navel oranges round and round, removing all the white
membrane. Slice enough for a layer into a crystal bowl. Sprinkle lightly
with powdered sugar, if needed, and freshly grated coconut (canned
Southern-style coconut may be used). Continue with orange slices, sugar,
and coconut to fill bowl. Pour ¼ cup or more Grand Marnier through
the layers and chill ambrosia an hour or two before serving.

WEEKEND BRUNCH FOR EIGHT

BLOODY MARYS*
ROAST CANADIAN BACON   EGGS IN TARRAGON CREAM
TOASTED ENGLISH MUFFINS   BUTTER   BLUEBERRY PRESERVES
BELGIAN ENDIVE SALAD
BRANDY FRUIT COMPOTE   CREAM CHEESE WAFERS
COFFEE

A weekend brunch, either on Saturday or Sunday, is a leisurely, casual kind of party, both for the hostess and the guests. Informal as this party is, there's a touch of elegance in the delicately seasoned eggs cooked in a chafing dish and the starkly simple endive salad. Perfect with these is the glazed Canadian bacon, which looks impressive when baked whole. Offer Bloody Marys or Screwdrivers to your arriving guests. And have ready also a pot of freshly made coffee for those who can't navigate without that first cup. Finish the party with an easy and delicious fruit compote and thin cream cheese wafers.

Do Ahead: This is such an easy menu, not too much needs to be done in advance. That's the beauty of chafing dish cookery. You do it more or less on the spot and the food tends itself while you are free to visit with guests. Anytime the week before, make the dough for the cookies so it can chill overnight before you bake them. Day before, wash salad materials and mushrooms for the egg dish. Chill in plastic bags. Make dressing for the salad. Check your chafing dish and supply of Sterno so that once you start cooking the eggs everything moves along smoothly. Next morning, prepare fruit compote as directed in recipe and chill for 2 hours before serving. Prepare Canadian bacon and roast for 1 hour so it will be out of the oven shortly before you serve. Start the chafing dish eggs about one-half hour before your guests arrive—boil the eggs *mollets* (soft, 5-minute boiled eggs) and sauté the mushrooms. Start the sauce. It can finish cooking gently in the chafing dish while you greet your guests. Fix salad, toast muffins, and make fresh coffee just before you serve.

ROAST CANADIAN BACON

Place a 2- to 3-pound piece of Canadian bacon in shallow roasting pan and rub well with ground cloves. Spread with about 2 tablespoons Dijon mustard. Pour 1 cup dry white wine into pan. Roast at 350° F. for 30 minutes, basting occasionally with wine and pan juices. Combine ½ cup apricot jam with a little of the pan sauce (not any fat, but there's usually very little) and spread over bacon. Roast for 30 minutes longer, basting with pan juices until meat is glazed. Transfer to a warm platter and cut into slices at the table.

EGGS IN TARRAGON CREAM

First a word about chafing dishes. Use a traditional chafing dish for this —not a candle warmer. By this I mean the double-boiler type that has an inner pan called the blazer in which actual cooking and browning are done and the outer pan or water jacket called a *bain-marie*. After foods are browned, sauces made, etc., in the blazer, it is set in the water jacket containing an inch or two of hot water to finish cooking or keep warm. Some chafing dish units or fondue sets have an open cup for the fuel and use canned Sterno. Do not use liquid chafing-dish fuel for this type unit. Other chafing dishes have burners, usually with a wick or some absorbent material. Use liquid fuel, not Sterno, with these.

8 soft-cooked Eggs Mollets (below)	1 cup heavy cream
½ pound fresh mushrooms	1½ teaspoons dried leaf tarragon
½ cup butter, divided	1 teaspoon salt
Lemon juice	Freshly ground black pepper
½ cup flour	Dash of nutmeg
3 cups chicken broth	English muffins, split and toasted

Eggs Mollets: Remove eggs from refrigerator ahead of time and let them reach room temperature. With large spoon lower eggs, one by one, into a saucepan of boiling water and simmer for 5 minutes. Whites will be coagulated and softly set, the yolks soft. Plunge immediately into cold water with a stream of cold water running over them until completely cooled. Crack shells gently and peel eggs.

Rinse mushrooms quickly and wipe dry with soft cloth or paper towels. Slice lengthwise. Melt 2 tablespoons butter in blazer pan of chafing dish placed directly over flame. Add mushrooms and cook, stirring about with a wooden spoon, until just tender, 3 to 5 minutes. Sprinkle with a few drops lemon juice. Remove from pan (if more convenient, these may be done ahead in a sauté pan). Melt rest of butter in blazer and blend in flour. Stir over heat for 2 to 5 minutes. Gradually add chicken broth, cream, and tarragon. Cook over medium flame, stirring constantly until sauce boils and thickens. It will take longer than on your kitchen range, but the gentle heat ensures a smooth, well-cooked sauce. Season with salt, a little freshly ground pepper, and a dash of nutmeg. Five minutes before you plan to serve, add peeled whole eggs and mushrooms, heat for 5 minutes longer. Place blazer over *bain-marie* or water jacket over an inch or two of hot water to keep warm. Serve over toasted English muffins.

TOASTED ENGLISH MUFFINS

There are varying opinions about how to toast English muffins. Some want them lathered with soft butter and toasted under the broiler; others prefer the muffins toasted crisp and dry. For this creamy dish, the latter is better. Allow one whole muffin for each guest and a few extras for the good blueberry preserves. Split muffins and lay cut side up on rack of broiler pan. Toast under broiler until crisp and brown. Provide a pot of soft butter for those who want it.

BELGIAN ENDIVE SALAD

This elegant, slightly bitter vegetable needs very little embellishment and tastes best with a simple vinaigrette dressing.

Ahead of time make Sauce Vinaigrette* (classic French dressing) and season it with a teaspoon each chopped fresh tarragon and dill or a generous pinch of each of the dried herbs. Separate leaves of about 6 heads Belgian endive and drop into cool water. Drain and gently blot dry on clean towel. Chill in plastic bag. To serve, arrange leaves in a shallow glass bowl and sprinkle with a handful of shredded radish or crisp raw carrot and minced parsley. Drizzle about ⅓ cup dressing over the salad. Serve rest in a bowl or decanter so guests may add more if they wish. Decorate with crisp curls of raw carrot.

BRANDY FRUIT COMPOTE

This recipe by gastronome Jim Beard, came to me through Jeanne Voltz, food editor of *Woman's Day* magazine.

> *1 can (6 ounces) frozen orange*   *8 fresh peaches*
>   *juice concentrate*   *Sugar to taste*
> *2 baskets fresh strawberries*   *½ cup brandy or cognac*

Ahead of time, defrost unopened can of orange concentrate. Wash and hull berries, blot dry on paper towels. Peel peaches, cut into halves, and remove stones. Place in shallow crystal bowl. Sprinkle lightly with sugar. Cover with strawberries and sprinkle lightly with sugar to taste. Stir brandy into liquefied, undiluted orange concentrate. Pour over fruits and mix gently. Cover and refrigerate for 2 hours. Stir now and then. Place on buffet with individual small bowls.

CREAM CHEESE WAFERS

Rich buttery cookies with the elusive flavor of cream cheese. Use whole nutmeg, freshly grated, if you have it.

> *1 cup butter, softened*   *1 teaspoon ground or freshly*
> *1 3-ounce package cream cheese*   *grated nutmeg*
> *1 cup sugar*   *¼ teaspoon ground cardamom*
> *1 egg yolk*   *½ teaspoon salt*
> *1 teaspoon vanilla*   *2½ cups sifted all-purpose flour*

Work together until thoroughly mixed and smooth the butter, cream cheese, sugar, egg yolk, and vanilla. Use your hands, a wooden spoon, or the mixer. Blend nutmeg, cardamom, and salt into flour and work it into the butter mixture until smooth. Shape on foil into 2 long rolls about 1½ inches in diameter. Wrap and chill overnight. Cut in slices about ⅛ inch thick and place on ungreased cooky sheets. Bake at 350° F. for 8 to 10 minutes. Do not brown, merely tan well. Overcooking spoils the delicate flavor and texture of these cookies. Makes 5 to 6 dozen.

QUICK BRUNCH FOR TWELVE

FRESH PINEAPPLE ON THE SHELL
SWEET CHERRIES
BAKED HAM OMELET
TOASTED ENGLISH MUFFINS AND JAMS
DANISH PASTRY STRIPS
COFFEE

Here's a menu so easy and quick it's sinful. It's equally good for a late supper. The foods are attractive and easy to manage on one plate, light but satisfying. I like to contrast the tartness of fresh pineapple with sweet cherries when they're available or strawberries served with a bowl of powdered sugar for dunking. A pleasant wine for this is Alsatian Gewürztraminer or California Rhine wine.

Do Ahead: Have the fruits prepared and arranged ahead of time and all ingredients ready for the ham dish. You can beat the eggs and pop the dish into the oven the minute your guests arrive. It will be ready by the time they've had a Bloody Mary* or a cup of coffee. For easy pickup service, butter the English muffins after they're toasted, then cut into halves. Cut Danish pastries into neat finger strips and arrange on a tray. If you can find the midget size pastries in your bakery, use those (or several days ahead, make Danish Kringle* and freeze them). And brew plenty of hot coffee to serve with the ham and muffins and more to go along with the pastry later on.

FRESH PINEAPPLE ON THE SHELL

Wash and dry 2 to 3 fresh ripe pineapples and lay on a board. With a heavy knife, cut in half lengthwise from bottom through the leafy crown. Cut halves lengthwise into 2 or 4 wedges, depending on size of fruit. Tear away any brown or unsightly leaves but leave a pretty green tuft on each wedge if possible. Cut away hard fibrous core from center of pineapple. Loosen fruit by cutting close to rind with small sharp knife or curved serrated knife. Keeping fruit in shell, cut crosswise into half-inch slices then lengthwise once or twice to make bite-size pieces. Put wedges on plate or tray and sprinkle lightly with powdered sugar if it seems needed. Cover with foil or plastic film and chill.

BAKED HAM OMELET

A baked omelet of sorts, enriched with diced ham and Jack and cottage cheese. It's easier to make, however, and much less temperamental. The recipe serves 12, but I usually make half the recipe again for seconds, and bake it after the first is out of the oven.

1 pound Jack or Muenster cheese *1 dozen eggs*
2 cups finely diced cooked ham *Salt and pepper*
½ cup melted butter or margarine *Tabasco*
½ cup sifted flour *1 pint small curd cottage cheese*
1 teaspoon baking powder

Ahead of time, shred cheese, dice ham and sauté it briefly in 1 tablespoon of the butter. Preheat oven to 400° F. and melt rest of butter in a large pyrex baking dish (9×13 inches). Sift flour with baking powder. Beat eggs and season lightly with salt and pepper (how much depends on the ham). Add 5 to 6 drops of Tabasco and stir in the flour, ham, Jack cheese, cottage cheese, and half the melted butter. Turn rest of butter around in dish to coat it evenly. Pour in egg mixture. Bake at 400° F. for 15 minutes. Reduce heat and bake for 10 to 15 minutes longer, until puffed and light golden brown on top. Serve at once from dish. Cut into 12 squares.

MIX-AND-SWITCH MENUS

The following two menus show how you can mix and switch recipes in this book in endless combinations and variations. Similar mix-and-switch menus will be found in other chapters.

SUNNY MIDDAY BRUNCH
(For Eight)

CHAMPAGNE AND ORANGE JUICE*
BRANDADE DE MORUE*   GRILLED CANADIAN BACON
TORTINO OF ARTICHOKES*   TOASTED VIENNA BREAD
BUNDT CAKE, GRAND MARNIER*
STRAWBERRIES   HOT COFFEE

A pleasing contrast of flavors for a festive occasion. Make the *bundt* cake and *brandade* the day before. Next morning hull 2 baskets of strawberries and splash with ½ cup Grand Marnier. Fix ingredients for *tortini* (omit prosciutto) and lightly brown sliced Canadian bacon in large skillet or broiler. Keep warm. Bake the tortini while you enjoy the champagne and brandade.

CLAM BRUNCH FOR EIGHT

SMOKED SALMON   DARK BREAD   CREAM CHEESE
CLAMS AND EGGS   TOASTED BRIOCHE* OR HOMEMADE BREAD*
MACÉDOINE OF FRUITS*   COFFEE

A delicious noonday feast for 8 friends who are especially fond of fish flavors. Start with drinks, if you like, and a pretty platter of thinly sliced smoked salmon. Garnish salmon with capers and lemon wedges. Accompany with the pepper mill, strips of thin pumpernickel bread, and cream cheese. Make the brioche or homemade bread ahead and freeze or use frozen brioche and bake bread from frozen yeast dough. More toasted brioche or bread taste great with the fruit and a second cup of coffee.

CLAMS AND EGGS

Make 6 cups Sauce Béchamel* using juice drained from 4 cans minced clams (8 ounces each) as part of the liquid. Season lightly with salt, freshly milled pepper, a little lemon juice, 2 teaspoons anchovy paste, several dashes Tabasco sauce, and ½ cup heavy cream. To serve, place in chafing dish and add 12 hard-cooked eggs, quartered, the clams, and ½ pound crisp-cooked bacon, cut into bits. Blend well, heat through, and top with minced parsley. Serve on freshly made toast.

II Luncheons

In many countries around the world, the middle meal is the main meal of the day. It's an occasion for entertaining perhaps as much or more than the evening repast. Here in America, families are scattered at noon, particularly in our large cities. That pleasant, unifying European custom of the big family meal at noon is not possible. Rather, midday is considered a time for ladies' luncheons. But why can't we use the middle of the day for some of our regular entertaining? There are only fifty-two weekends in which to have friends in for dinner, a patio supper, and the like. Some of our favorite people take off regularly for their weekend spots, so the years speed along and we don't get together as often as we wish.

Entertain more often at noon with a sociable buffet luncheon. Invite some of your husband's associates for luncheon at home instead of the club. They'll love it. Get several couples together you can't see on weekends for a relaxing pause in the middle of the day. You'll be surprised how much less involved it is than a dinner party. Liquor is no problem, since you probably won't want much of it. A glass of sherry, a Bloody Mary, or a sparkling vermouth cassis. Or champagne for special occasions. Your business guests should be refreshed and uplifted, ready for their afternoon appointments. Luncheon foods are lighter, too, and served in smaller quantities. A big meat or fish salad, cold fish or chicken with a lively sauce, a good soup or bisque, all the delicious egg and cheese dishes, less pretentious desserts. The menus in this chapter will give you some fresh ideas along these lines for ladies' luncheons, couples' luncheons, committee and business get-togethers, and the newish drop-in luncheons.

LUNCHEON FOR A V.I.P.
(For Eight)

CHILLED ROSÉ WINE
COLD HALIBUT, MEXICANO   DEVILED CRAB QUICHE
ZUCCHINI VINAIGRETTE
ICED ONION RINGS
RASPBERRY PEAR MERINGUE
COFFEE   TEA

A pretty luncheon to honor a distinguished guest. It was planned for eight ladies, but men would enjoy it equally. A chilled rosé is attractive and refreshing with these foods. A French Provence and a California Grenache rosé both are good, and there are many others. I use pastel linens for the buffet and two smaller tables with bouquets of tiny red roses mixed with white baby's breath and feathery greens. They provide nice background for the cool green and white main course dishes and for the red and white dessert.

Do Ahead: You may make pastry for the quiche several days ahead and chill it. The day before, make the meringue shells, the zucchini vinaigrette, and poach the halibut. Defrost frozen crab meat overnight in refrigerator. Roll pastry shell and chill it. Early next morning, assemble and glaze the meringue. Fix onion rings and make the Mexicano sauce for halibut. Make quiche last thing and bake it to be ready 10 or 15 minutes before luncheon is served.

COLD HALIBUT, MEXICANO

4-pound piece fresh or frozen   *½ cup dry white wine*
*   halibut*   *1 bay leaf*
1 slice lemon   *Water to cover fish*
1 slice onion   *Sauce Mexicano (below)*
Sprig of parsley   *Lemon slices*
1 tablespoon salt

If frozen halibut is used, defrost in refrigerator. Tie fish loosely in cheese-cloth, leaving long ends for handles; place in large roasting pan or fish poacher. Combine remaining ingredients except sauce and lemon garnish and heat to boiling. Simmer for about 10 minutes and pour over fish. Seal pan tightly with foil or lid and steam-poach fish in oven at 350° F. for about 6 minutes per pound or by Jim Beard's foolproof directions, which allow 10 minutes' cooking time for each inch of fish's thickness. If fish is 2 inches at thickest part, allow 20 minutes. Fish will be opaque but moist. Lift from liquid and cool slightly. Untie cheesecloth, lift fish by the long handles, and carefully flip it over onto a platter. Cover with foil or plastic wrap and chill. When ready to serve, skin fish if necessary, wipe platter clean. Spoon sauce Mexicano generously over fish. Serve extra in a sauceboat. Garnish platter with lemon slices.

SAUCE MEXICANO

Halve, seed, and peel a very soft-ripe avocado. Mash with fork. Add 1 tomato, peeled, seeded, and finely chopped, ¼ cup minced white onion, 1 tablespoon vinegar, 1 tablespoon salad oil, plenty of salt, and 1 cup dairy sour cream. Mix well and season to taste with 1 to 2 tablespoons finely chopped, seeded, canned green chiles. (If made ahead, cover with foil pressed directly on surface. Add few drops green food color later if needed.)

DEVILED CRAB QUICHE

Pastry* for 10-inch pie
½ pound frozen Alaska king crab
   meat, thawed, or 1 7½-ounce
   can
Lemon juice
½ cup minced green onion
2 tablespoons butter or margarine
1½ cups sliced mushrooms
2 teaspoons flour
¼ cup dry white wine

2 tablespoons minced parsley
4 eggs
1 cup dairy sour cream
½ cup milk or half-and-half
½ teaspoon salt
Freshly ground pepper
Generous dash nutmeg
1 tablespoon Dijon mustard
½ cup shredded Swiss cheese
¼ cup grated Parmesan cheese

Make pastry dough ahead and thaw crab meat overnight in refrigerator. Roll chilled pastry ⅛ inch thick and 2 inches larger than pie plate or quiche pan. Fit carefully into pan without stretching dough. Turn under ½-inch overhang in pie pan and pinch into a fluted edge. Or double overhang forward in quiche pan and roll into a sort of fat, rounded edge. Chill. Drain thawed crab (save the good liquid—it has flavor). Break crab into chunks and sprinkle with a few drops lemon juice. Cook onion in melted butter until soft. Stir in mushrooms and cook for 2 to 4 minutes. Sprinkle in flour, wine, and parsley. Mix and add to crab meat. Stir lightly. Beat eggs with sour cream and milk and stir in seasonings and crab liquid. Spread crab and Swiss cheese in pastry shell, pour in the egg mixture, and sprinkle evenly with Parmesan. Bake at 375° F. for 30 to 35 minutes, or until filling is slightly puffed and set. Cool for 15 minutes before cutting into 8 wedges. If baked ahead, reheat at 350° F. for about 10 minutes.

ZUCCHINI VINAIGRETTE

Almost any crisp cooked vegetable is good with this zipped-up vinaigrette sauce, but zucchini is especially effective and seems available the year round in most markets.

Add to 1 cup Classic French Dressing (Sauce Vinaigrette*) 1 tablespoon white wine, 2 tablespoons each finely chopped parsley, green pepper, sweet pickle relish, canned pimiento, and green onion. Trim ends from 6 to 8 medium zucchini (about 6 inches long) but do not peel. Cut each lengthwise into 4 to 6 flat slices. Cook in boiling salted water for 3 to 4 minutes only, until still slightly crisp. Drain and lay in shallow dish. Cover with the vinaigrette sauce and marinate for several hours or overnight. Arrange neatly in center of salad platter with white Spanish onion rings (see Iced Onion Rings*).

RASPBERRY PEAR MERINGUE

Meringue is left in oven, turned off overnight to produce beautifully crisp white dessert shells.

5 egg whites
¼ teaspoon salt
1½ cups superfine sugar
1 package (10 ounces) frozen raspberries, defrosted enough to separate
2 tablespoons cornstarch

¼ cup sugar, divided
1 can (29 ounces) Bartlett pear halves
2 3-ounce packages cream cheese
1 teaspoon grated lemon peel
3 tablespoons sour cream
Whipped cream

Beat egg whites with salt until peaks form. Gradually beat in superfine sugar, 1 tablespoon at a time, until meringue stands in stiff, sharp peaks. Cut brown paper to fit baking sheets and draw 8 circles, each about 3 inches across. Brush with oil. Spread meringue within circles, building it up on sides to form shells, or pipe meringue round and round through pastry tube into 8 individual meringues. Preheat oven to 450° F. for 15 minutes. Put meringue in oven, close door, and turn off heat. Leave meringue in oven without opening door, at least 5 to 6 hours or overnight, to dry out and become crisp. Remove from paper and put on serving platter.

To complete dessert, drain raspberry syrup into small saucepan. Blend cornstarch and 2 tablespoons sugar. Stir into syrup. Stir over low heat until clear and thickened. Gently stir in the berries. Cool, stirring occasionally. Drain pears. Soften cream cheese with fork and blend in remaining 2 tablespoons sugar, lemon peel, and sour cream. Spread over bottom of meringue shells. Place pear half in each meringue and spoon cooled raspberry filling on top. Decorate with whipped cream if desired.

1798507

WEEKEND LUNCHEON FOR COMMITTEE OF EIGHT

BLOODY MARYS OR ICED JUICES
YOGURT GLAZED CHICKEN   SPINACH RICE SALAD
FRENCH BREAD
FRESH FRUIT AND CHEESE OR CARROT WALNUT CAKE
COFFEE

Many couples I know work together on committees—for the local church or school, the property owners' association, political and conservation groups. And often, policies can be discussed and settled over a Saturday or Sunday luncheon. Sometimes a convivial drink is served such as a chilled Rhine wine or California Semillon, again only chilled juices, or a friendly cup of coffee to get everyone started. The menu might be merely a big hearty salad such as Niçoise* or a hot dish and salad like this menu. Both the glazed chicken and the rice salad loaded with spinach and other bits of crunch are easy make-aheads. Pears, apples, or peaches for out-of-hand eating with some good cheese make a perfect dessert. But little squares of the easy, one-bowl carrot cake are always eagerly accepted with the last cup of coffee.

Do Ahead: Make the carrot cake the day before and oven-poach chicken breasts. Cook rice for the salad and toss it with the French dressing. Early next morning, prepare vegetables and add to rice salad. Make yogurt sauce for chicken, assemble chicken dish to be glazed for a few minutes before serving. Make Bloody Marys just before luncheon.

BLOODY MARYS OR ICED JUICES

For each Bloody Mary allow 4 ounces tomato juice, a jigger of vodka, Worcestershire, and lemon juice to taste. Shake over ice. A refreshing Virgin Mary is made the same except no vodka is used. V-8 or grapefruit juice served over ice cubes makes an excellent light luncheon starter.

YOGURT GLAZED CHICKEN

Chicken breasts are poached ahead and glazed at the last minute in a quick yogurt sauce.

4 whole chicken breasts, split
Salt and freshly ground pepper
2 onion slices
2 lemon slices
2 whole cloves
2 sprigs parsley
1 teaspoon cornstarch

½ cup dry white wine or chicken broth
1 cup plain yogurt
2 tablespoons minced shallots
¾ cup mayonnaise
½ cup grated Parmesan cheese

Season chicken with salt and pepper and place in shallow baking pan with onion and lemon slices, cloves, and parsley. Add wine or broth and cover tightly with foil. Oven-poach at 350° F. until tender and springy, about 30 minutes. Strain off liquid and save it. Cool chicken, cover, and refrigerate. Remove skin and pull meat from bones in long meaty strips. Lay in shallow baking dish. Mix cornstarch with the wine or broth (first remove any fat from it) and blend with yogurt, shallots and mayonnaise. Spread evenly over chicken and sprinkle with Parmesan. Set in 400° oven until hot and bubbly, about 10 minutes. Run under broiler a minute or two to glaze with flecks of brown.

SPINACH RICE SALAD

The variety of wonderful salads you can make with rice seems endless. This one has lots of crunchy texture and is pretty to look at.

1 cup converted white rice
1½ cups cold water
1 teaspoon salt
1 bay leaf, broken up
1 slice lemon
½ cup Classic French Dressing*
Freshly ground pepper
½ cup red onion slices, quartered

½ cup diced green pepper
¼ cup chopped parsley
2 cups chopped fresh spinach
1 can pimientos, diced
4 slices crisp cooked bacon, crumbled
Small leaves spinach
2 medium tomatoes, quartered

Place rice, water, salt, bay leaf, and lemon in heavy pan with tight lid. (If you do not have this type pan, which steams rice Oriental style, follow cooking directions on label.) Cover and heat to boiling. Immediately turn heat to very lowest. Steam rice without raising lid or stirring for 25 minutes. Remove from heat and let stand for 5 minutes, covered. Fluff rice with fork and remove lemon and bay leaf. Toss gently with about half the dressing and a few grindings of pepper. Cool. Add onion and diced and chopped vegetables. Toss gently until mixed, adding more dressing, salt and pepper if needed. Cover and chill. At serving time, mix in bacon bits and spoon salad into shallow salad bowl rimmed with small, crisp spinach leaves. Place quartered tomatoes around edges.

CARROT WALNUT CAKE

This is unbelievably tender and moist. You may frost it, if you like, but it needs no adornment.

2 cups sifted unbleached white flour	2 cups sugar
2 teaspoons soda	1½ cups light salad oil
2 teaspoons cinnamon	3 cups grated or finely shredded raw carrots
1 teaspoon nutmeg	2 teaspoons vanilla
4 eggs	¾ cup chopped walnuts

Resift flour with soda and spices. In large bowl of electric mixer, beat eggs and sugar lightly on low speed. Add oil, then rest of ingredients except walnuts. Blend for a few seconds on low speed, then turn mixer to high and beat for 4 minutes, or until batter is light, shiny, and creamy-looking. Stir in nuts. Pour into greased and floured oblong pan, 9×13 inches. Bake at 325° F. for 1 hour or until top springs back when lightly touched. Cool in pan on wire rack and cut into small "pick-up" squares.

SALAD BAR LUNCHEON FOR SIXTEEN

HOT CLAM CUP

SALMON MOUSSE   CURRY STUFFED TOMATOES

GOLDEN EGG PLATTER

SESAME BISCUITS   FRENCH ROLLS

HONEYDEW BLUEBERRY WEDGES

COFFEE   ICED TEA*

A buffet table laden with an assortment of colorful salads makes a tempting summer luncheon especially for the ladies. The mousse and egg salad make twelve servings each. These are not full-size luncheon servings, and need not be in view of the variety of foods offered. For a guest list this size, several dishes are usually easier for the hostess to manage than one huge one. Everyone will surely find something to his liking.

The salmon mousse is pretty and pink and always a luncheon favorite. Make it with more expensive lobster or crab if you wish. The principle and method are about the same. Vary the seasoning to suit the fish you use. Everything can be done much in advance except bacon for the egg salad, the clam soup, and sesame biscuits. These require only a few minutes. If wine is wanted, serve a white Rhône or a California Chardonnay.

Do Ahead: The day before make salmon mousse and shrimp salad for the tomatoes. Chill overnight. Boil eggs for the salad and wash and dry lettuce and cucumbers. Chill in plastic bags. Make Golden Vinaigrette* and the blueberry sauce. Next morning, peel and hollow tomatoes, drain and fill with shrimp salad. Chill. Oven-broil bacon* and slice onion into ice water to chill. Put together ingredients for the clam soup and have ready to heat for a few minutes just before serving. Assemble egg salad. Cut melons into wedges and let chill during luncheon. Make tea for iced tea, recrisp French rolls, and bake biscuits. Keep them warm. Assemble dessert after luncheon dishes are cleared away.

HOT CLAM CUP

Combine in large saucepan: 1½ quarts bottled clam juice (6 bottles), 1 quart double-strength, fat-free chicken broth, 3 cups dry white dinner wine. Heat to boiling and season sharply with lemon juice—2 or 3 tablespoons—Lawry's Seasoned Salt, a generous dash of nutmeg, and several drops of Tabasco. Simmer for a few minutes. Serve hot in small mugs.

SALMON MOUSSE

*2½ cups clear chicken broth,
   divided
1 teaspoon dried tarragon leaves
1 lemon slice
2½ envelopes unflavored gelatin
2 tablespoons grated onion
¼ cup fresh lemon juice
3 or 4 dashes Tabasco sauce
Salt*

*1 tablespoon minced fresh dill or
   1 teaspoon dried dill weed
2 cans (1 pound each) red salmon
   (4 cups) or 2 pounds (4 cups)
   fresh Poached Salmon**
*¾ cup mayonnaise
1 cup heavy cream, whipped
Sprays fresh dill or watercress
Lemon twists*

Pour 2 cups chicken broth into saucepan and add tarragon and lemon slice. Simmer gently for about 5 minutes. Put remaining ½ cup cold broth in small bowl and sprinkle with gelatin, let stand until gelatin is softened. Remove lemon from hot broth and stir in gelatin. Season with grated onion, lemon juice, Tabasco sauce, salt if needed, and dill. Be generous with Tabasco and dill, as flavor will be blander when whipped cream is added. Drain salmon, remove any skin and bones, and flake. Stir into gelatin. Whizz in blender, in 2 batches, until smooth. Chill until thickened but not set. Fold in mayonnaise. Whip cream until thick and fluffy, fold in. Taste mousse and add additional lemon juice, salt, or dill if needed. Turn into 8-inch ring or fish mold rinsed in cold water. Cover with plastic film and chill overnight. Unmold onto a chilled glass plate and decorate with sprays of fresh dill or watercress and lemon twists.

Lemon Twists—Cut lemon crosswise into paper thin slices. Slash each slice to center on one side. Twist cut edges in opposite directions.

CURRY STUFFED TOMATOES

4 cups cooked tiny cocktail
  shrimp
1 can (6½ to 7 ounces) light
  meat tuna
2 cups finely chopped celery
¼ cup drained capers
1 cup mayonnaise
2 teaspoons curry powder

1 tablespoon lemon juice
1 teaspoon grated onion
Few drops Tabasco sauce
16 firm-ripe tomatoes, uniform
  size
Salt
Parsley

Combine shrimp, flaked drained tuna, celery, and capers. Mix mayonnaise with curry powder, lemon juice, grated onion, and Tabasco sauce to taste—you may need more seasoning than is specified. Pour just enough dressing over salad to moisten well. Mix lightly and chill in covered container. Peel tomatoes. Impale on long kitchen fork. Hold and turn over a flame a few seconds until skin bursts. Slip off skin under cold running water. Scoop out centers and turn tomatoes upside down to drain. Chill. To serve, salt tomato shells lightly and fill with shrimp salad. Arrange on large salad platter. Top each with a small spray of parsley if you wish.

GOLDEN EGG PLATTER

Bacon and eggs for lunch in an easy, show-off salad.

1 dozen hard-cooked eggs
2 cucumbers
Boston or Bibb lettuce
1 pound lean bacon

1 sweet red onion
Salt
Freshly ground pepper
Golden Vinaigrette*

Cook eggs ahead of time. Place in saucepan and cover with cold water. Heat to boiling. Cover with tight lid, turn off heat, and let eggs stand for 15 minutes. Slide pan back and forth now and then to move eggs and keep yolks centered. Crack shells gently and hold eggs under cold running water to cool. Chill in plastic bags. Wash cucumbers and score by running tines of fork down cucumber from tip to tip all around. Chill. Wash lettuce, separate and dry leaves. Chill in plastic bag. Spread bacon on rack over shallow broiler pan. Oven-broil in hot oven (400° F.) until crisp, about 15 to 20 minutes. Blot with paper towels if necessary, wrap in foil, and set aside. Slice onion into paper thin rings in bowl. Sprinkle lightly with salt and cover with ice water. Let stand for 1 hour. To serve, line a large salad platter with small lettuce leaves. Peel eggs and slice with egg slicer. Mound half of them in center of lettuce. Sprinkle with salt and pepper, half the bacon, crumbled. Drizzle with a few spoonfuls of the vinaigrette. Slice rest of eggs on top. Sprinkle with salt and pepper and rest of crumbled bacon. Slice cucumbers thinly and arrange with onion rings around eggs. Drizzle salad all over lightly with vinaigrette. Serve rest of dressing in a separate bowl. Fill a small bowl with extra lettuce leaves and place near the salad and dressing (it's easier for guests to take fresh lettuce leaves for their plates than try to wrestle out leaves from under an arranged salad, I've discovered).

SESAME BISCUITS

Open 3 packages refrigerator biscuits and separate. Dip each biscuit in melted butter—you will need 4 to 6 tablespoons. Sprinkle tops of each biscuit with sesame seeds and place 2 inches apart on cooky sheet. Bake as label directs. Serve hot in napkin-lined basket. Butter isn't necessary for these rich little biscuits. However, provide a tub of soft butter for those who prefer French rolls or want more butter on the biscuits.

HONEYDEW BLUEBERRY WEDGES

Combine in saucepan 1 quart fresh or frozen (unsweetened) blueberries, ½ cup sugar, or to taste—it varies with the berries—mixed with 1 teaspoon cornstarch, ½ cup port wine. Stir and heat to boiling. Simmer just until sauce has thickened slightly. Remove from heat and add 2 tablespoons lemon juice. Taste and add more sugar or lemon juice if necessary. Don't make it too sweet—it must have a light, fresh quality. Cool, cover, and refrigerate. To serve, cut 2 or 3 chilled honeydew melons into wedges and arrange on large dessert platter or tray. Set dessert plates and bowl of blueberry sauce nearby.

SALAD LUNCHEON FOR EIGHT

WINE SPRITZERS
BEEF SALAD PROVENCE
CHEESE BREAD
RASPBERRY CHARLOTTE TART
COFFEE

A perfect menu for a leisurely Sunday luncheon—maybe after a game of tennis or a bird walk. It's light but filling and couldn't be easier. You need cooked roast or boiled beef for the salad, so do as our thrifty French friends do—plan this party after you've had a splendid roast beef dinner. Or buy good roast beef at the delicatessen. The warm cheese bread can be fashioned from your own yeast dough or a hot roll mix. I find frozen bread dough very good and use it frequently for this type of loaf. The pretty berry tart is really an easy sort of quick charlotte made of puréed raspberries in whipped cream piled into a shell made of ladyfingers instead of pastry.

Do Ahead: Day before, roast the beef and cool it. Make the Mustard Vinaigrette and prepare the tart. Potatoes and eggs for the salad can be boiled the day before or early in the morning so they can be cool by lunchtime. Cheese bread can be baked the day before and reheated in foil. Or start it early enough before the party to rise, bake, and cool briefly before it is served.

WINE SPRITZERS

Chill bottles of dry white wine—Muscadet or California Blanc Fumé is good. For each drink, pour about 4 ounces chilled wine over ice cubes in tall highball glasses. Add a strip of lemon peel and club soda.

BEEF SALAD PROVENCE

Attractive garnishes and a colorful presentation are an integral part of this gardeny-looking salad.

*4 cups diced cold roast or boiled
  beef
Mustard Vinaigrette (below)
8 new potatoes, boiled (3 to 4
  cups when sliced)
1 cup thinly sliced celery or
  young fennel
8 hard-cooked eggs
8 thinly sliced radishes
⅓ cup chopped sour pickles
1 large sweet red onion*

*1 green or red sweet pepper,
  sliced into rings
Salt and freshly ground pepper
2 cucumbers, peeled and thinly
  sliced
4 firm-ripe tomatoes, peeled and
  quartered
Small lettuce leaves
1 cup black olives
Mayonnaise*

To prepare beef, cut cold roast or boiled beef (trimmed of all fat) into thin slices. Cut into ½-inch strips, then into squares. Put into a large bowl with about ¼ cup of the vinaigrette. Marinate for several hours. Boil whole new potatoes in salted water just until tender. Drain and cool. Peel and slice into bowl with meat. Add celery, 4 of the eggs, peeled and quartered, radishes, and pickles. Peel onion, slice thinly, and drop 2 or 3 slices into a bowl of ice water. Quarter rest of slices, separate, and add to salad. Toss with just enough vinaigrette to moisten salad well but not make potatoes soggy. Season with salt and pepper. Cover and refrigerate. Prepare green pepper and cucumbers and peel tomatoes. Chill in plastic bags. At lunchtime, line a large salad plate with small lettuce leaves and mound meat salad in the center. Cover all over with sliced eggs (use an egg slicer for nice even slices) and black olives. Arrange green peppers and onion rings, quartered tomatoes, and cucumber slices around. Add 2 tablespoons mayonnaise to rest of dressing. Serve in separate sauceboat alongside.

MUSTARD VINAIGRETTE

To 1½ recipes Classic French Dressing* (Sauce Vinaigrette) add 1 tablespoon Dijon mustard, pinch of dry mustard, 1 tablespoon minced fresh parsley, and ½ teaspoon each tarragon and rosemary. Blend.

CHEESE BREAD

This may be baked in a loaf pan like the typical spiral bread, but it's handsome coiled in a round cake pan.

1 loaf frozen bread dough, or
½ recipe Homemade Bread*
dough or 1 package hot
roll mix
½ cup sesame seeds
1 cup shredded sharp Cheddar
cheese

2 tablespoons soft butter
¼ cup chopped green onions
2 tablespoons minced parsley
Few drops Tabasco sauce
1 egg, beaten lightly

Defrost frozen dough overnight in refrigerator. Let homemade bread dough rise as directed until ready to shape. Prepare hot roll mix by package directions, let rise. Toast sesame seeds in dry skillet or with a teaspoon butter over very low heat until gold in color. Stir continuously —and don't let them burn. Save out 1 tablespoon for top of loaf, mix rest with cheese, butter, onions, parsley, and Tabasco. Knock down risen dough with your fist to deflate it and place on board. Roll into a long rectangle about 9×16 inches. Brush all over with beaten egg and let dry for a few minutes. Spread evenly with cheese filling. Roll up tightly from long side, pulling and stretching dough as you roll, and sort of press dough down to enclose filling. Pinch edges together to seal completely, form into a ring, and pinch ends together to seal. Lift carefully into a greased 9-inch round cake pan, turning it so seam is down. Make 6 to 8 diagonal slashes around ring about ½ inch deep. Let rise until dough is light, about 30 minutes. Brush with beaten egg and sprinkle with sesame seeds. Bake in hot oven (400° F.) for 40 to 50 minutes, or until nicely browned. Turn out on rack to cool. Cut slightly warm loaf into thick wedges with sharp serrated knife. (I usually cool loaf completely, slice thickly, reassemble in foil and heat at 400° F. for about 10 minutes.)

RASPBERRY CHARLOTTE TART

The filling is a raspberry mousse and may be chilled in a charlotte mold if you prefer. This is prettier and easier to serve.

2 packages (10 ounces each)
  frozen red raspberries
½ cup granulated sugar
1 envelope unflavored gelatin
2 tablespoons framboise
  (raspberry liqueur) or Grand
  Marnier

2 teaspoons lemon juice
1 cup whipping cream
2 tablespoons powdered sugar
16 to 20 ladyfingers
½ cup crushed almond
  macaroons*
Fresh berries for top

Defrost raspberries by package directions. Crush one package berries with fork or whiz in blender to a coarse purée—do not liquefy. Empty into saucepan and add juice drained from second package. Mix granulated sugar and gelatin and stir into purée. Stir over very low heat until gelatin is melted. Add liqueur, lemon juice, and drained berries. Chill until syrupy-thick but not firm. Meanwhile, mix cream and powdered sugar and chill for 30 minutes to 1 hour. This gives the cream extra body. Line a 9-inch pie plate with split ladyfingers, letting the ends extend over the top in a pretty scalloped rim. Cover bottom of plate with more ladyfingers. Cut and fit in pieces when necessary to cover bottom completely. Sprinkle shell with macaroon crumbs, saving out a few for the top. Beat cream until thick and fluffy but not dry. Fold it into thickened raspberry purée. Spoon into ladyfinger shell and sprinkle with remaining crumbs. Chill until set, several hours or overnight. Decorate with a few whole berries if they're available. Cut into 8 wedges and serve as you do a pie.

Note: Strawberries, blueberries, peaches, nectarines or canned or cooked pineapple may be used with appropriate liqueurs.

AUTUMN LUNCHEON FOR EIGHT

DRY SHERRY

RAW VEGETABLES   CURRY MUSTARD SAUCE   GREEN OLIVES

BULGAR PILAF WITH CHICKEN

ONION CHEESE STICKS

APRICOT ASPIC

WITH

MACÉDOINE OF FRUITS

HOT TEA   COFFEE

This menu was planned for ladies, perhaps your symphony or library committee. But men will find it equally appealing. The nutty wheat pilaf is a change from rice and makes a pleasing one-dish luncheon when combined with chicken.

Do Ahead: Cook chicken the day before so you can get rid of all the fat and have the flavorful broth for your pilaf. Make the beautiful apricot aspic, which serves as both salad and dessert, in advance also, but prepare the macédoine of fruits 2 or 3 hours before the luncheon. After you sauté the bulgar (cracked wheat) and vegetables, they cook later with little or no attention on top of the stove or in the oven. A Moselle or California Riesling would be pleasant with this luncheon.

DRY SHERRY

Sherry is a cheering drink on the first cool day of autumn. Serve a light dry cocktail sherry (Tio Pepe is brittle dry, the amontillado and manzanilla are less so) in stemmed glasses. Big bitey green Spanish olives are the perfect accompaniment. Crisp raw vegetables with a nip of sauce served in the living room before luncheon taste good with it too.

RAW VEGETABLES, CURRY MUSTARD SAUCE

Cut cauliflower and broccoli flowerets into manageable pieces or slices, carrots and celery into sticks. Wash and chill in plastic bags. Season 1 cup mayonnaise (or half mayonnaise, half yogurt) with 1 teaspoon curry powder, 1 teaspoon soy sauce, 2 teaspoons prepared mustard, and a little grated onion. Chill. Set the bowl of dipping sauce in center of a shallow bowl or tray. Arrange vegetables around it. Scatter a few ice cubes through the vegetables to keep everything crisp and moist. Serve in the living room before luncheon.

BULGAR PILAF WITH CHICKEN

*1 broiler-fryer chicken cut into
    pieces, plus 1 whole breast or 2
    thighs
1 onion stuck with 2 cloves
1 teaspoon coriander seeds
2 lemon slices
1½ teaspoons salt
2 sprigs fresh parsley
1 quart cold water
½ cup butter or margarine*

*2 onions, chopped
2 cups bulgar (cracked wheat)
    from health food store
1 teaspoon dried sweet basil
Pinch cayenne pepper
2 tomatoes, cut in wedges
½ cup chopped fresh parsley
Salt and freshly ground pepper
½ cup shelled pine nuts or toasted
    slivered almonds*

Day before, place chicken, onion with cloves, crushed coriander seeds, lemon, salt, parsley, and water in large heavy kettle. Heat to simmering. Cover and cook gently until tender, about 45 minutes. Cool, uncovered. Strain stock and measure 3½ cups for bulgar. Cover and refrigerate. Wrap chicken breasts, thighs, and legs in foil and refrigerate. Save bony pieces and any leftover stock for soups or sauces.

An hour or two before luncheon, heat butter in large heavy skillet (Dutch-oven type) or cook-and-serve pan. Add onions and cook gently until soft and golden. Add bulgar and stir over low heat until it smells toasted and takes on a rich golden color. Stir in the broth, skimmed of its fat and heated, sweet basil, and cayenne. Cover tightly, turn heat to lowest, and steam bulgar for 15 minutes. Gently stir in tomatoes and parsley. Cover and steam for 15 minutes longer or until liquid is absorbed. Remove skin and fat from chicken and pull meat from bones in thick strips. Taste pilaf and add salt and freshly ground pepper if needed. Toss with chicken and nuts. Transfer to casserole or heatproof platter if your cooking pan can't go to the table. Cover and keep warm in 350° F. oven until ready to serve. Add a little hot broth as needed to keep pilaf moist but still flaky.

ONION CHEESE STICKS

Melt ¼ cup butter or margarine in an oblong pan (13×9 inches) and cover evenly with ¼ cup minced sweet onion. Place 2 cups biscuit mix (your own recipe or packaged mix) in bowl and stir in ¾ cup shredded sharp Cheddar cheese, 1 teaspoon celery seed, a dash each of seasoned salt and seasoned pepper and about ⅔ cup milk. Mix to a soft dough and knead a few turns on a floured board. Roll into an oblong about 10×6 inches and cut in half crosswise. Cut into strips 1×3 inches long. Place in pan and turn in butter-onion mixture to coat evenly. Bake at 425° F. about 15 minutes, until sticks are crisp and golden. Makes 20.

APRICOT ASPIC

1 can (1 pound, 14 ounces) *¼ cup lemon juice*
 apricot halves   *2 cups canned pineapple juice*
3 envelopes unflavored gelatin *(not syrup)*
½ cup sugar   *Macédoine of Fruits (below)*

Drain apricot syrup into saucepan and add water if needed to make 1½ cups liquid. Sprinkle gelatin evenly over the top and add sugar. Stir over low heat until gelatin is melted. Purée apricots in blender and blend into hot syrup. Stir in lemon and pineapple juices. Cool or quick-chill in freezer until mixture is syrupy-thick but still liquid. Pour into 6-cup ring mold rinsed first in cold water. Cover with plastic wrap and chill overnight. Unmold on chilled platter and fill with honeyed fruits.

MACÉDOINE OF FRUITS

Halve and seed 2 cups black grapes. Pare and section 2 oranges. Peel, seed, and slice 2 peaches. Combine all with 2 cups canned or fresh pineapple tidbits. Combine and shake together in glass jar ¼ cup honey, 2 tablespoons each fresh lime juice and sherry, 1 tablespoon toasted sesame seeds. Pour over fruits and chill.

MIDSUMMER DROP-IN LUNCHEON FOR EIGHTEEN

VERMOUTH ORANGE BLOSSOMS
COLD PICKLED SALMON   DILL OR YOGURT MAYONNAISE
BASKET OF ASSORTED DARK BREADS
MUSHROOM CHEESE TART   BEAN SALAD MIMOSA
MELON AND FRUIT PLATTER   MACAROONS*
COFFEE   TEA

The drop-in luncheon is a leisurely, come-and-go affair, served over several hours, usually eleven-thirty to three o'clock. It's more flexible and informal than a regular luncheon. You can invite more guests with this kind of party, since (hopefully) they don't all arrive at the same time or stay the full stated hours of your invitation. Food should be the "fork or pickup kind" that will look pretty and taste fresh over several hours.

Do Ahead: You can pickle the salmon a week in advance and let it mellow in the refrigerator. Make the cookies anytime during the week. To serve eighteen, you will need three of the mushroom tarts, which can be made a few days ahead and frozen. However, I prefer to make the pastry several days in advance, refrigerate, and then prebake the day before the luncheon. At the same time I sauté mushrooms and green onions for the filling, measure and combine rest of filling ingredients, cover them tightly, and refrigerate overnight. First thing next morning, I fill and bake the tarts to be warmed briefly just before serving. They puff up a little less than fresh from the oven, but they cut more easily and the flavor is even better. Cook the green beans and eggs for the salad the day before also and prepare the French dressing and mayonnaise sauce.

About 2 hours before the luncheon, fix the vermouth drink, the melons and fruits, and garnishes for the salmon platter. Chill everything. Have plenty of back-up extras so you can keep the serving platters on the buffet looking fresh and attractive all during the luncheon.

VERMOUTH ORANGE BLOSSOMS

Combine in glass jars with screw tops: 3 cans (6 ounces each) frozen orange juice concentrate, 4½ cups cold water, 2 tablespoons fresh lemon juice, and 1 bottle (⅘ quart) dry vermouth. Mix well and chill. Shake well with a few ice cubes and pour into cold pitcher. Serve in small glasses. Makes 24 to 28 cocktail-size (⅓ cup) glasses.

COLD PICKLED SALMON

One big piece of salmon on a platter is spectacular-looking for a summer party, but it's more difficult to cook and serve than salmon steaks. Both taste the same, so let your situation and cooking abilities determine which you'll use.

2 quarts water, or to cover fish	*3 pounds each, or several small*
2 tablespoons mixed pickling	*steaks) (See note)*
spices	*1 lemon, thinly sliced*
1 onion, sliced	*3 tablespoons chopped fresh dill*
1 carrot, sliced	*(or 1 tablespoon dried dill)*
2 sprigs parsley	*6 tablespoons sugar*
2 teaspoons dill seed	*Sliced cucumbers, cherry*
1 tablespoon salt	*tomatoes*
¾ cup vinegar	*Dill or Yogurt Mayonnaise*
4 to 6 pounds fresh salmon (one	*(below)*
piece, or 2 large fillets of 2 or	

Put water in pan large enough to hold salmon (cut large piece in two if necessary) and add pickling spices, 2 onion slices, carrot, parsley, dill seed, salt, and vinegar. Heat to boiling, then simmer gently for 10 minutes. Add fish tied loosely in cheesecloth. Cook gently—don't allow the water to boil, but just to ruffle the surface slightly—until fish looks whitish and opaque. It takes about 10 minutes for steaks, about 15 to 20 minutes for the fillets or large piece. Do not overcook, as it's going to be in pickling liquid for several days. Lift out fish or pour off liquid and save it. Cool fish enough to handle, then place in shallow glass dish with rest of onion slices, lemon, and dill. Add sugar to pickling liquid and pour over fish. If it doesn't cover fish, heat more water and vinegar (2 parts water, 1 part vinegar) and add to dish. Place plate on top of fish to keep it submerged. Cover and chill for several days.

To serve, remove skin and bones from steaks and cut fish into neat

2-inch pieces. Mound on large platter. For large piece, carefully lift top
half of salmon off and pull out backbone. Skin fish, put back together,
and place on platter. For boned fillets, simply skin. Slice carefully but
keep slices together and shape of fish intact. Ladle a little pickling
liquid over fish to keep it moist and shiny. Decorate platter with sliced
cucumbers, cherry tomatoes, and sprays of fresh dill if you have it.
Serve with Dill or Yogurt Mayonnaise.
Note: Other fish, such as swordfish or halibut, may be used.

DILL MAYONNAISE

Season 2½ cups mayonnaise with 2 tablespoons chopped fresh dill or
2 teaspoons dried dill weed and a little lemon juice. Chill.

YOGURT MAYONNAISE

Combine 1 cup each mayonnaise and plain low-fat yogurt and season
with 2 teaspoons Dijon-type mustard and 2 teaspoons each minced
fresh parsley, tarragon, chives, and a few snips Oriental garlic if you
have it in your herb garden (looks like chives but has more exotic
flavor).

MUSHROOM CHEESE TART

This is enough filling and pastry for one 9-inch glass pie pan. You will
need 3 pies for this party.

Pastry (Pâte Brisée*)	*3 eggs*
4 green onions and tops, sliced	*1 cup half-and-half (milk and*
3 tablespoons butter or margarine	*cream)*
1 pound fresh mushrooms	*Freshly ground pepper*
1 teaspoon salt	*Generous dash nutmeg*
1 teaspoon fresh lemon juice	*¾ cup grated Swiss cheese*
1 tablespoon flour	*Paprika*

Roll pastry ⅛ inch thick and 2 inches larger all around than your pan.
Roll pastry onto rolling pin, lift over pan and unroll. Allow pastry to
settle into pan easily. Without stretching it, press neatly on bottom and
sides of pan. Trim overhang ½ inch larger than pan, fold it under,
and press to the rim in a sort of fat rounded edge. Pinch into a fancy
fluted edge with your fingers or press with tines of fork. Prick bottom of
pastry with fork and line with foil. Fill with dry beans to hold pastry

sides in place as it bakes. You can also protect the rim from over-
browning with a band of foil. Prebake shell at 400° F. for 10 minutes.
Remove foil and beans and bake for 5 to 10 minutes longer, just until
it begins to color. Cool.

Cook onions in butter until soft and golden in large heavy enameled
or stainless steel skillet (your trusty black iron pan will darken the
mushrooms). Trim mushrooms and rinse quickly or wipe with damp
paper towels. Slice lengthwise and add to onions. Cook and stir over
moderate heat for 2 to 3 minutes, then mix in salt and lemon juice.
Cover and simmer gently for about 2 minutes. Sprinkle with flour and
cook uncovered until mushroom liquid has thickened. (May be prepared up to here day before. Cover with plastic wrap pressed closely
onto mushrooms, then cover dish. Refrigerate.) Beat eggs just enough
to blend, then stir in half-and-half and seasonings to taste. Turn mushrooms into prepared pie shell and add egg mixture. Sprinkle wth cheese
and stir through lightly with fork without touching pastry. Dash with
paprika. Bake at 350° F. for 30 to 35 minutes, until puffed and lightly
browned. Cool at least for 15 minutes before cutting. If baked ahead,
warm up in 350° F. oven for about 10 minutes. Makes 6 servings.

BEAN SALAD MIMOSA

Wash and trim 4½ pounds fresh young tender green beans and cut into
2-inch pieces. Drop into a large kettle of boiling water salted with 1
tablespoon salt. Cook briskly, uncovered, for 5 minutes. Cover loosely
and cook for 5 to 10 minutes longer, raising lid often, until beans are
still crisp-tender. Drain and place at once in glass dish or bowl. Cooked
this way, they should still be beautifully green. Add ½ teaspoon each
dried tarragon and sweet basil leaves, a generous dash of nutmeg to
1½ cups Classic French Dressing.* Stir into beans, one tablespoon at
a time, just enough dressing to make beans shiny. There should be none
in bottom of dish—too much makes beans heavy and soggy. Cool, then
cover and refrigerate. They may be stored in a plastic bag. Shake and
turn occasionally to marinate beans. Hard-cook and chill 4 eggs. Just
before serving chop egg whites coarsely and add to beans with a bunch
of green onions, sliced. Place beans in glass bowl rimmed with small
leaves of Boston or Bibb lettuce if you like. Drizzle with a little dressing,
then drift sieved or finely chopped egg yolks over the top. Divide egg
yolks into 3 little plastic bag parcels after you chop them so you can
add a little to beans each time you replenish bowl on buffet table.

MELON AND FRUIT PLATTER

Arrange pared crescents of honeydew, cranshaw, or cantaloupe, or some of each, attractively on a platter with strawberries-on-the-stem and tiny bunches of seedless green grapes. Tuck in wedges of lime for the melon and provide a little bowl of brown or powdered sugar for those who want it for their berries. One cranshaw and one honeydew or 3 cantaloupes are adequate for this luncheon.

GAMBLE HOUSE LUNCHEON
(For Thirty-Five)

SHERRY OR CHILLED VIN ROSÉ

TOMATO PIQUANT SOUP

BUILD-A-SALAD   FRESHLY BAKED BREAD

POPPY SEED DRESSING   CREAMY PINK DRESSING

PAKLAVA

COFFEE   TEA

Historic Gamble House was built in 1908 by internationally famous architects Greene and Greene. Located in Pasadena, California, it is now a cultural Heritage Landmark and an outstanding example of the American Craftsman movement. The Wednesday buffet luncheons put on by its Docent Council offer the fortunate thirty-five who can get a reservation an opportunity to share the traditional hospitality of this highly individual old home. This menu and recipes are from the cookbook *Luncheon/Gamble House,* compiled by the Docent Council.

The decorations and serving appointments for the Gamble House luncheons are always special and often include some of the lovely pieces which belonged to the original owners, David and Mary Gamble. For the luncheon above, the salad greens were presented in Mary Gamble's huge cut-glass punch bowl, the other addables in beautiful old crystal and silver compotes. On occasion, the desserts are served on the rare old plates seen in the butler's pantry.

Preceding the luncheon, guests sip sherry or chilled vin rosé in the spacious teak-paneled hall behind the famed Tiffany glass doors or on the terrace overlooking a magnificent sweep of gardens. It's an altogether pleasing and memorable experience. You can duplicate their menu for a successful buffet luncheon for one of your groups. But, unfortunately, you can't duplicate the Gamble House—that pleasure you must experience on the spot!

Do Ahead: The salad dressings may be made several days in advance. Cook the turkey rolls and ham the day before, cool and refrigerate before cutting into small cubes. Two days ahead, remove *fillo* dough (also called phyllo dough or strudel dough) from freezer and defrost overnight in the refrigerator. One day ahead, shape fillo dough into *paklavas* and refrigerate overnight. Bake early next morning. Defrost frozen bread dough overnight in refrigerator. Next morning, shape bread and let rise and bake so it can cool for at least 1 hour before luncheon. Wash and chill greens, prepare rest of vegetables and soup. Broil and crumble bacon.

TOMATO PIQUANT SOUP

This recipe makes 12 mugs of soup. For the Wednesday luncheons, the amounts are usually tripled or quadrupled.

1 can (8 ounces) tomato sauce	*1½ teaspoons salt*
2 cups condensed beef bouillon	*2 teaspoons sugar*
5½ cups water	*¼ teaspoon basil*
1 quart tomato juice	*4 or 5 drops Tabasco sauce*
½ teaspoon horseradish	

Mix all ingredients in large kettle and simmer until steaming hot. Taste for seasoning. You may want to add more Tabasco and basil if you like it zippier. Serve hot in mugs.

BUILD-A-SALAD

This varies with the season. The day I lunched at Gamble House, this was the colorful assortment offered: Diced ham and turkey, julienne strips of Swiss cheese, julienne strips of green and red pepper, halved cherry tomatoes, sliced green onions, crumbled bacon, alfalfa sprouts, the salad greens, and 2 dressings. Sliced celery or cucumber, carrot strips, shrimp, tuna chunks, Cheddar chunks, sliced avocado, julienne beets, hard-cooked eggs are other suggestions for this type salad.

Bowl of Greens: Allow 8 to 10 heads of an assortment of greens, usually a mixture of romaine, iceberg, Boston, or butter, spinach, and some chopped parsley. Wash, dry, and chill. Break greens into bite-size pieces into crystal punch bowl. Set a stack of service plates next to the greens with rest of the salad makings following it.

Diced Turkey: Roast by package directions 2 frozen turkey rolls or a frozen breast of turkey. Cool and dice.

Diced Ham: Sometimes the Docents bake a boneless ham. Otherwise, they purchase thickly sliced ham at a good delicatessen, dice and place in compote. About 3 pounds of ham is adequate.

Julienne of Swiss Cheese: Usually about 2 pounds of sliced Swiss cheese are purchased, then quickly cut into julienne strips.

Julienne of Red and Green Pepper: Three or 4 large sweet peppers are enough. Use the 2 colors when possible. Wash, seed, and cut into thin lengthwise strips.

Cherry Tomatoes: Wash about 3 baskets chilled cherry tomatoes and cut into halves.

Sliced Green Onions: Wash and slice 2 bunches green onions and a little of the tops.

Crisp Bacon: Broil or oven-bake 2 pounds bacon. Drain on paper towels and crumble.

Alfalfa Sprouts: Sprouts of various kinds, alfalfa, lentil, and the more familiar soybean sprouts, are available in health food stores and many supermarkets. They add a lot of crisp texture and good food value for little money. The Docents use them, particularly lentil and alfalfa, in salads and sandwiches, often in place of more time-consuming lettuce. Loose bean sprouts are found in the produce sections, the others usually in cartons. A 4-ounce carton of alfalfa sprouts, which makes 2 packed cups, goes a long, long way and is plenty for each guest to have a healthy sprinkle on her salad for this luncheon.

CREAMY PINK DRESSING

This is served in a glass bowl at the end of the salad buffet. You might halve this 2-quart recipe and double the poppy seed dressing since the Docents usually provide 2 quarts of dressing for their salad luncheons.

1 quart mayonnaise
1 bottle (12 to 14 ounces) chili
  sauce (the tomato type)

½ cup pickle relish
1 medium onion, minced
½ pint dairy sour cream

Mix all ingredients and chill. Keeps well refrigerated.

POPPY SEED DRESSING

1 egg
¼ cup sugar
¼ cup lemon juice
1 tablespoon poppy seeds
1 teaspoon dry mustard

1 teaspoon paprika
½ teaspoon onion salt
1½ cups salad oil
¼ cup honey

Combine first 7 ingredients and blend well with beater or wire whisk. Add by droplets ¼ cup oil, continuing to beat constantly. Slowly beat in rest of oil, beating continuously. Stir in honey and beat well. Chill. Makes 2 cups.

FRESHLY BAKED BREAD

Many interesting breads, rolls, and muffins are served at the Gamble House luncheons. The simplest are the yeast loaves baked from frozen bread dough. One loaf is served at each table for four. It's placed on a small board with a good knife so that each guest may slice her own. The loaves are slightly warm but cool enough to slice. Frozen bread dough is available in the frozen foods cases, in most markets (or freeze your own bread dough in loaves and bake later). Follow package directions for thawing and baking.

PAKLAVA

This is the Armenian spelling of the dessert called *baklava* in Greece. Docent Jean Devirian, editor of the Gamble House cookbook, worked out this unusual and fairly easy way to handle the tissue-thin leaves of fillo (*phyllo*) dough. Try it, it's much easier than the traditional layered baklava and a lighter dessert. Don't be discouraged if your first attempts aren't perfect. Your skill improves with practice. Frozen fillo or strudel dough can be found in Middle East markets and specialty shops.

*1 pound package frozen fillo
(phyllo) dough
3 cups sugar
1½ cups water
½ cup honey*

*½ pound (2 cubes) butter
2 tablespoons sugar mixed with
1 teaspoon cinnamon
½ pound thinly sliced walnuts*

Place frozen fillo dough in refrigerator overnight to thaw. Have everything else prepared and arranged for ease in using before you remove dough. It is tissue thin and fragile, and dries out and cracks incredibly fast. Although Jean Devirian does not suggest it, I found that a dish towel slightly dampened, not wet at all, kept the dough moist while I worked. I put one folded, slightly damp towel on the board, laid the dough not being worked on over it and covered it with another slightly damp towel while I worked on one thin sheet on the board. If you're fast as Jean is, just keep the unused leaves wrapped tightly in waxed paper and foil while you work.

First, make the syrup. Mix in saucepan sugar, water, and honey. Boil gently until slightly thickened, 3 to 5 minutes. (I add a tablespoon of lemon juice when I make it.) Set aside. Have ready 2 cooky sheets with ½-inch sides (they're usually called jelly roll pans). Melt butter and set beside cooky sheets along with a pastry brush. Mix sugar and cinnamon in small bowl and set beside cooky sheets. Set bowl of sliced walnuts alongside. Remove fillo dough from package and unroll it on board. You will find you have a folded stack of about 15 or so tissue-thin leaves or sheets of pastry. With sharp knife, cut layers in half lengthwise at the fold into 2 rectangles. Return one half, rerolled and carefully wrapped in foil or original package, to refrigerator. Lay rest on dampish towel, as described. Beginning at corners, carefully lift off one sheet and lay it on the board. Cover rest with dampish—but not wet—towel or foil to seal out air. Using both hands, gather or ripple the sheet of dough as you would crinkle tissue paper into a long, narrow pleated strip. Move both hands along length of dough to keep strip an even 1½ inches wide. Coil strip loosely into a pinwheel about 3½ inches across. Do not crush or force the coils together in a tight little round, but rather loosely coil them so they barely touch. Lift coils with spatula to cooky sheet and with brush, lightly "lay" on butter to cover dough completely. This seals the dough and stops it from breaking and cracking. Sprinkle with cinnamon-sugar. Continue to make coils, butter them, sprinkle with cinnamon sugar until you've used all the leaves in the first stack of dough. Each cooky sheet will hold 9 to 12 paklava. When all are buttered and sugared, sprinkle evenly and lavishly with sliced walnuts. Bake in 375° F. oven until they are light tan and crispy—feel them—about 20 minutes. Remove from oven and dribble 1 tablespoon of the syrup over each paklava. Then go back and dribble more syrup over each roll until they are well sauced. You may not use all of the syrup. These should be shaped the day before, covered with foil, and refrigerated. Make syrup the day you plan to bake the paklava, however. Make more paklava with the other half of dough or wrap it in original package and return to freezer until you're ready to use it. (One pound fillo dough makes 30 to 32 paklava.)

MIX-AND-SWITCH MENUS

FANCY LUNCHEON FOR TWELVE

WINE SPRITZERS*
LOBSTER MOUSSE   CHICKEN BREASTS, CIRCASSIAN*
HERB BUTTER BISCUITS   SALADE COMPOSÉE*
PAPAYA SHERBET ON THE HALF SHELL*
HOT COFFEE

Everything's delightfully cold and make-ahead except the hot biscuits. With the luncheon, serve a California Riesling or a Mosel wine like Urziger Würtzgarten.

LOBSTER MOUSSE

Follow recipe for Salmon Mousse* substituting bottled clam juice for the chicken broth and 4 cups cooked lobster meat for the salmon. Replace dill seasoning with fresh or dried tarragon and a generous pinch each of thyme and marjoram. Decorate platter with sliced cucumbers and serve with a bowl of Chef's Mayonnaise* flavored with tarragon and grated lemon peel.

HERB BUTTER BISCUITS

Make Zephyr Hot Biscuits* or use 3 packages refrigerated biscuits. Melt butter in bottom of baking pan, toss in minced chives and parsley. Turn biscuits in herb butter to coat evenly and bake as directed.

BRIDGE LUNCHEON FOR EIGHT

SHRIMP RICE SALAD   POPPY SEED ROLLS
CHOCOLATE WALNUT TORTE
HOT TEA   HOT COFFEE

Serve salad and rolls with hot tea for luncheon; the torte with coffee after the bridge game.

SHRIMP RICE SALAD

Follow directions for Spinach Rice Salad,* replacing spinach with 2 cups chopped celery and the bacon with 1½ pounds cooked, cleaned shrimp. After rice is tossed with half the French dressing, add ¼ cup mayonnaise and 1 teaspoon curry powder to rest of dressing. Toss with rice, vegetables, and shrimp. Garnish platter with tomato quarters and sliced hard-cooked eggs.

CHOCOLATE WALNUT TORTE

Make Chocolate Pecan Cake* batter and omit pecans. Bake in 2 (9-inch) round layers at 350° F. for 35 to 40 minutes. Cool and split carefully into 4 layers. Combine and chill for at least 1 hour 3 tablespoons powdered sugar and 1½ cups heavy cream. Beat until stiff and fold in ½ cup ground walnuts, 2 teaspoons vanilla. Spread between layers and on top. Decorate top with shaved chocolate.

MEN-ARE-INVITED LUNCHEON
(Planned For Eight)

MARTINIS OR GIBSONS
SOUPE AU PÍSTOU*   FRENCH ROLLS
TUNA SALAD PROVENÇAL
APPLE TART, NORMANDY*   COFFEE

Any time of day men love soup. Add an apple pie and you have a feast to their tastes. The day before, make the earthy soup but wait until next day to add the garlic-herb paste. Cook potatoes for the salad, also make pastry for tarts. With men on deck, you'll need two tarts. Bake next morning to serve warm. Assemble salad and chill it. Drink a California Zinfandel or Corbières.

TUNA SALAD PROVENÇAL

Make Salade Niçoise,* omitting cooked green beans. Replace them with a package of frozen artichoke hearts cooked and chilled in a little of the salad dressing.

III   Al Fresco Parties

Literally, al fresco means in the cool, and that's what these al fresco meals are all about. Casual, in some cases, a bit elegant in others, but all are relaxed, informal, hearty, and happy affairs.

Who knows, perhaps a picnic was the first buffet? When I think of a picnic, I see a gay cloth spread on a grassy slope near a stream—with foods galore covering the whole cloth. There are cold meats or a chicken, good breads for sandwiches, the ubiquitous deviled eggs, crisp finger vegetables, colorful fruits, a cake or cookies, and cold lemonade or bottles of wine or beer. Perhaps you picture a picnic in a park beneath giant trees? Or spread under a bright umbrella on the sand at the beach? No matter, they're all fun. The English are among the world's greatest picnickers, and I've planned a fairly simple English picnic with Cornish pasties for the main dish and their favorite seedcake for dessert. Another is a nostalgic American Fourth of July that will take you on a childhood journey back to a small town picnic, complete with baked ham, fried chicken, chocolate cake, and homemade ice cream.

On the elegant side is a Mediterranean patio party featuring an unusual cold Turkish chicken with a walnut sauce, hot lemony shrimp, and beautifully cool Greek oranges.

The poolside buffet with spicy grilled ribs and sausages, black beans and rice with a colorful *gazpacho* salad and watermelon for dessert is pure fun. So is the Mexican fiesta. It begins with Margaritas, proceeds through a delicious chicken dish cooked with pumpkin seeds and chiles, and finishes with lemon sherbet spiked with Kahlúa.

These menus can be served indoors as well as out. But everything tastes twice as good served in the open air. And these parties were planned with hearty, outdoor appetites in mind.

POOLSIDE SUPPER FOR EIGHT

SANGRÍA
POTTED CREAM CHEESE
GLAZED BEEF OR PORK RIBS   ITALIAN SAUSAGES
BLACK BEANS AND RICE
GAZPACHO SALAD
WATERMELON

A hearty supper for outdoor appetites. After hours of swim and sun everyone is twice as hungry as usual. An icy glass of the *sangría* will be welcome after the swim along with a nibble of the peppery cheese spread and later with the meat and beans. The sangría will serve 8, but it might be wise to have another batch chilling in the refrigerator. Spanish melon, cantaloupe, or cranshaw might be served along with the watermelon. Or, you might stuff the watermelon as I have suggested below.

Do Ahead: Soak the black beans two days ahead and cook them the day before. Their rich flavor improves on standing. In the morning make the cream cheese spread and its pepper sauce topping. Chill the melon and sangría makings. Two or three hours before supper, marinate ribs and poach sausages. Prepare the gazpacho salad and chill it. Grill the ribs and brown sausages over charcoal. Or oven-bake the ribs and brown sausages lightly in skillet while the rice cooks.

SANGRÍA

2 bottles dry red wine (a Napa
*   California Burgundy or*
*   Zinfandel or a dry Spanish or*
*   Italian wine)*
¾ cup sugar
1 cup fresh lemon juice
2 oranges, thinly sliced

2 lemons, thinly sliced
2 ounces Triple Sec
2 ounces brandy
2 bottles (7 ounces each) club
*   soda*
Ice

Combine all ingredients except soda and ice and chill. At serving time, pour into large pitcher or glass bowl over ice cubes. Add soda. Makes 8 to 12 servings.

POTTED CREAM CHEESE

Mash 12 ounces cream cheese until soft and blend in 2 tablespoons grated red radishes (about 4) and 1 tablespoon grated green onions. Pack into a mold that's wide and shallow so you'll have lots of top surface. This amount fits exactly into 3 fluted (3½-inch) tart pans and the molds make a pretty design when turned out on a plate. Chill for several hours. Mix together ½ cup A 1 Sauce, 1 tablespoon canned green chiles, forced through a sieve, or *salsa jalapeño* (Ortega) and a few drops Tabasco. It should be very hot to contrast with the creamy cheese.

Unmold cheese onto plate and spread hot sauce over the top and let it run down sides slightly. Serve with crackers or vegetable sticks. Provide spreaders so that with each bite of cheese you cut into a bit of the hot sauce topping. Matzo crackers are excellent with this.

GLAZED BEEF RIBS

Beef ribs or the bones cut from a standing ribs of beef (not short ribs, which need braising) are not often seen in the average supermarket. They're tender and delicious, however, and worth looking for. Ask your market man to save them for you when he makes an eye-of-the-rib roast. One or 2 ribs are an adequate serving with the hearty black beans and a slice or two of sausage. Use pork spareribs if you can't find beef ribs.

8 beef ribs, cut from uncooked　　*½ cup catsup*
　　rib roast (4 or 5 pounds)　　*¼ cup red wine vinegar*
Salt and pepper　　*2 tablespoons grated onion*
1 tablespoon dried rosemary　　*1 tablespoon Dijon mustard*
　　leaves　　*¼ cup beef broth*
½ cup A 1 Sauce

Rub ribs with salt, pepper, and rosemary. Place in shallow glass dish. Combine remaining ingredients, mix well, and pour over ribs. Marinate for 2 or 3 hours, turning occasionally. Remove from marinade and place in shallow metal roasting pan, using the curve of the ribs as rack. Roast at 350° F. for 1 hour to 1 hour 15 minutes, until glazed and tender. Baste every 20 minutes. For charcoaled ribs, place drained ribs, bone side down, 6 inches above coals. Grill for 30 to 40 minutes, turning often. Baste with marinade after about 20 minutes. Cook until meat is tender and glazed.

GLAZED PORK RIBS

Allow 3 or 4 ribs per person. Leave whole and rub with salt, pepper, and ground ginger. To marinade above, add 1 tablespoon sugar and 1 clove garlic, puréed. Pour over ribs and marinate for several hours. Drain and cook at 350° F. for 1 hour. Drain off fat. Baste with marinade and cook for 1 to 1½ hours longer, turning and basting often. Cut into single riblets. For charcoaled ribs, place over coals or weave on spit after ribs have baked one hour and fat is drained. Grill until tender and glazed, about 30 to 45 minutes, basting after the first 15 to 20 minutes.

ITALIAN SAUSAGES

A few slices of these are perfect with the black beans and contrast handsomely with the beef ribs.

Prick with fork 4 or 5 (1½ pounds) fresh Italian sausages—use some hot and some mild ones. Place in skillet and cover with cold water. Heat barely to simmering, then poach gently for about 10 minutes. Drain, cool, and refrigerate. When ready to serve, brown lightly in hot skillet or lay on charcoal grill to tinge lightly with brown. Cut into diagonal slices and place on warm platter with ribs.

BLACK BEANS AND RICE

Red beans also are served with rice in many Latin countries, particularly Brazil and the Caribbean. Black beans have a more distinctive flavor, however, and are usually available in larger supermarkets or Latin American specialty shops.

1 pound black beans	1½ quarts water
1 small ham hock or ¼ pound chunk salt pork	2 to 3 teaspoons salt
2 onions	1 cup dry red wine
2 cloves garlic	2 tablespoons salad oil
1 bay leaf	Freshly ground black pepper
Pinch oregano	Cayenne pepper
	Fluffy Dry Rice (below)

Wash and pick over beans. Soak overnight in water to cover beans by 1 inch. Drain beans, add fresh water, and put in large heavy kettle with ham hock or salt pork, 1 onion, chopped, 1 clove garlic, minced, the bay leaf, and oregano. Heat to boiling, then lower heat and simmer gently until beans are tender, 2 to 2½ hours. Slow cooking is the Latin secret of their beautifully cooked beans, usually done in a heavy clay pot. Another trick is to keep the kettle half off the burner to keep liquid at a gentle, bare simmer. Add salt and wine the last half hour of cooking. When beans are tender, heat oil in skillet. Add remaining onion, sliced, and the garlic clove, minced. Cook gently until soft and add to beans. Scoop out about a cup of beans, add to skillet along with a little bean liquid. Mash with wooden spoon and fry until mixture is smooth. Pour back into bean pot. It should give the liquid a rich, slightly thickened texture. If there's any meat on ham bone, shred it and add to beans. Taste and add salt if needed, freshly ground pepper, and a few flicks of cayenne. Serve in a heavy, earthy-looking casserole alongside a similar dish of rice so guests may spoon beans over rice in proportions they prefer.

FLUFFY DRY RICE

If you have a heavy pan with a good tight-fitting lid, cook rice by this method. This is actually the Chinese way and never fails to produce flaky, dry rice, each grain fluffy and separate. Otherwise, cook rice by directions on package.

2 cups long grain white rice, not processed	3 cups cold water
	2 teaspoons salt

Wash rice through several waters until water is clear looking. Drain and put in heavy pot with tight-fitting lid. Add water and salt (you may add ½ cup more water if you prefer softer rice). Heat to boiling. Immediately turn heat to very lowest (or completely off on electric units) and let rice steam without stirring or raising lid for 25 minutes. Stir lightly with fork. Cover and let stand for 5 minutes. May be set in oven at 300° F. to keep warm. Makes 6 cups.

GAZPACHO SALAD

Vegetables and herby wine-flavored dressing are layered in salad bowl
and chilled for several hours before dinner.

⅓ cup red wine vinegar
1 teaspoon salt
1 clove garlic, crushed
½ teaspoon dried basil
½ teaspoon dried oregano
¼ teaspoon dried rosemary
1 bay leaf, broken
Freshly ground pepper
3 tablespoons dry red wine

1 cup olive oil (or other salad
oil)
2 onions, thinly sliced, separated
into rings
2 green sweet peppers, sliced
into thin rings
2 cucumbers, thinly sliced
5 large firm-ripe tomatoes, sliced
Bibb lettuce

Combine first 10 ingredients in bowl or covered jar. Mix or shake until
well blended. Two hours ahead, in large glass salad bowl alternate
layers of onion, green pepper, cucumber, and tomato. Drizzle each layer
with a little of the dressing. Cover with plastic film and refrigerate. Wash
and dry lettuce, chill in plastic bag. To serve, put lettuce in a salad bowl
near marinated salad, a stack of salad plates, and the extra dressing
nearby. Guests serve themselves lettuce, marinated salad, and dressing ad
lib.

WATERMELON
(Plain, Spiked, or Stuffed)

Melons are so good served simply with salt or a wedge of lime or lemon
I seldom dress them up. For this buffet, though, if you want to make a
dramatic dessert, spike the melon or stuff it. To spike it, cut a 2-inch plug
out of melon, pour in some gin, sherry, or port. Replace plug, wrap
melon in foil, and chill. Cut in slices or wedges to serve. For a stuffed
watermelon, cut a thick lengthwise slice off one side. Cut out melon from
the rind in pretty oval scoops with a kitchen tablespoon (not a measur-
ing spoon). Remove seeds and combine scoops in large bowl with scoops
of honeydew or cantaloupe to make a pretty contrasting mixture. Add a
few seasonal berries. Combine 1 cup fresh orange juice and ¼ cup sugar
in small saucepan. Heat to boiling and simmer for a minute or two. Add
2 tablespoons apricot brandy or white crème de menthe, cool, and pour
over melon scoops. Chill. Place melon shell on large tray and fill with the
chilled melon, berries and liquid.

BARBECUE LAMB FEAST FOR EIGHT

PEEL-AND-DUNK SHRIMP   HOT PINK MAYONNAISE
BUTTERFLIED LEG OF LAMB
BARLEY PILAF   GHIVETCH
EXOTIC FRUIT COMPOTE
COFFEE

A leg of lamb grilled over charcoal is perfect for an outdoor feast, but it's difficult to carve attractively. To avoid this problem, ask your meat man to bone the lamb for you (unless you're good at this) so it can be cut open and laid back like a book or butterfly. It makes a flattish roast, roughly 2 to 2½ inches thick, that takes on rich flavors when marinated before you grill it. And, it slices easily and beautifully. With it serve the barley pilaf. If you haven't tried this grain, please do. It has a pleasant nutty flavor and texture that's good contrast for the lamb. If you prefer not to venture, serve Butter Brown Potatoes* or Rice Pilaf with Pine Nuts.* While the lamb cooks, keep your guests busy and happy with the spicy peel-and-dunk shrimp and whatever libations you provide. Wine or beer would be good or the usual highballs and cocktails.

The *ghivetch,* a colorful Balkan mixture of vegetables baked and served cold, makes an interesting menu change also. To end this hearty feast, the exotic fruit compote is appropriate. Add some crisp cookies, if you like, such as the Vanilla Crescents* or Cream Cheese Wafers* sprinkled with sesame seeds.

When the lamb is cooked, transfer it to a carving board and place on one end of the table or a serving cart with warm plates. Have your husband or host for the evening slice it and serve each guest. Place the barley and vegetable dish on the patio table set with gay cloth or mats, napkins, and silver where guests may serve themselves. A good Beaujolais, such as Fleurie or Moulin-à-vent, or a California Gamay would be pleasant to drink with this meal.

Do Ahead: If you plan to serve cookies and they're the refrigerator type, make dough at least 2 days in advance and bake cookies the following day. Prepare and cook the ghivetch the day before the party so it can chill overnight. Make marinade for lamb, pour over lamb, and marinate overnight. Cook unpeeled shrimp and chill overnight in spicy liquid. Next day make mayonnaise dunk for shrimp. Assemble fruit bowl so it can chill for about 2 hours before dinner. Remove lamb from refrigerator at least an hour before you plan to start cooking it. Start charcoal grill so coals will be ready about an hour before you plan to serve. Get barley casserole ready so it can bake in oven while the lamb cooks.

PEEL-AND-DUNK SHRIMP

This is a favorite way to cook and serve shrimp along our Southern Gulf—in the shell, to be peeled and dunked by each guest. Southerners cook shrimp with their own blend of herbs and spices. I've substituted mixed pickling spices which include many of their favorite seasonings. Shrimp may be served hot and dipped in melted butter or cold, as I've suggested here, with a sharp mayonnaise dunk.

Combine in large kettle or pot 2 tablespoons mixed pickling spices, 3 garlic cloves, 2 sliced lemons, 1 sliced onion, handful of celery leaves, 1½ tablespoons salt, and at least 2 quarts water. Heat to boiling and add 3 pounds washed, unpeeled large shrimp. When water boils again, reduce heat and simmer shrimp for 5 to 7 minutes, depending on size, or until shells are pink. Cool shrimp in spicy liquid, then pour into bowl with spices and enough liquid to cover them. Cover with foil and refrigerate overnight. Drain and pile in a large bowl or napkin-lined basket. Serve with bowl of Hot Pink Mayonnaise. Guests peel their own shrimp and dunk in the sauce. Provide a big bowl or basket for the shells and tons of paper napkins.

HOT PINK MAYONNAISE

Season 2 cups mayonnaise to taste with Worcestershire sauce, Tabasco, crushed garlic, and a little catsup to color pink.

BUTTERFLIED LEG OF LAMB

Directions are given here for charcoaled lamb. It may be cooked in the broiler and oven. Most important to remember, either way, serve it pink and juicy. If overcooked, it will be dry and rather tasteless.

1 large (6- to 7-pound) leg of lamb, boned and butterflied
2 cloves garlic, split
Thick slice lemon
2 teaspoons salt
Freshly ground black pepper
1 teaspoon crumbled dried rosemary leaves

Seeds of 2 or 3 cardamom pods
¼ teaspoon nutmeg
½ teaspoon ground cloves
½ cup finely chopped onion
2 tablespoons lemon juice
¼ cup red wine vinegar
⅔ cup olive or other salad oil

As suggested, have meat man bone leg of lamb, and cut it so it may be laid out flat, butterfly style. Place in glass or ceramic dish and rub all over with garlic, lemon, salt and pepper. Put garlic in small bowl or mortar and blend with wooden spoon or pestle with the rosemary, cardamon seeds, nutmeg, and cloves. Rub well into surfaces of lamb. Combine remaining ingredients and pour over lamb. Cover and marinate overnight in refrigerator. If convenient, turn meat occasionally, to marinate evenly.

To cook, drain off marinade and save it for basting. Scoop out the onions, as they char easily. Place lamb, skin or fat side up, on grill 8 to 10 inches from medium-hot coals. Grill, basting with marinade, until well browned on one side, about 20 minutes. Do not cook too fast. Turn and grill for another 20 minutes to brown fat side. Test with a sharp knife to estimate how much longer to cook meat. Timing will depend on thickness of meat and the coals, but 5 to 15 minutes longer should be about right for juicy pink lamb. Transfer to a carving board and cut into ½-inch-thick slices. Serve hot.

Oven-Cooked Butterflied Lamb—Drain marinade and onions from lamb. Place lamb in broiler pan (not on rack) with skin or fat side down. Place pan as far as possible from heat and broil until browned, about 10 minutes. Baste and turn. Broil second side for about 10 minutes. Place pan in hot oven (400° F.) and cook, basting with pan juices and marinade, for 15 to 20 minutes longer. Remember, you are not roasting a bone-in leg of lamb, but rather a sort of thick lamb steak. Overcooking will make it dry and uninteresting.

BARLEY PILAF

Cashews, which have a texture rather like pine nuts and pistachios and are less expensive than either, add an exotic taste and texture to the barley.

½ cup butter or margarine	*Freshly ground black pepper*
1 large onion, chopped	*½ cup finely chopped green*
2 cups pearl barley	*onions*
5 cups (approximately) hot	*¼ cup finely chopped parsley*
chicken broth	*1 cup lightly salted toasted*
1½ teaspoons salt	*cashews*

Heat butter in large heavy skillet and add onion. Cook until soft and golden. Add barley and stir about over low heat until grains are coated with fat and lightly tanned but not brown. Transfer to a large (2-quart) buttered casserole and add about ⅔ of the boiling chicken broth or enough to cover barley generously. Season with salt and pepper. You may need more salt later—it depends on the broth. Cover dish tightly and bake in 350° F. oven for 25 to 30 minutes. Stir lightly with fork and stir in green onions, parsley, and rest of broth. Cook for about 15 minutes longer or until broth is absorbed and barley grains are puffed and tender. Adjust seasonings. Keep warm in slow oven until ready to serve. Toss in whole cashews just before serving.

GHIVETCH
(Balkan Vegetable Dish)

This Rumanian vegetable stew has many of the ingredients you find in the popular *ratatouille* of France and *caponata* of Italy—tomatoes, peppers, zucchini, garlic, olive oil. This dish is lighter, however, since the vegetables are baked, not fried. They will stay colorful and crisp-tender if you don't overcook. Vary the ingredients according to the market's bounty. And serve hot or cold. I prefer it cold, particularly for this menu.

2 cups diagonal slices fresh green beans
1½ cups diagonal slices carrot (3 or 4 carrots)
1 cup diagonal slices green celery
3 or 4 small unpeeled zucchini, sliced thickly on diagonal
1 small head cauliflower, broken into flowerets
1 green sweet pepper, cut into ½-inch strips
1 red sweet pepper, cut into ½-inch strips
4 firm-ripe tomatoes, cut into wedges

½ cup olive oil
2 teaspoons salt
2 large cloves garlic, crushed
½ teaspoon dried leaf tarragon
½ teaspoon dried marjoram
½ teaspoon fennel seeds
Pinch of dill seeds
¼ cup chopped parsley
Freshly ground black pepper
1 cup beef bouillon
Lemon wedges and cruet of wine vinegar

Wash and prepare vegetables and pile into a shallow baking dish (about 9 × 13 inches). Pour a spoonful or two of the oil over them and mix it through with your fingers until they are coated and shiny. This helps vegetables retain color. Heat rest of oil with remaining ingredients (except lemon and vinegar) to boiling and pour over vegetables. Mix well and cover tightly with lid or foil. Bake at 350° F. for about 45 minutes, or only until crisp-tender. To help retain color, do not raise lid during cooking. Cool in covered dish. Taste and adjust seasonings. Chill overnight. Serve with lemon wedges or a cruet of wine vinegar, or both.

EXOTIC FRUIT COMPOTE

Easy to make, delicious, and appealing.

4 navel oranges
1 cup fresh California dates
1 cup preserved kumquats
3 large, brown-flecked bananas
½ cup orange marmalade

¼ cup Cointreau
2 tablespoons anisette liqueur
1 cup fresh orange juice
½ cup blanched almond slivers,
lightly toasted

Peel oranges, slice into cartwheels, and arrange neatly in shallow crystal bowl. Cut dates from pits into matchstick slivers. Cut half the kumquats into slivers. Sprinkle half the dates and kumquats over oranges. Peel bananas and slice thickly on the diagonal. Arrange over the oranges. Sprinkle with rest of the fruit slivers and the whole kumquats. Mix marmalade, liqueurs, and orange juice and pour over fruits. Cover and chill for 2 or 3 hours. Top with toasted almonds just before serving. Serve with crisp cookies if you like.

PASTY PICNIC FOR EIGHT

ICE CHEST OF RAW VEGETABLES
CAMBRIDGE SAUCE
CORNISH PASTIES   MUSTARD PICKLES
HARD-COOKED EGGS
BECKY'S FRUIT ICE CREAM
ENGLISH SEEDCAKE   COFFEE

Pasties make a delicious out-of-hand meal that's good warm or cold. My Cornish mother-in-law taught me how to make these savory meat turnovers, and I frequently serve them for special family occasions or guests. She used part kidney suet in her pastry; I prefer part butter. Mustard pickles are traditional with pasties, and the sharp contrast of flavors is excellent. We like to drink beer with this meal, while others feel a good red wine is the best choice. Put plenty of ice in an ice chest or two (you can buy lightweight, inexpensive ones at supermarkets and drugstores) and pack with your favorite raw vegetables, the Cambridge sauce, eggs, and beer. The other foods, dishes, and a colorful picnic cloth can go into a regular hamper. The ice cream goes along in its own freezer.

Do Ahead: Make pastry and bake seedcake several days ahead. The day before: Prepare pasties and set on cooky sheets. Wrap in foil and freeze. Hard-cook eggs, make Cambridge sauce, and clean vegetables and pack in plastic bags. Mix the ice-cream makings and refrigerate overnight. Next morning: Bake pasties so they'll be fresh out of the oven when you pack them. Cool slightly, wrap in foil, then in layers of newspapers. They will stay warm for several hours. You can also reheat them on the picnic grill in their foil wrap while coffee is being made. Slice vegetables, cut into sticks, etc., and pack in plastic bags. Freeze ice cream, repack, and wrap in heavy towels or canvas and newspapers.

ICE CHEST OF RAW VEGETABLES

Use whatever you like and what's best in the markets. And prepare plenty, for these are to be munched on with a drink or glass of beer before you eat the pasties and along with them later. Pick-up sticks of celery, carrot, and green peppers are always popular. Also, crisp young radishes and cherry tomatoes, half-moons of raw white turnip, slivers of fennel, flowerets of broccoli and cauliflower. Sticks or slices of unpeeled cucumber are good if they're young and small and unwaxed. Otherwise peel them. Pack into plastic bags with a few ice cubes, then into the ice chest. On the picnic table arrange everything in neat groups in a large shallow bowl. Add a few ice cubes to keep everything crackle crisp. Set bowl of Cambridge sauce alongside for dunking.

CAMBRIDGE SAUCE

Actually a mayonnaise sauce with Cambridge seasonings. Sieve a hard-cooked egg into 1½ cups mayonnaise. Blend in ½ teaspoon dry mustard, 2 minced anchovy fillets, ½ teaspoon dried tarragon, 2 teaspoons each minced shallot and drained capers. Season with a speck of cayenne pepper and a few drops tarragon vinegar if sauce seems to need more sharpness.

CORNISH PASTIES

Some recipes add turnip or carrot, but that's heresy in the Bateman family. The original thrifty pasty was long on potatoes and short on meat—we like them meaty.

Regular Pastry* (5 cups flour) or   *Freshly ground pepper*
    double recipe Quick Puff Paste*   *¼ teaspoon leaf thyme*
3 pounds beef round steak   *½ cup minced parsley*
3 to 4 medium potatoes   *6 tablespoons butter (or use part*
1½ cups chopped onion   *chopped kidney suet)*
Salt   *1 egg yolk*

Make pastry ahead and chill. Trim meat and cut into small cubes less than ½ inch each. Put in large bowl. Pare potatoes, slice thin, then dice. Add to meat. Stir in onion and season well with about 1½ teaspoons salt, plenty of freshly ground pepper, crumbled thyme, and parsley. Cut pastry into 8 equal pieces for ease in handling and roll each about ¼ inch thick and cut into an 8-inch round. Brush edges with water. Put a compact mound of filling on half of each pastry, leaving a margin all around. Dot with butter. Fold pastry over to enclose filling and pinch edges together to seal or press with tines of fork. Prick top with fork. With wide spatula lift pasties carefully to cooky sheets and brush with egg yolk beaten with a tablespoon water. Bake at 400° F. for about 15 minutes. Reduce heat to 350° F. and bake for 30 to 40 minutes longer, until crust is browned and meat is tender.

To Freeze Pasties: Place pasties on cooky sheets and do not glaze with egg wash. Wrap in foil and freeze overnight. Unwrap and brush with egg wash. Bake at 400° F. for 20 minutes, then at 350° F. for 40 to 50 minutes.

MUSTARD PICKLES

Mother Bateman made her mustard pickles when tiny pickling cucumbers, button-size onions, and green tomatoes were in season. Homemade pickles are very worth while so watch your markets for these vegetables if you want to make your own. A good recipe for mixed mustard pickles can be found in such basic cookbooks as the *Fannie Farmer Cook Book*. They can also be purchased in fine foods shops and large supermarkets.

HARD-COOKED EGGS

What's a picnic without these? Take along plenty of salt and pepper. They're also great with a dab of the Cambridge sauce. Cover one dozen eggs with cold water. With cover on pan slightly ajar heat to boiling. Cover pan tightly, turn off heat, and allow eggs to stand for 15 minutes. Crack shells under cool water so eggs will peel easily later. Put in plastic bag and refrigerate.

BECKY'S FRUIT ICE CREAM

If you don't have a crank-turned ice-cream freezer, serve strawberries and heavy cream, unwhipped, instead. This recipe makes a gallon of incomparable ice cream. Reduce amounts for a smaller freezer.

3 large oranges
Juice of 2 large lemons
2 large bananas
1 can (8 ounces) crushed
    pineapple
1 (10-ounce) box frozen red
    raspberries (optional)

2 large eggs
3 cups sugar
1 quart half-and-half
1 cup heavy cream, whipped

Grate peel from 2 oranges and add to juice of all 3. Put in blender container with lemon juice, sliced bananas, and pineapple. Whiz in blender (in 2 batches if necessary) just until mushy but not completely liquefied. If you use the raspberries—they do add an exquisite color and fragrance —purée them with other fruits and add the juice of another lemon. Beat eggs with sugar and blend in half-and-half. Combine with fruit purée and chill for several hours or overnight. Fold in whipped cream.

To freeze: Have ready crushed ice and coarse (rock) salt—5 to 6 parts ice to 1 part salt. This smaller proportion of salt to ice takes ice cream longer to freeze but gives it a finer texture. Scald ice-cream can, rinse in cool water, and set in the ice-cream bucket. Fit dasher into place and fill can about ¾ full with cream mixture. Put on lid and secure the hand-crank attachment. Test by turning a few times. Pack bucket with alternate layers of crushed ice and salt to slightly above the level of cream. Let stand for 5 minutes. Put a pan under side drip spout to catch draining salt water. Begin turning crank slowly and steadily. Add more salt and ice as ice melts. After cream is frozen to a mush, in 5 to 10 minutes, turn crank more rapidly until ice cream is stiff and crank will barely turn. Drain off water. Wipe ice and salt from lid and remove it. Lift out dasher, scrape it and pack ice cream down with a spoon. Cover with foil, then replace lid and plug the opening with a cork. Repack bucket with layers of ice and salt. Cover with a heavy cloth and newspapers and allow ice cream to ripen for several hours.

ENGLISH SEEDCAKE

This traditional English cake is more or less a poundcake with the haunting flavor and aroma that caraway seeds give. Add seeds to poundcake mix if you're pressed for time.

*1 cup (2 sticks) butter or
    margarine
6 eggs, separated
2 cups sifted all-purpose flour
½ teaspoon salt*

*Pinch of nutmeg
1 cup sugar
1 teaspoon vanilla
2 teaspoons caraway seed
Powdered sugar*

Allow butter to soften until workable. Separate eggs while cold and allow them to stand while you prepare rest of ingredients. Sift flour with salt and nutmeg. Cream the butter until light, then beat in sugar until mixture is light in color, fluffy and creamy in feel. Add egg yolks, one at a time, and beat hard after each addition. Beat for at least 2 minutes, until mixture is very light and fluffy. Using a rubber spatula or wooden spoon, gradually blend in flour, vanilla, and caraway seeds. Beat egg whites with separate (or clean) beaters until stiff and shiny but not dry. Gently fold into batter. Spoon into greased and floured small (9-inch) tube pan or Turk's-head mold. Bake at 350° F. for 60 to 70 minutes, or until cake shrinks slightly from sides of pan. Cool for 10 minutes, then turn out onto a wire rack to cool. Dust with powdered sugar. Wrap in foil and allow to ripen for several days. Serve in thin slices.

MEXICAN FIESTA FOR EIGHT

MARGARITAS   TOSTADITAS
SEVICHE IN AVOCADO SHELLS
POLLO EN PIPIÁN   GREEN CORN CASSEROLE
FRIJOLES REFRITOS   WARM TORTILLAS
MEXICAN BEER
LEMON SHERBET, KAHLÚA   COFFEE

Spicy and hearty Mexican food is always suitable for an outdoor party. This menu is a bit adventurous and includes several dishes that might be new to some of your guests. Invite friends who enjoy new flavors or are *aficionados* of Mexican foods. The chiles used here in most cases are the milder, less *picante* canned green chiles, which are easy to use and available almost everywhere. Let the fiesta start with Margaritas, which seem to have become almost as popular as martinis for a predinner drink in warm weather. With them, or as a first course, seviche served in avocado half shells is a pretty and provocative appetizer.

The *pollo en pipián* is a sort of uncomplicated *mole* made with green chiles, almonds, *tomatillos* (unique Mexican green tomatoes) and pumpkin seeds (*pepitas*) in a rather delicate sauce. With it serve a baked fresh corn casserole patterned after the marvelous green corn tamales made in both Mexico and our Southwest when fresh corn is in season. Though you don't need them with this menu, no Mexican fiesta is complete without beans and tortillas. Have at least a taste of creamy refried beans with a dab of sour cream for each guest. And warm tortillas. In the Southwest, fresh or fresh-frozen corn tortillas are available in Mexican stores and supermarkets. Around the country, canned and frozen tortillas can be purchased. If you do serve them, heat just before the other foods are ready. Or ask your guests to participate. Let each warm his own tortilla on a hot griddle.

If you want a salad or something crisp, add a platter of chilled shredded lettuce, topped with chopped tomatoes and a few pork cracklings (called *chicharrones* in Mexico). Dress with salt, pepper, and a little vinegar.

I use colorful Mexican pottery for this supper, Mexican handmade glasses, and a coarse, hand-woven table runner and napkins, all of which we've picked up on our various trips down there. Fantastic Mexican paper flowers in hot pinks, orange, and yellows would be fun to use—or a piñata—though I usually end up with sprays of our scarlet bougainvillaea, which says Mexico in a hurry, and our black pottery angel candlesticks from Oaxaca. Lots of green leaves interspersed with fresh lemons, limes, and small pineapples also make pretty and easy table decorations for a Mexican fiesta. Cold Mexican beer is the perfect drink for this party. And suggest Mexican cottons or other casual attire for your guests—they'll have more fun.

Do Ahead: Make lemon sherbet a day ahead so it can freeze overnight in the lemon shells, or buy a good lemon sherbet if you prefer. Beans, which always improve in flavor when made in advance, can be done several days ahead—or a week or more, frozen and reheated. Do the blender part of the pumpkin sauce the day before and finish it next day after you brown the chicken. The corn casserole and seviche must be prepared the day of the party. Make seviche first so fish can marinate 4 or 5 hours in the lime juice. Husk corn, cook grits, and assemble the casserole. Refrigerate until about an hour and 15 minutes before serving. Brown chicken and complete sauce. Heat chicken in sauce on top of the range or in the oven while casserole cooks the last half hour.

MARGARITAS

Serve these tequila cocktails very, very cold, and please, don't make them sweet—they lose their punch. Rub the rims of stemmed cocktail glasses with cut lime (or lemon) and twirl in coarse sea salt or kosher salt to coat well. Regular salt can be used but doesn't make such a pretty frosty rim. Set glasses upright and let rim dry. For each cocktail, pour over cracked ice in pitcher or martini mixer: 1½ to 2 ounces tequila, ½ ounce Cointreau or Triple Sec liqueur, and the juice of ½ lime or 1 tablespoon fresh lemon juice. Stir like crazy until very, very cold. Strain into the salt-rimmed glasses.

SEVICHE IN AVOCADO SHELLS

Several tropical countries have their favorite marinated "raw fish." This one is Mexican and uses juicy big Mexican limes called *limones*. Fear not, the fish is not raw, but cooked completely by the action of the acid in the lime juice.

> 2 pounds boneless, very fresh
> white-meat, firm-fleshed fish
> (sea bass, Spanish mackerel,
> red snapper, all are fine)
> 2 cups fresh lime juice (8 to 10
> big limes) (lemon juice may be
> used but doesn't give same
> flavor)
> Salt
> 1 onion, finely chopped
>
> 2 tomatoes, peeled, seeded, and
> chopped
> 1 to 2 tablespoons Mexican hot
> sauce (taco sauce or salsa
> jalapeña) or 2 to 3 tablespoons
> (milder) canned green chiles,
> chopped
> Chopped parsley or cilantro[1]
> 4 avocados

Cut fish into small cubes and place in shallow, nonmetallic dish. Cover with lime juice. Marinate for several hours in the refrigerator until fish becomes white and opaque like poached fish. Stir occasionally. When fish is completely cooked by the juice, season to taste with salt, the onion, and tomatoes. Add hot sauce to taste. Taco sauce or sauce from the *jalapeña* chiles is much hotter than the canned green chiles, so season accordingly. Chill.

To serve, cut 4 soft-ripe avocados into halves lengthwise, twist halves slightly, separate, and lift out seed. Rub cut surface of avocado with lime juice and sprinkle lightly with salt. Drain seviche (save a little of the liquid) and taste it. Should taste fresh, brisk, and rather hottish. Add more seasoning if needed. Heap into avocado halves set on small plates or in scallop shells. Drizzle with a little of the liquid and top with a little chopped parsley or *cilantro*. Serve with *tostaditas* (crisp-fried tortilla pieces) or corn chips.

[1] *Cilantro*—fresh green coriander leaves called cilantro in Mexico and used in many of their sauces. In Chinese markets it is called Chinese parsley. Use sparingly. It has a definite, unusual flavor not to everyone's liking.

POLLO EN PIPIÁN

My own rather simple version of chicken in pumpkin seed sauce from many recipes I've tried.

¼ cup pumpkin seeds[1] (pepitas)
¼ cup blanched almond slivers
½ teaspoon cuminseeds
2 cups chicken broth
2 chicken fryers (2½ to 3 pounds each)
Lemon juice
Salt and freshly ground pepper
2 tablespoons salad oil

2 tablespoons butter or margarine
1 large onion, chopped
2 cloves garlic, minced
½ teaspoon cinnamon
2 tablespoons chopped parsley
1 can (4 ounces) green chiles, rinsed, seeded, and chopped
1 can (10 ounces) tomatillos[2]

In small dry skillet, toast pumpkin seeds and almonds lightly over low heat until almonds are sort of golden-looking. Stir and watch carefully. Do not let them burn. Put in blender with cuminseeds and 1 cup chicken broth. Whiz until puréed. Set aside.

Cut chicken into serving pieces, blot dry, sprinkle with lemon juice, salt and pepper. Heat oil and butter in large heavy frying pan. Add chicken pieces in single layer—do not crowd in pan—and cook gently until browned on all sides. As it is browned, remove pieces to a shallow baking dish that can go to the table. Continue until all are browned. Pour off all but 2 tablespoons fat, add onion, and cook until soft. Stir in garlic, cinnamon, and 1 cup of broth. Cook gently for 2 or 3 minutes. Put in blender and add parsley, chiles, and drained tomatillos. Whiz until puréed. Return to frying pan and add puréed seeds, almonds, and broth. Cook and stir over low heat until sauce is hot and blended. Pour over chicken. To serve, heat in moderate oven (350° F.) until hot through, about 30 minutes.

[1] *Pumpkin Seeds*—Hulled, untoasted pumpkin seeds, usually called *pepitas,* are sold in health food stores, specialty shops, and many supermarkets. Mexicans use them in numerous sauces, particularly *mole verde.*
[2] *Tomatillos*—A variety of Mexican green tomato (not an unripe tomato at all). They are sold fresh in many Western markets and in cans in Mexican and specialty shops as *tomatillos enteros.* Their flavor is unique and there is no substitute for them. They're used in various sauces—*moles, salsa, verde,* etc.

GREEN CORN CASSEROLE

Fresh corn tamales are special, even in Mexico, and are usually reserved for fiestas. They are tricky to make, time-consuming, and require ingredients I'm not sure are available everywhere. This unauthentic casserole I dreamed up incorporates the good flavors of the Mexican green corn *tamal*—fresh sweet corn, cooked hominy grits, which have a delicate parched corn flavor akin to *masa* dough used in tamales, and green chiles and cheese. Good with grilled meats, too.

4 ears fresh corn
4 cups milk
1 teaspoon salt
1 cup hominy grits
¼ cup butter or margarine
2 teaspoons sugar
1½ cups aged Swiss cheese, shredded

1 can (4 ounces) green chiles, seeded and chopped
3 eggs
½ cup grated sharp Cheddar cheese

Cut kernels from corn. With back of knife, scrape out milky substance and add to kernels. You should have about 2 cups scraped corn. Heat milk, salt, and corn just to boiling and slowly stir in grits. Cook and stir over medium heat until smooth and thickened, about 5 minutes. Beat in butter, sugar, Swiss cheese, and chiles. Beat eggs lightly and stir a little of the hot mixture into them. Stir back into hot grits. Blend smooth and turn into a greased shallow 2½-quart casserole. Sprinkle Cheddar on top. Let stand for 30 minutes. Bake in 350° F. oven until firmish and golden on top, about 1 hour. Serve warm from dish.

FRIJOLES REFRITOS

Mashed beans rather than refried beans (*frijoles refritos*) might convey a better picture of these moist, velvet-rich beans that show up at practically every Mexican meal—from breakfast on.

1 pound pinto or Mexican pink beans (or red beans)
2 quarts water
2 teaspoons salt

1 clove garlic, mashed
½ cup bacon drippings or lard, divided
Dairy sour cream

Cook beans by directions for Pinto Beans* until nearly tender, about 1½ to 2 hours. Season with salt, garlic, and ¼ cup drippings or lard. Cook gently until very tender—30 minutes to 1 hour. In a large heavy skillet, heat rest of the drippings or lard and add a cupful of the beans. Mash and stir with a big wooden spoon, then stir in some of the bean liquid. Stir until smooth. Add more beans and liquid, mash and stir until you've added all the beans and liquid. Mixture should be creamy smooth and moist—and smell heavenly. Add more salt if needed. Serve in a pottery casserole with a bowl of sour cream on the side. Add a basket of warm tortillas if they're available in your markets.

WARM TORTILLAS

If frozen tortillas are used, defrost enough to separate. Dampen your fingers and rub lightly over surface of tortilla. Put on hot, dry griddle, one at a time, and turn almost immediately—before it becomes crisp. Tortillas must be kept soft and pliable. Remove from griddle in a few seconds by lifting one edge with your fingers as the Mexicans do. Pile in a warm bowl or pan lined with a clean towel or napkin. Fold towel over to cover tortillas and keep warm as each one is heated.

LEMON SHERBET, KAHLÚA

An unusual combination you must try to appreciate.

8 large lemons for shells (optional)	Dash of salt
	1 tablespoon zest of lemon peel
1⅓ cups sugar	¾ cup lemon juice
2 teaspoons unflavored gelatin	2 egg whites
2½ cups milk	Kahlúa (Mexican coffee liqueur)

Prepare lemon shells if you plan to use them. Cut a thin slice from the sides of 8 large lemons (or cut tops from large oranges if you prefer). Scrape out pulp with a spoon. Press juice from the lemon pulp and use it in the sherbet. Add more if needed. Combine in saucepan sugar, gelatin, and milk. Stir over low heat until gelatin is melted. Add salt and lemon zest (if you don't have a lemon zester that removes the yellow peel in thin, thin strips, remove peel with grater). Set aside to cool. Stir in lemon juice and pour into 1 large or 2 smaller freezing trays. Freeze until mushy-firm. Put mushy sherbet in chilled mixer bowl with egg whites. Beat until light and fluffy. Freeze again until firm enough to mound, then

heap into lemon shells. Freeze overnight. Arrange on a platter lined
with shiny green leaves. Set dessert plates and spoons nearby with a bottle
of Kahlúa. Guests drizzle it over their sherbet, ad lib.

INSIDE-OUT BUFFET FOR TWELVE

TARAMOSALATA
CRACKER BREAD OR VEGETABLE STICKS
SLICED TOMATOES AND ROASTED SWEET PEPPERS
CHICKEN BREASTS, CIRCASSIAN
LEMON SHRIMP   STUFFED MUSHROOMS
ARMENIAN BREAD
GREEK ORANGES   KOURABIEDES
ITALIAN COFFEE

This is a switch we call our inside-out party. We dine outdoors in our
bricked courtyard, but the buffet is set in the dining room just inside.
And most of the food is prepared ahead in the kitchen. For this summer
party, I made a floor-length cloth for our round dining table from a gay
flower-splashed wash-and-wear sheet. From another sheet I made match-
ing shorter cloths for the three tables we set up outdoors. With bright
summer flowers and leaves from our garden and fat blue candles everywhere, the dining room and courtyard looked like one big, cool garden.

Mediterranean foods seem especially appealing for an outdoor party.
We offered highballs with the *taramosalata,* but I also had a pitcher of
icy, very dry no-sugar Sangría,* which some of our guests drank both
before and during dinner. For others we had a light red Greek or Spanish wine and a chilled California Chablis.

Do Ahead: Almost all the food can be made in advance. Make the
cookies and bread a week ahead if you wish. Freeze bread in foil and reheat it to serve warm for dinner. However, the dough can be refrigerated up to 24 hours, and the bread's wonderful baked the day of
the party. You can roast the peppers several days in advance—they improve in the refrigerator. Plan to prepare the chicken breasts, walnut
sauce, and oranges the day before, the stuffed mushrooms and taramosalata the morning of the party.

You may vary this menu and do less cooking if your time is limited.
Roasted peppers are available in most Italian delicatessens and you can
buy the Armenian bread or use crisp French rolls. A bowl of fresh
strawberries chilled for an hour with a few spoonfuls of good brandy

Weekend brunch with Bloody Marys and creamy eggs in a chafing dish.
(*Photo courtesy Sterno, Inc.*)

Luncheon for a V.I.P. with cold halibut, warm crab quiche, and beautiful raspberry pear meringues. (*Photo courtesy Pacific Kitchen, Seattle.*)

and a little orange juice would make an easy replacement for the Greek oranges.

I baked the mushrooms just before dinner while the bread heated. At the last few moments, my husband quickly cooked the shrimp in a huge black skillet on our patio grill while I put the cold food platters, the warm bread, and mushrooms on the buffet. Wineglasses, silver, and napkins were already in place on the tables. After dinner I took the big crystal bowl of cool-looking Greek oranges outside on a tray and served them in the pretty blue glass dishes we use for fruits. Cookies were passed, and later Italian coffee and demitasse cups were brought out. A very successful party and worth the effort.

TARAMOSALATA

The Greeks make this with carp or mullet roe, which can be purchased in Armenian and Greek specialty stores. Otherwise, make it with red caviar (salmon roe), available in all supermarkets.

6 tablespoons lemon juice
⅓ cup chopped onion
4-ounce jar taramo (carp roe)
2 slices firm white bread
1 cup olive oil

Minced parsley
Armenian cracker bread or
  sesame crackers, and sticks of
  fennel and celery

Put lemon juice, onion, and *taramo* in blender. Remove crusts from bread and dip bread quickly in water and squeeze dry (if salmon roe is used, do not dip bread in water, and use 3 slices). Add to blender and whiz until smooth. Gradually blend in enough oil to make paste smooth, thick, and creamy. Pour into bowl, cover, and chill. Mound on serving dish and sprinkle with minced parsley. Serve with pieces of cracker bread or unsweetened sesame crackers and crisp sticks of fennel and celery. Decorate plate with black olives.

SLICED TOMATOES AND ROASTED SWEET PEPPERS

Wash and dry 6 firm green and red bell peppers and lay them on a gas burner directly over the flame turned medium high. Do only 2 or 3 at a time. Turn frequently with tongs or 2 spoons until the skins look burned and charred. (You may put peppers under the broiler for 10 to 12 minutes to char skins if you prefer. Turn often.) Lift peppers into sink and rub off skin under cold running water. Drain and dry on paper towels. Cut lengthwise into one-inch strips, cutting out seeds and membranes. Place in refrigerator dish and add 2 crushed cloves garlic and turn them in about ⅓ cup olive oil or just enough to make them shiny. Too much makes peppers heavy and soggy. Cover and refrigerate overnight or for several days.

To serve, arrange on a large platter in neat rows with 4 sliced big beefsteak tomatoes. These flavorful tomatoes need no dressing, but you may drizzle with a little olive oil, salt and freshly ground pepper, a few snippets of sweet marjoram, and bright parsley. Splash the whole platter with a few drops of lemon juice at the last moment.

CHICKEN BREASTS, CIRCASSIAN

This cold chicken with walnut sauce is a classic dish of the Circassian Turks and usually made with a whole chicken. It's much easier to make and serve with meaty chicken breasts only.

1 small onion, sliced
1 carrot, sliced
3 or 4 sprigs parsley
Generous dash cayenne pepper
2 whole cloves
2 cups chicken broth
4 whole chicken (fryer) breasts

1 teaspoon salt
3 slices firm-type white bread
1½ cups walnuts
Sweet Hungarian paprika
Lemon juice
Greek olives
Parsley

Combine in large shallow kettle the onion, carrot, parsley, cayenne, cloves, and broth. Add chicken, skin-up, cover and simmer gently for about 25 minutes. Add salt and cook for 15 to 20 minutes longer, until chicken is tender and white. Cool chicken, wrap in foil and refrigerate. Strain broth, saving carrot and onion. Boil broth rapidly if necessary to reduce to 1½ cups. Remove crusts and tear bread into pieces. Drop half of it into blender with half the walnuts. Whiz until finely ground, but light and powdery-looking. Empty blender and repeat with rest of bread and walnuts. Add half the stock, carrot, and onion. Blend for a few minutes. Add rest of bread-walnut mixture and stock and blend to a smooth paste. Season to taste with a good sweet Hungarian paprika, a little lemon juice, and salt if needed. Blend until smooth. Pull skin from chicken and lift meat from each breastbone in one piece. With sharp knife, slice thinly on the diagonal, or pull apart in long strips. Arrange neatly on large serving platter and spoon walnut sauce over it to mask completely. Cover with plastic wrap and chill until ready to serve. Decorate platter with black Greek olives and parsley.

LEMON SHRIMP

Simplicity itself with the true flavor of shrimp enhanced. Sauté quickly in olive oil lightly scented with bay leaves and garlic, then splash with lemon juice.

Shell, devein, and rinse 3 pounds jumbo shrimp (12 to 15 per pound) leaving tails intact. Blot dry on paper towels and lay in flat tray. Sprinkle with the juice of 2 large lemons and about 1 tablespoon sea salt or kosher salt. Cover and refrigerate until just before serving time. Ahead of time heat slowly for 2 or 3 minutes ½ cup olive oil with 2 crumbled bay leaves (Turkish) and a split clove of garlic. Set aside. To cook, blot shrimp lightly with paper towels. In a large, heavy 12-inch skillet, heat 2 or 3 tablespoons of the flavored oil (discard garlic) and add enough shrimp to cover bottom of pan. Cook and stir over a brisk heat until shrimp becomes pink and opaque, just 4 or 5 minutes. Remove to large serving platter, cover with foil, and keep warm. Continue to cook rest of shrimp, adding and heating oil each time. Sprinkle lightly with more fresh lemon juice, a little melted butter if you wish, and a shower of bright, minced fresh parsley. Serve at once with fat lemon wedges. Great with the warm Armenian bread.

STUFFED MUSHROOMS

Rinse 12 large mushrooms and blot with paper towels. Pull out stems and rub mushrooms with olive oil. Chop stems and cook with ½ cup minced onion, 1 minced clove garlic in 1 tablespoon olive oil and 2 tablespoons butter. When vegetables are soft and moisture has reduced, add 2 tablespoons minced parsley, 1 cup fine, soft bread crumbs, and 4 thin slices *prosciutto,* chopped. Toss for a few seconds, until crumbs are lightly browned. Season lightly with salt and pepper (prosciutto is salty), a pinch of crumbled oregano, and a few drops lemon juice. Rub mushrooms with olive oil and mound filling into them. Set in shallow baking dish and sprinkle tops with freshly grated Parmesan. Bake in hot oven (400° F.) for about 15 minutes.

ARMENIAN BREAD

This delicious flat loaf, which is different from *pita* with the balloonlike pocket, can be purchased in Middle East bakeries. But it's so much easier to make than most yeast breads I hope you'll try it. Dough can be refrigerated up to 24 hours. To approximate the baker's crisp crust, bake bread in the morning. Reheat in foil at 400° F. for 10 minutes or so with the top of foil opened loosely.

1¼ cups milk (or use all water)   Olive oil
1 cup very warm water   6 cups sifted, unbleached
2 packages active dry yeast   all-purpose flour
1½ tablespoons sugar   1 egg yolk
1½ teaspoons salt   ¼ cup sesame seeds

Heat milk just until bubbles form around edges, then cool to lukewarm. Rinse large bowl of electric mixer in hot water then add the very warm water. Sprinkle in yeast and sugar and stir to blend well. Stir in warm milk, salt, and ¼ cup olive oil. Blend on low speed of mixer. Add 3 cups flour and beat at medium speed for 5 minutes. Remove bowl from mixer and work in 2½ cups flour with a heavy wooden spoon, beating dough against sides of bowl. Sprinkle the ½ cup flour on board, turn dough onto it, and knead until it's smooth and feels springy and stretchy, about 5 minutes. Cover with plastic wrap and let rest for 20 minutes. Pound dough with your fists and knead for a few seconds to work out the air bubbles. Divide into 2 equal balls. Flatten each on greased cooky sheet into a flat round cake about 10 to 12 inches across. If you wish, pull a 3- to 4-inch piece of dough from middle, shape into a ball. Oil it and replace to give baked loaf a sort of two-level effect. Rub lightly with olive oil and let stand at room temperature for 20 minutes. (To refrigerate dough, cover rounds with plastic wrap and refrigerate from 2 to 24 hours. Remove chilled dough, uncover, and let stand at room temperature for 10 minutes before baking.) In either case, brush dough with egg yolk beaten lightly with a tablespoon water and sprinkle each loaf with 2 tablespoons sesame seeds. Bake in moderate oven (350° F.) for 30 to 40 minutes, or until crust is a deep golden brown. Cool on wire racks. Reheat as suggested. Cut in wedges or cut each loaf in half, then cut into oblong pieces. Makes 2 loaves.

GREEK ORANGES

The original recipe uses whole oranges and boils and drains the slivered peel several times. This way is simpler and the peel has more of the orange essence. Halved or thickly sliced oranges, though not as elegant as whole ones, are easier to eat for a buffet supper.

Allow 12 medium oranges or 8 to 10 large ones. The only work involved here is making the slivered peel. And that's easy with an orange or lemon zester (Philip Brown, popular food writer and lecturer, gave me one and I couldn't cook without it). This handy gadget makes 5 needle-thin slivers of the peel with each downward stroke the length of the orange. The whole orange is done in seconds, giving you 2 to 3 tablespoons slivers. You will need 1 cup slivers. Without a zester, pare orange part of peel off from white membrane in strips and scrape away any remaining membrane with tip of spoon. Stack several strips together on cutting board and cut into thin, thin julienne strips. Cover with cold water and boil for 10 minutes. Drain and rinse. Combine in deep saucepan 3 cups sugar, 2 cups water, and the peel. Boil briskly until syrupy, about 10 minutes. Pare oranges, cutting off all white membrane. Cut each into halves crosswise or into 4 thick slices. Place in large bowl. Pour boiling syrup over oranges and let stand for 10 minutes. Pour syrup back into pan and boil again for 10 minutes. Add a few drops red coloring to make the syrup a pinky-gold if you wish. About ¼ cup Grand Marnier or other orange liqueur may be added. Pour over oranges. Cool and chill. Serve oranges very cold with some syrup and peel over them.

KOURABIEDES

Elegant little shortbread cookies with a clove in each.

1 cup unsalted butter
½ cup powdered sugar
2 egg yolks
1 teaspoon vanilla

3 cups sifted all-purpose flour
½ teaspoon baking powder
4 dozen whole cloves

Beat butter and sugar together until light and creamy. Beat in egg yolks and vanilla. Sift together flour and baking powder and work it into the creamy mixture to make a soft dough. Work with wooden spoon or hands until smooth. Shape into 1-inch rolls on waxed paper and chill for at least 1 hour. Cut into 1-inch slices and shape into flattish balls. Place 1 inch apart on ungreased cooky sheets and stick a whole clove in each. Bake at 325° F. until pale gold in color, about 20 minutes. Cool on wire racks. Traditionally, these are sprinkled with sifted powdered sugar, but I prefer them plain. Makes about 4 dozen.

Greek Anise Cookies—Sometimes, I divide the dough in half and add a few drops of anise extract to half of it. The combination of anise and cloves is delicious.

ITALIAN COFFEE

It's difficult to duplicate at home the aromatic flavor of espresso as made in Italian restaurants in a large electric urn which forces steam under pressure through powdered coffee. If you have a small home-type espresso machine, use it by all means. Follow manufacturer's directions, which usually suggest 8 tablespoons fine grind Italian roast coffee to 1½ cups cold water. Otherwise, use a good Italian dark-roasted coffee, available either in cans or freshly roasted and ground, from a specialty coffee shop (and use good bottled water for a superior flavor). Make it very strong and black in a drip coffee maker and serve in demitasse cups (see Black Coffee*). Sugar, strips of lemon peel, or anisette may be offered with it.

NOSTALGIC FOURTH-OF-JULY PICNIC
(Expandable—but planned for 12)

HIBACHI HOT DOGS   POTATO CHIPS
PICKLES   OLIVES   CELERY   CHERRY TOMATOES
COKES   BEER   LEMONADE
SPICY GLAZED HAM   COLD FRIED CHICKEN
RYE BREAD   HOMEMADE BREAD*   FRENCH ROLLS
BUTTER   MUSTARD
TRESA'S POTATO SALAD   OVERNIGHT COLESLAW
SWEET-SOUR BEAN SALAD
HOMEMADE ICE CREAM   CHOCOLATE PECAN CAKE
COFFEE   ICED TEA*

The Fourth of July to me is like Christmas and Thanksgiving, a time for family celebrations and favorite, traditional foods. One of my happiest childhood memories recalls the annual July-Fourth picnic held on the shady church lawn in our small town. Everyone participated. Each mother brought her own special ham or cake, pickles and such to spread on the long tables the men had fashioned with boards laid over wooden sawhorses. If ever there was a lavish buffet, that was it. What fun it was to wander among the gaily covered tables laden with goodies from other kitchens. We always looked for Tresa's potato salad with the pretty egg slices all over the top. And Mrs. Whitely's pickles were the crispest in town. Everyone tried to taste my mother's chocolate cake. And sample, rather sparingly, the (strange and exotic to our simple young palates) roast chicken flavored with rosemary and stuffed with spicy Italian sausages our Italian neighbor brought.

We still have family picnics on the Fourth, but not with such a lavish display of food. Many of the old favorites, however, are included in the menu suggested here—baked ham glistening with spices and mustard, fried chicken, chocolate cake, and homemade ice cream. These recipes are not at all unusual—there's plenty of that kind elsewhere in the book —but they are all unusually good and timeless in their appeal. Many of these foods can be purchased at the delicatessen if you prefer, but they aren't the same as homemade. Or, for this kind of celebration, you might do as we do. Assign different family groups to make one or two dishes—one to bake the ham, another to fry the chickens, and so on. That way it's not much work for anyone.

Do Ahead: Everything, just about. If you make bread, bake it a week or more in advance and freeze it. Bake the ham two or three days in advance. Fry the chickens the day before and chill them—they taste better than hot. Make potato salad also, or cook potatoes and boil the eggs, then make salad the following morning. Make slaw and bean salad and refrigerate overnight. This is like Christmas; you'll have to do some juggling in your refrigerator space. Make the cake the day before also and frost it. Combine the ingredients for the ice cream and chill overnight. Freeze next morning. Pack the celery, pickles, etc., in plastic bags and carry to the picnic in an ice chest or two along with the salads and meats.

HIBACHI HOT DOGS

The youngsters usually do these and pass them around for everyone to nibble on with potato chips and a glass of beer or lemonade. Plan on one or two hot dogs for each person if the picnic lasts for several hours with the usual ball game, races, and so forth. Grill frankfurters on the hibachi over charcoal until brown. Cut into bite-size chunks and spear on picks. Pass with a dip made of catsup, hot prepared mustard, and chili powder to taste.

SPICY GLAZED HAM

This was the way my mother cooked her nonprocessed whole ham— simmered a long time in a spicy liquid then glazed. My revised method gives some of the old-fashioned ham taste to our modern convenience hams. It's worth the little effort, I think.

1 (6-pound) fully cooked boneless	*2 tablespoons cider vinegar*
ham	*1 bay leaf, broken in pieces*
White pepper	*½ dozen whole cloves*
2 cups apple cider	*1 cinnamon stick, broken in pieces*
Brown sugar	*Prepared mustard*

Place ham in roasting pan and rub all over with white pepper. Heat to boiling apple cider, ¼ cup brown sugar, vinegar, bay leaf, and whole spices. Simmer for about 5 minutes and pour over ham. Cover with foil and bake in 300° F. oven for about 1 hour or 10 to 12 minutes per pound. Baste occasionally. To glaze ham, remove foil and drain off most of the liquid. (Save it for a sauce when you serve ham hot.) Lather ham liberally with about 2 tablespoons prepared mustard, then sprinkle thickly with brown sugar. Dampen with a little of the spicy liquid. Cook at 425° F. for about 30 minutes or until glazed, basting frequently. Cool and slice thinly for sandwiches.

COLD FRIED CHICKEN

When properly done, tender and succulent fried chicken with a light crisp crust is one of America's great dishes. When it's greasy and soggy or cooked to death, it's pretty poor. There are dozens of ways to fry chicken—in the oven, dipped in milk and crumbs, rolled in corn meal, sizzled in deep fat—you name it. This is my favorite way.

Start with whole, very fresh fryers about 2½ pounds each. I like to cut them apart at the joints—poultry shears are a great help—and use the back for stock. Precut supermarket fryers are usually hacked apart, not necessarily at the joints, and this makes a difference in the appearance and taste of the finished chicken. If you don't want to bother, buy legs, breast, and thighs, allowing 2 to 3 pieces for each person. Rub chicken all over with fresh lemon juice and season with salt and freshly ground pepper. If you like more seasonings, add seasoned salt and a little marjoram. Let chicken stand for about 1 hour. Heat ½ inch fat in a large heavy skillet. There are varying opinions on the fat to use. I like half vegetable shortening or light oil and half butter heated in a black cast-iron skillet. Drop chicken pieces into a heavy brown paper bag containing flour and a generous dash of nutmeg. Shake to coat pieces evenly, then shake off the excess flour. Place in hot fat, the dark meat first, in a single uncrowded layer so chicken can brown evenly. Cook over medium heat until golden brown and crisp on the bottom, about 15 minutes. Turn pieces, add a little more butter if needed, and brown a little more slowly on second side. If it's cooked slowly and with constant attention, chicken will be done by the time it's browned all over and crisp. Otherwise, cover pan loosely so steam can escape and cook chicken for 10 to 15 minutes longer. When tender, remove lid and turn chicken back and forth to recrisp skin. Drain on crumpled paper towels. Cool, then place in covered dish or foil and refrigerate.

TRESA'S POTATO SALAD

6 large potatoes (about 2 pounds)
Salt
6 hard-cooked eggs
2 tablespoons prepared mustard
1 to 2 teaspoons sugar
2 to 3 tablespoons wine vinegar

¾ cup mayonnaise
½ cup finely chopped onion (see note below)
Freshly ground pepper
1 teaspoon celery seeds
Paprika

Cook potatoes in the jackets in boiling salted water until tender. Drain and return pan to heat for a few seconds to dry potatoes thoroughly. Cool. Peel eggs and mash 4 of the yolks with mustard, 1 teaspoon sugar, and 2 tablespoons vinegar. Stir into mayonnaise. Peel potatoes and cut into cubes. Chop 4 egg whites and add to potatoes with onion. Mix gently with enough of the dressing to make salad mound well, but not enough to make it wet and soggy (I harp on this soggy salad business a lot, but it's important). Season with about 1 teaspoon salt, plenty of freshly ground pepper, and the celery seeds. Taste and add more sugar, vinegar, and salt if needed. Heap into bowl, cover, and chill. To serve, sprinkle with paprika and cover with the 2 eggs, peeled and cut into neat slices with an egg slicer.
Note: I usually add 2 tablespoons minced fresh parsley and 2 or 3 green onions, finely chopped, though these are not in the original recipe.

OVERNIGHT COLESLAW

This stays crisp and crunchy to the last bite.

*1 head green cabbage, thinly
    shredded
2 sweet white onions, peeled,
    thinly sliced
¼ cup sugar
1 teaspoon prepared mustard*

*½ teaspoon dry mustard
1 cup cider vinegar
1½ teaspoons salt, or to taste
1 teaspoon celery seeds or
    caraway seeds
¾ cup salad oil*

Prepare cabbage. Separate onion into rings. In refrigerator container or bowl, layer cabbage, onion slices, and sugar. Combine remaining ingredients in saucepan and heat to boiling. Pour over cabbage layers. Cover and refrigerate overnight. To serve, toss slaw to mix well and add more salt if needed.

SWEET-SOUR BEAN SALAD

My mother considered herself Irish though she had a Dutch grandmother. The sweet-sour tang of this favorite bean salad is no doubt Dutch inspired. The *garbanzos* are my modern touch. Mother used green beans and yellow wax beans.

*3 pounds fresh (or 3 cans of 1
    pound each) cut green beans
1 can (1 pound) garbanzo beans
1 can (4 ounces) pimientos,
    drained and diced
1 green sweet pepper, seeded and
    diced
1 sweet red onion, peeled, sliced,
    separated into rings
1 clove garlic, crushed*

*1 teaspoon salt
½ cup cider vinegar
½ cup tarragon vinegar
⅔ cup sugar
½ cup salad oil
1 tablespoon chopped fresh dill
    (or 1 teaspoon dried dill)
Freshly ground black pepper
½ cup crumbled crisp-cooked
    bacon (optional)*

Cook fresh green beans in boiling salted water until crisp-tender. Drain, blanch quickly in cold water, then cool. Or, drain and rinse canned green beans and garbanzos. Combine in large refrigerator container with pimientos, green pepper, and onion. Combine dressing ingredients in glass jar, cover, and shake until well blended. Pour over salad and mix

well. Taste and add more salt and pepper if needed. Refrigerate overnight—or several days. At serving time, heap into shallow bowl and top
with crisp bacon if you like.

HOMEMADE ICE CREAM

Though we sometimes had a French custard ice cream, most often it
was the American or Philadelphia type ice cream made with cream,
sugar, and flavoring—no eggs. Next to vanilla, banana and fresh strawberry were our favorites. The original old recipe used all heavy cream—
too rich for my taste nowadays.

1 quart light cream	*Pinch of salt*
1 vanilla bean, split (or 1	*1 cup plus 2 tablespoons sugar*
tablespoon vanilla extract)	*1 pint heavy cream*

Combine light cream, split vanilla bean (add extract later if used), salt,
and sugar in saucepan. Steep over very low heat or, preferably, in top of
double boiler for about 10 to 15 minutes. Do not allow cream to boil—
merely get it warm enough to melt sugar and release the flavor essence
from the vanilla bean. Remove from heat and scrape seeds out of the
vanilla bean into the hot cream (discard bean) or add extract. Add
heavy cream and cool. Cover and chill overnight. Fill a prepared
2-quart ice-cream freezer ¾ full with chilled mixture. Follow general
directions for freezing and packing given in Becky's Fruit Ice Cream.*
When frozen, wrap in heavy canvas or layers of newspapers and carry to
the picnic.

Banana Ice Cream—Reduce light cream in recipe above to 3 cups.
Force 3 large ripe bananas through sieve and add to chilled cream mixture before freezing. Omit 1 tablespoon vanilla extract and add 1 teaspoon nutmeg.

Strawberry Ice Cream—Reduce light cream in recipe above to 3 cups.
Half-freeze vanilla ice cream (above) flavored with half the amount of
vanilla. Wipe lid of freezer can and carefully remove it. Stir 2 cups
crushed, sweetened strawberries into cream. Replace lid and finish freezing.

CHOCOLATE PECAN CAKE

Pecans were plentiful in our area and we put them in everything—cakes, the famous pecan pie, cookies, sweet rolls. This rich buttermilk chocolate cake is made from scratch the old-fashioned way and is one of the best I've ever tasted.

4 eggs, separated	1 teaspoon vanilla
3 squares unsweetened chocolate, cut into pieces	1 cup buttermilk
2 cups sifted cake flour	1 teaspoon soda
⅛ teaspoon salt	1 cup chopped pecans
2 cups sugar, divided	Chocolate Cream Frosting
¾ cup butter (we used the real McCoy for this)	(below)

One half hour ahead of time, remove eggs from refrigerator. Separate them and drop whites into small bowl of electric mixer. Drop yolks into cup or small bowl. Melt chocolate in small saucepan over low heat. Resift flour with salt. Grease and flour 3 (9-inch) round layer-cake pans. Beat egg whites until soft peaks form. Gradually beat in ¼ cup sugar, beating until whites are stiff but still moist-looking. Set aside. Cream butter in large bowl of mixer until soft. Gradually beat in 1¾ cups sugar, beating at medium-high speed until mixture is creamy, light, and very fluffy. Drop in egg yolks, one by one, and beat well after each is added. Mixture should be as light as whipped cream. Blend in vanilla and slightly cooled chocolate. With rubber scraper, lightly blend in ⅓ of the flour. Mix buttermilk and soda and blend ½ of it into batter. Repeat with flour, buttermilk, and flour. Beat again for a few seconds, until batter is shiny and looks like satin. Gently fold in pecans and stiffly beaten egg whites. Spoon into prepared pans and spread evenly. Bake at 350° F. for about 30 minutes, or until sides shrink slightly and top springs back when gently touched. Remove from oven and let stand on wire racks for about 5 minutes. With small flexible spatula, gently loosen and free cakes around edges, then invert. Let stand for a few seconds, then gently lift pans from cakes. Cool cakes and fill and frost with chocolate cream frosting.

CHOCOLATE CREAM FROSTING

This unusual and easy frosting was the invention of the late, imaginative food writer, Helen Evans Brown. She called it Fabulous Frosting, when it first appeared in her *Patio Cook Book,* and rightly so. It's luscious and creamy, becomes firm enough to wrap for a picnic cake, yet it never hardens. And it freezes beautifully.

This is double Helen's recipe: Melt 2 packages (6 ounces each) semisweet chocolate bits in double boiler over hot, not boiling, water. Blend in 1 cup dairy sour cream and a pinch of salt. (I add 2 to 4 tablespoon powdered sugar, 1 teaspoon vanilla, or a little dark rum.) Stir smooth and spread on cake.

MIX-AND-SWITCH MENUS

TERRACE SUPPER FOR EIGHT

MELON WITH PROSCIUTTO

POACHED SALMON   HERB MAYONNAISE*

PEAS AND TOMATOES   PEPPER RICE SALAD

MERINGUE PRALINÉ

COFFEE

Nothing's more cool-looking than a platter of cold salmon prettily garnished and served with a lively mayonnaise sauce. With it are other cool dishes, all rather elegant. For an easy appetizer, serve wedges of your favorite melon—Spanish, cranshaw, honeydew—wrapped in thinly sliced *prosciutto.* To accompany the cold salmon, cook tiny peas and heat gently in butter for 2 or 3 minutes with cherry tomatoes. Serve warm. Make the meringue layers, pastry cream, and praliné the day before. Also cook rice and marinate it for the salad. In the morning poach salmon, cool it, and make sauce and garnishes. Serve a white Rhône wine (Hermitage, perhaps) or a California Chardonnay.

POACHED SALMON

Poach a 5- to 6-pound piece or a small whole salmon by recipe for Cold Halibut, Mexicano,* adding another ½ cup white wine and 2 teaspoons dried tarragon. Cool, place on platter, and remove skin. Garnish with thinly sliced cucumbers, quartered hard-cooked eggs, and lemon wedges. Serve with Herb Mayonnaise.*

WATERCRESS RICE SALAD

Make Spinach Rice Salad,* substituting 1 cup chopped watercress leaves for the spinach, ½ cup chopped green onion for the red onion. Omit tomato garnish. Ring with watercress.

MERINGUE PRALINÉ

Make and cool meringue layers described in Gâteau Dacquoise.* Make Praliné.* Make Pastry Cream* (Crème Pâtissière) and flavor with 2 table-spoons each rum and praliné. Whip 1 cup heavy cream and fold half of it into pastry cream. Spread between meringue layers. Swirl top layer with whipped cream and sprinkle with ¼ cup crushed praliné.

PRALINÉ

Stir over moderate heat in small heavy saucepan until sugar dissolves ½ cup granulated sugar, ⅛ teaspoon cream of tartar, and ¼ cup water. Stir in ½ cup chopped blanched almonds (or walnuts, filberts, or pe-cans) and boil *without stirring* until syrup is a rich caramel color, 3 to 4 minutes. Do not overcook or let syrup become dark or it will be bitter. Pour at once onto a cold cooky sheet or marble slab. Cool until hard and brittle. Break into pieces and crush coarsely with rolling pin or put in blender and whiz until fine. Store in tightly covered jar. Makes 1 cup.

NEIGHBORHOOD PATIO FEAST FOR EIGHT

NUTS AND SEEDS*   GUACAMOLE   COLD BEER
POLPETTE   BEANS BORRACHOS
ITALIAN OR ONION ROLLS   GAZPACHO SALAD*
ICE CREAM   CARROT WALNUT CAKE*   COFFEE

A fun party of hamburger and beans that borrows from several national cuisines. Make the spirited beans at least a day in advance—their flavor is richer. Fix the nuts and seeds the day before and make the easy carrot cake. Next day layer and refrigerate the bowl of tomatoes, cucumbers, green peppers, and onions for the gazpacho salad, and shape the delightful Italian hamburgers. Guacamole is better if made an hour or two before serving. Use your own favorite recipe for this popular avocado dunk. Mine includes soft-ripe avocado coarsely mashed with a fork, chopped onion, tomatoes, and Mexican hot sauce to taste.

BEANS BORRACHOS

Cook 2 pounds of your favorite beans—pinto, pink, black, or red kidney —by recipe for Pinto Beans.* Cook lightly, but not until crisp, 1 pound lean bacon cut in pieces. Drain bacon. In ½ cup drippings cook until soft 2 large onions, 2 cloves garlic, and tomato, all chopped. Add 1½ cups beer or dry red wine and simmer for 5 minutes. Pour over beans in large casserole. Season with salt if needed, freshly milled pepper, and Tabasco or chopped chiles to taste. Stir in half the bacon, top with rest. Bake at 350° F., adding bean liquid if needed, until beans are bubbly hot and flavors rich and mellow, 45 minutes to 1 hour.

POLPETTE

Crumble 2 slices firm white bread into ½ cup bouillon or red wine. Mix 2 pounds lean ground chuck beef with 1 minced clove garlic, 2 tablespoons minced parsley, grated peel of 1 lemon, salt to taste (about 1½ teaspoons), plenty of freshly milled pepper, and a dash of nutmeg. Squeeze bread almost but not completely dry and add to meat with 2 lightly beaten eggs. Blend and shape lightly into 8 patties. Dust with flour. Cook on greased hot griddle on outdoor barbecue until browned but juicy inside. Or place in hinged wire grill (these meat cakes are softer than the average hamburger patty) and cook over hot coals. Serve with warm, prebuttered Italian or Kaiser (onion) rolls.

IV Dinners

The dinner menus in this book I think of as the most formal of all the parties. They're really not formal, of course, since the idea here is to give you menus you can prepare ahead—even if it takes a week or more at odd times—and serve without help, in most cases. But, the dinners are all dressier than the other parties.

They're planned with a first course, usually served in the living room on the coffee table or placed on the dining table before guests are seated. Incidentally, all the dinners suggest tables for sit-down dining, though the food is served buffet. A main course and dessert follow. You won't find many quick sautés or delicate fish dishes (much as I love them) with sauces that need last-minute attention or that suffer from waiting. Those belong in the more intimate dinners for two or four, or even six when critical timing can be more closely watched. Nor will you find a single airy, hot soufflé in the whole book. Instead, the main course for these parties is usually a meat dish with a vegetable that can be served rather easily, such as the wine-simmered Veal Mediterranean with Pine Nut Pilaf. Or, as in the Pot Au Feu, the meat and vegetables are all served together on one huge platter.

The salads I've suggested are not often the bowl of tossed greens but usually a cold vegetable mixture. Or a light composed salad of Belgian endives or celery root rémoulade. The desserts are frequently a conveniently frozen-ahead sherbet or *bombe* with a fruit sauce. Pies and cakes or rich tortes I've reserved for the holidays and dessert parties. Except for the co-operative dinner for twenty-four, in which everybody gets into the act, most of the dinners are planned for eight. The bigger parties for twelve, eighteen, twenty-four, and so on will be found among the more casual luncheons, late suppers, and cocktail buffets.

The importance of planning for a successful buffet dinner cannot be stressed enough. Every detail must be thought out carefully and fully. What can be made ahead and frozen? When should it be prepared? When to put it on to cook? How much refrigerator and freezer space is involved? Can it be done with one oven, or should I change the menu? And just as important as all these considerations is the appearance of the dish. Will it look beautiful on the buffet table? Can it be served easily and rather neatly by the host or hostess or the guests themselves? And can it wait a reasonable time and not be ruined? All these questions, and more, went through my thinking and planning for these menus and have been put to the actual test. The **Do Ahead** section with each menu I think you'll find a big help in planning and executing a successful party.

SIT-DOWN BUFFET FOR EIGHT

ICED GINGER SHRIMP

VEAL MEDITERRANEAN   PINE NUT PILAF

SALADE COMPOSÉE

RIBBON BOMBE   SCARLET SAUCE

COFFEE

A comfortable, gracious way to entertain more than four guests for dinner in small quarters. The menu is a colorful one of Mediterranean inspiration—all make-ahead, wiltproof, and waitproof. Two small tables in pink and yellow cloths with small baskets of flowers might echo the gay cloth of the dining table and its mixed French bouquet of cornflowers, white daisies, and red carnations. Arrange the main course and salad on the big table and serve the striking dessert on the sideboard or the buffet table after everything has been cleared away. With the main course, drink a Frascati or California white Chianti.

Do Ahead: Make the ginger shrimp a couple of days in advance and chill. Assemble the easy *bombe* the day before so it can freeze overnight. Asparagus and artichokes for the salad platter may be cooked and marinated the day before or early the morning of the party. Cook eggs and prepare rest of salad materials. Brown the veal and assemble the rest of the casserole. Either cook it completely to be reheated at dinnertime, or put on to cook 3 hours before serving. Several hours before dinner prepare strawberry sauce for bombe. Toast pine nuts and sauté onions and rice for the pilaf. Start pilaf cooking one half hour before dinner.

ICED GINGER SHRIMP

Serve this in the living room on the coffee table with cocktail plates and picks or forks. The shrimp are spectacular when heaped over a bed of finely crushed ice in a large silver or crystal bowl.

Heat to boiling: 2 quarts water, 1 sliced onion, 1 sliced lemon, 1 clove garlic, halved, ¼ cup diced candied ginger (or a thick slice of fresh gingerroot if you live near an Oriental market). Simmer for 10 minutes. Add 2 pounds unpeeled large shrimp, lower heat, and simmer shrimp for 5 minutes only. Add 1½ teaspoons salt. Cool slightly, then peel and devein shrimp. Refrigerate in ginger liquid overnight or several days. Remove from liquid and serve plain (for the calorie watchers) or with a dipping sauce of ½ cup each mayonnaise and sour cream spiked lightly with soy sauce and Dijon mustard.

VEAL MEDITERRANEAN

A mirepoix of fresh vegetables in the French style and some unusual seasonings associated with Greek cooking make this oven veal stew a memorable one. Make it ahead, if you wish, and reheat.

3½ pounds boneless veal shoulder cut in 1½-inch cubes	1 cup finely diced onion
2 teaspoons salt	½ cup finely diced carrot
Freshly ground pepper	½ cup finely diced celery
¼ cup flour	2 cloves garlic, crushed
¼ cup olive or light salad oil	1 cup chopped, peeled tomato (or drained, canned tomato)
2 tablespoons butter	2 cups dry white wine
½ teaspoon dried thyme leaves	1 cup beef bouillon or stock
½ teaspoon cinnamon	1 pound fresh small mushrooms
1 teaspoon crushed fennel seeds	Minced parsley
¼ cup minced parsley	

Season veal well with salt and pepper, then dredge in flour. In large heavy skillet, brown slowly, a few pieces at a time, in 4 tablespoons of the oil and butter mixed. Remove browned veal to large (4-quart) casserole. Add crumbled thyme, cinnamon, fennel, and parsley, stir until well mixed. Heat rest of fat and gently cook onion, carrot, and celery until soft but not brown. Stir garlic, tomato, wine, and bouillon into pan and scrape up browned bits from bottom. Pour over veal and mix well. Cover tightly and braise gently at 250° F. for 2½ hours. Add mushrooms and more stock and salt and pepper if needed. Cover and cook for 30 minutes longer. Skim off fat and top veal with minced parsley.

PINE NUT PILAF

Any stock or seasonings may be used for this, but only unprocessed, raw long grain rice will give you flaky dry pilaf—each grain beautifully separate—as it's cooked in Turkey and other Middle East countries.

2 cups raw long grain rice
⅓ cup butter or margarine
1 bunch green onions, chopped
  (whites only, use tops for
  garnish)

3½ cups rich chicken stock,
  boiling hot
Salt
½ cup shelled pine nuts, lightly
  toasted

Wash rice through several waters; drain and dry on paper towels. Heat butter in large heavy pan that has a tight lid. Add onions and stir-fry a minute or two, until soft. Toss rice into pan and stir-fry only until it is coated and shiny with fat but not brown. Pour in hot stock and add about 1 teaspoon salt (it depends on stock seasonings, so more may be needed). Mix well, cover pot tightly and turn heat to very lowest or place pan in 325° F. oven. Cook until rice is tender, dry, and flaky, 25 to 30 minutes. Let stand for 10 minutes off the heat, then fluff up with fork. Stir in ¼ cup chopped green onion tops and the pine nuts.

SALADE COMPOSÉE

In the composed or arranged salad, a decorative vegetable and salad course in one, the components may vary. Use the best vegetables of the season. Canned or frozen can be substituted.

Cook 2 pounds fresh asparagus (or 1½ pounds small whole green beans) in boiling salted water until crisp-tender. Drain. Cook and drain 1 package frozen artichoke hearts. Lay vegetables in shallow glass dish and drizzle with Caper Dressing (below) to coat well. Cover and refrigerate. Chill a small head cauliflower broken into flowerets. Hardcook and chill 4 eggs. At serving time, arrange the vegetables in neat rows on a pretty platter, separating and decorating the groups with quartered eggs, tomatoes, and ripe olives. Pour the dressing lightly over salad and frame platter with small leaves Boston lettuce.

CAPER DRESSING

Add to Classic French Dressing* (Sauce Vinaigrette) an extra pinch of
dry mustard, 2 teaspoons minced shallot, and 2 tablespoons drained capers. Blend.

RIBBON BOMBE

For the stunning ribbonlike effect, press contrasting layers of sherbet
into mold one atop the other rather than around the sides of the mold as
is done traditionally. Any contrasty flavors and colors can be used.
Very easy!

1 pint raspberry sherbet　　　　　　*1 pint lime sherbet*
1 pint pineapple sherbet　　　　　　*Scarlet Sauce (below)*

Chill tall or dome-shaped metal 6-cup mold. Soften raspberry sherbet
slightly with wooden spoon and press into bottom of mold in even layer.
Set in freezer for at least 30 minutes to firm up. Soften pineapple sherbet slightly and press into mold in even layer on top of raspberry layer.
Firm up again in freezer. Spread softened lime sherbet on top of pineapple layer. Cover mold with foil and freeze overnight. Make scarlet
sauce several hours before dinner and chill. To unmold, moisten a
chilled dessert platter. Dip mold its full depth in and out of warm water
for a few seconds. Invert plate on mold and, holding both firmly, reverse
them with a flip. Shake mold to loosen *bombe*. Return to freezer to firm
up again. If you like, decorate base of bombe with a ribbon of whipped
cream. Cut into slices or wedges and top each serving with a spoonful
of sauce.

SCARLET SAUCE

Wash, dry, and hull 1 pint of fresh strawberries. Put in blender with
½ cup orange marmalade. Whiz until smooth. Add 2 tablespoons brandy
or an orange liqueur if you prefer. Chill. Makes 2 cups.

DINNER WITH AN ENGLISH ACCENT
(For Eight)

HOT SCALLOP SHELLS

STEAK AND KIDNEY PIE

BROCCOLI AND CELERIAC RÉMOULADE

ASSORTED CHEESES   APPLES OR PEARS

SLICED FRENCH ROLLS   BUTTER

CHESTNUT TRIFLE

COFFEE

My husband comes from an English family and dotes on meat pies, so we try to have this sort of party at least once during the winter season, often at holiday time. Scotch and Bourbon highballs are provided, but most of our guests seem to prefer and expect the fine dry sherry, usually Tio Pepe, we serve preceding this dinner. Guests are seated at two small tables in the living room and the main course and cheeses arranged on the dining table. I serve the scallop shells in the living room from a tray—a nice way to announce that the main course will be ready shortly. To enjoy with the rich meat pie and cheeses, we pour a regional red Bordeaux, perhaps from the St. Émilion area or a California Cabernet Sauvignon. Later the trifle and coffee service are placed on a chest in the living room for guests to serve themselves at leisure.

Do Ahead: Make pastry for the meat pies several days ahead. The day before, brown beef and kidneys and braise briefly. Refrigerate. Early next day, cook celery root and broccoli and prepare rémoulade sauce and French dressing and chill them. In the afternoon, make the custard cream and complete the trifle. Roll pastry for meat pies, assemble, and refrigerate until ready to bake. Just before you're ready to dress for the evening, toss vegetables with the dressings and fix the scallop shells. Refrigerate everything. Put the meat pies in the oven about an hour and fifteen minutes before you plan to serve them. This is usually just before the first guests arrive.

HOT SCALLOP SHELLS

Rinse 1½ pounds bay or sea scallops in cool water and blot dry on paper towels. Cut into small cubes. Generously butter 8 individual scallop shells or ½-cup size ramekins and sprinkle each with about 2 teaspoons dry bread crumbs. Divide scallops among shells and sprinkle each with a few drops lemon juice, salt and pepper, a few snipped chives, and 1 tablespoon heavy cream. Cover with a tablespoon dry crumbs and drizzle over with 2 teaspoons melted butter. Bake in a hot oven (425° F.) for 8 to 10 minutes, or until scallops are plumpish and tender, the buttery crumbs slightly crisp and golden.

Baking Note: If you have two ovens, bake these separately about 25 minutes before meat pies are done. In one oven, raise oven temperature for shells. Remove pies for 8 to 10 minutes while scallops bake. Return pies to oven and finish baking at 350° F. while guests are busy with the first course.

STEAK AND KIDNEY PIE

Use the pastry you prefer—one suggested below or regular piecrust dough made with part butter. A puff paste type is more traditional. You may cook the meat completely and then bake the pie briefly to brown the crust. However, it has a richer meld of flavors if you cook it longer under the crust and less beforehand. The recipe makes 2 pies, enough for 8 full-meal servings plus extras.

Sour Cream Puff Paste, Quick* *Puff Paste,* or 2 packages (10* *ounces each) frozen puff pastry* *shells*	*3 cups sliced mushrooms* *½ teaspoon dried thyme leaves* *½ teaspoon dried marjoram*
3 pounds round steak	*2 tablespoons minced parsley*
1 pound lamb kidneys	*3 to 4 cups rich beef broth*
Salt, freshly ground pepper, flour	*2 teaspoons Escoffier Sauce*
4 tablespoons butter or margarine	*Robert (in gourmet section of*
2 tablespoons salad oil	*supermarket)*
2 onions, chopped	*1 egg, beaten*

Make pastry ahead and chill. Trim fat and connective tissue from steak and cut into strips about 1×1½ inches. Trim kidneys and soak for a few minutes in cool water. Drain and cut into small cubes. Blot dry.

Season with about 1½ teaspoons salt, plenty of freshly ground pepper, and dredge lightly in flour. In large heavy skillet heat part of butter and oil. Add meats, a single layer at a time, and cook and stir until well browned.

Remove browned meats to large bowl. Add more fat as needed until all meat is browned. Heat rest of fat and add onions. Cook and stir until soft. Stir in mushrooms and cook for a minute or two. Return meats to pan and sprinkle with herbs and parsley. Add about half the broth and the sauce Robert. Stir up all brown glaze from bottom of pan, cover, and braise meat for 20 to 30 minutes. Cool completely and refrigerate, covered.

To assemble and bake: Divide filling between 2 shallow (1½-quart) casseroles or deep pie dishes. The 10-inch pie dish about 1¾ inches deep is ideal. Pour in rest of broth and add more if needed to almost cover meats. (If frozen puff paste shells are used, thaw them ahead just enough to separate, but do not allow dough to become soft; press shells together at edges and roll into a sheet for each pie.) Divide dough and roll into 2 rounds about 2 inches bigger than the dish and a little thicker than is used for a regular pie. Cut a 1-inch strip from each and press around edge of dish. Top with pastry round cut to fit top. Moisten edges and press to pastry strip to seal. Pinch into a fluted edge. Cut hole in center of pies. Decorate tops with leaves or diamonds cut from pastry scraps, stuck in place with egg wash. Brush pastry all over with beaten egg. Bake in preheated 350° F. oven for 1 hour to 1 hour and 15 minutes. Pastry should be a rich golden brown, the meat tender. Serve warm in husky wedges.

BROCCOLI AND CELERIAC RÉMOULADE

In France, raw celeriac cut in pin-size slivers and marinated in a mustard mayonnaise is a popular first course. For a do-ahead buffet, cubes of the vegetable cooked briefly and marinated are much easier. Broccoli dressed with vinaigrette is delicious, and the two make a pretty salad platter that's perfect with the rich meat pie.

Peel 2 to 3 medium celery roots (celeriac) and cut into ½-inch cubes. Drop into lightly salted water and squeeze in a few drops lemon juice. Cook in boiling salted water only until crisp-tender, 3 to 5 minutes. Drain and mix gently with 1 tablespoon salad oil. Cool and refrigerate, covered. Separate tops of 1½ pounds fresh broccoli into small flowerets. Trim and peel stems. Slice crosswise into rounds about ⅓ inch thick. Cook in boiling salted water, stems on the bottom and flowerets on top, until crisp-tender, 5 to 7 minutes only. Drain and mix gently with 1 tablespoon salad oil. Cool and refrigerate, covered. Blend 1 cup mayonnaise with about 2 tablespoons Dijon mustard and a little lemon juice. Combine celery root with 1 cup slivered crisp celery and enough of the mayonnaise just to moisten well. Don't overpower vegetable with too much dressing. Season as needed with salt and freshly ground pepper. Mix broccoli with just enough Classic French Dressing (Sauce Vinaigrette)* made with half lemon juice to moisten well. Season as needed. Chill until serving time. Mound celery root in a shallow bowl or platter and sprinkle with minced parsley. Circle with broccoli. Decorate platter with cherry tomatoes if they're in the markets.

CHESTNUT TRIFLE

One of the most delicious and elegant of English sweets and perfect for a special holiday dinner. This is no trifling dessert despite the name, but layers of ladyfingers and a rich custard cream laced with Madeira, candied fruits, and preserved chestnuts.

¼ cup diced candied cherries	Syrup from chestnuts
2 tablespoons diced candied orange peel	1 package ladyfingers (about 4 ounces)
½ cup Madeira or cream sherry	½ cup heavy cream
2 tablespoons brandy	1 tablespoon powdered sugar
2 cups English Custard Cream* (Crème Anglaise)	8 whole candied cherries
½ cup coarsely chopped preserved chestnuts (marrons glacés)	

Marinate candied fruits in Madeira and brandy for at least 1 hour. Make custard cream and cool to room temperature, stirring frequently. Drain wine from fruits into a bowl and add 2 to 3 tablespoons syrup from chestnuts. Stir fruits and chestnuts into custard cream. Split ladyfingers and toast lightly for a few seconds under the broiler. Lay half of them in a shallow crystal bowl and sprinkle with half the wine mixture. Cover with half the custard, then another layer of ladyfingers, wine mixture, and custard. Cover with plastic film and chill. Chill heavy cream and powdered sugar together. Beat until thick. Cover trifle with the whipped cream forced through a pastry bag using rosette tip. Decorate top with whole cherries.

IMPRESSIVE SIT-DOWN BUFFET FOR EIGHT

VERMOUTH CASSIS
BRANDIED CHICKEN LIVER PÂTÉ
TOMATO TONNATO
CHICKEN IN MUSTARD SAUCE
LEMON ASPARAGUS   HOMINY SOUFFLÉ
FROZEN APRICOT VELVET
DEMITASSE

This buffet is surprisingly easy to do but rather impressive. With the vermouth, serve chicken liver pâté in a little crock with hot toast fingers or sliced French rolls. While the hot foods are being heated and finished, arrange the tomato tonnato on individual salad plates and place on the dining table, set with silver, napkins, glasses—and flowers, of course. When guests have finished the first course, they help themselves to warm plates and hot foods on the buffet. Serve the pretty dessert at the table after the main course is cleared away. And the demitasse in the living room. A chilled Pouilly-Fuissé or a good California Chablis would be nice to drink with this dinner.

Do Ahead: Make pâté a couple of days in advance. Chill. Day before— make frozen dessert and tonnato sauce for first course. Hard-cook the eggs. Next day—clean lettuce and asparagus, peel tomatoes, and prepare everything for mustard sauce. Roast the chickens and cool them. An hour or so before dinner, cook hominy grits for soufflé and make mustard sauce. Cut up chicken and add it to sauce. Complete soufflé, cover, and refrigerate. About 20 minutes before the soufflé is done, cook asparagus and assemble the tomato tonnato.

VERMOUTH CASSIS

The classic French recipe uses ½ jigger each dry French vermouth and *crème de cassis* (currant liqueur) over 2 or 3 ice cubes in highball glasses. Fill ¾ full with soda or seltzer. I prefer a jigger of vermouth, a little less cassis.

BRANDIED CHICKEN LIVER PÂTÉ

1 pound chicken livers
½ cup butter, softened
2 tablespoons brandy or cognac
½ teaspoon salt
Freshly ground black pepper
Dash of ground cloves
½ teaspoon dried tarragon

½ cup chicken broth
2 tablespoons Madeira
4 green onions, chopped
Generous dash of nutmeg
1 teaspoon anchovy paste
Few drops lemon juice
Minced parsley

Cut livers in halves, blot dry, and sauté in 2 tablespoons of the butter until lightly browned. Sprinkle with brandy; when it's warm, flame it. When flames die, season livers with salt, freshly ground pepper, cloves, and tarragon. Add broth and simmer gently for 6 to 8 minutes. Drain livers into blender container, saving broth. Add Madeira, about ¼ cup of the broth, and the onions. Whiz until mixture is smooth. Pour into bowl and work in more broth if needed. Add nutmeg, anchovy paste, and butter. Texture should be a good spreading consistency after the butter cools and becomes firm again. Adjust seasonings and add a few drops lemon juice. Pour into small crock or jar and cover with a little melted butter. Cover with foil and refrigerate overnight or several days. Remove butter film and serve in crock with toast or sliced French rolls. Or unmold onto a plate and sprinkle with minced parsley.

TOMATO TONNATO

This popular tuna sauce is good on many things besides cold veal. As a dip for vegetables, for instance. Or, as suggested here, spooned over tomatoes and hard-cooked eggs.

1 can (6½–7 ounces) white meat
*   tuna*
8 canned anchovy fillets, chopped
2 tablespoons lemon juice
1 tablespoon capers and a few
*   drops of their vinegar*
½ cup olive oil

8 hard-cooked eggs
3 large, firm-ripe tomatoes,
*   peeled*
Small lettuce leaves
Capers
Green Spanish olives

Combine tuna, anchovies, lemon juice, and capers in blender container. Whiz until smooth, stopping motor often to push mixture into blades with narrow rubber spatula. Gradually blend in olive oil until sauce is

smooth and creamy. Chill in covered jar overnight. To assemble, peel
eggs and slice tomatoes rather thickly. Arrange small lettuce leaves on
8 salad plates. Cover with tomato slices and eggs cut in halves lengthwise. Spoon tuna sauce over each and sprinkle with a few capers. Decorate each plate with 2 or 3 olives.

CHICKEN IN MUSTARD SAUCE

My adaptation of a delicious, mustardy chicken I've enjoyed in Burgundy. Make the sauce in an attractive pan that can go to the table and
serve the chicken in it.

*2 whole fryer chickens (about
    2½ pounds each)
Salt and freshly ground pepper
6 tablespoons butter
2 (or more) tablespoons Dijon
    mustard
3 tablespoons chopped shallots*

*2 cups sliced mushrooms
Few drops lemon juice
1 tablespoon flour
1 cup chicken broth
1 teaspoon grated lemon peel
1 cup heavy cream*

Dry chicken with paper towels and season with salt and pepper. Blend
3 tablespoons soft butter and 1 tablespoon mustard to a paste and
spread over chicken. Place in shallow flameproof roasting pan and roast
at 400° F. for about 1 hour. Baste occasionally. Cool and cut into
pieces at joints—2 legs, 2 thighs, 2 pieces of breast, 2 wings for each
chicken. Set aside backs for soup or snacks. Melt rest of butter in
heavy pan big enough to hold chicken later. Add shallots and cook
gently until soft. Stir in mushrooms and cook for 2 or 3 minutes. Sprinkle
with a few drops lemon juice and the flour. Stir with a wooden spoon,
then blend in chicken broth. Cook and stir until sauce thickens—it will
be thin. Add lemon peel, 1 tablespoon mustard, and cream. Stir until
smooth. Add chicken and any juices, but not fat, from roasting pan.
Mix well and taste sauce. Add salt and pepper and more mustard if
needed. It shouldn't be bland, but subtle and rich with mustard flavor.
Do this much an hour before dinner. At serving time, cook over very
low heat just until chicken is hot through, about 10 to 15 minutes. Do
not allow it to boil.

HOMINY SOUFFLÉ

Hominy grits, a form of coarsely ground, hulled dried corn, have a rich yet sort of delicate parched-corn flavor that's unique. For a change from rice or potatoes I often make grits into such dishes as gnocchi, gratins with cheese, or this voluptuous, non-temperamental soufflé.

3 cups milk	*½ cup butter or margarine*
3½ cups water	*1 cup grated sharp Cheddar*
2 teaspoons salt	*cheese*
1½ cups packaged hominy grits	*6 eggs, separated*

In large kettle, heat milk, water, and salt to boiling. Stir in grits with wooden spoon. Lower heat and stir until they are thick and smooth and fluffy, about 5 minutes. Beat in butter, half the cheese, and egg yolks one at a time. Grease a large shallow baking dish, about 2-quart size. Beat egg whites until stiff but not dry—the peaks will bend over slightly. Fold quickly into hot grits. Spoon into dish and smooth off top. Sprinkle with rest of cheese. Cover and set aside for 30 minutes—or refrigerate if it needs to wait for an hour. (You lose a little of the puffiness but none of the delicious flavor.) Bake at 350° F. until puffed and golden, 45 minutes to 1 hour.

LEMON ASPARAGUS

Trim 4 pounds fresh asparagus and cook in boiling salted water by directions for Fresh Asparagus.* Drain and toss with about 4 tablespoons butter mixed with 1 to 2 tablespoons fresh lemon juice.

FROZEN APRICOT VELVET

This is simply pure sweet fruit puréed and frozen, yet it tastes and looks like a creamy mousse. A little gelatin and egg white give lightness and the creamy texture. Dozens of variations are possible from this basic recipe. Purée melons, berries, peaches, and such at the peak of the season. Sweeten and freeze. Use later to make a sherbet like this one, or layer with whipped cream for a parfait, or fold in whipped cream for an elegant mousse.

3 to 4 pounds fresh ripe apricots   *2 packages unflavored gelatin*
   (or peaches or nectarines) or 2   *4 tablespoons fresh lemon juice*
   cans (29 ounces each) apricots   *2 tablespoons apricot brandy*
½ cup pineapple juice   *1 egg white*
1 cup sugar (little less for canned   *Whipped cream*
   fruit)

Peel and quarter fresh fruit and drop into pineapple juice. Add sugar. (For canned fruit, drain and add sugar and pineapple juice.) Purée in blender or force through food mill or strainer and pour into a saucepan. Soften gelatin for 5 minutes in lemon juice. Add to purée. Stir over very low heat until gelatin and sugar are completely melted. Do not cook fruit. Add brandy. Taste and add more lemon juice or sugar if needed. Pour into freezer tray or shallow pan and freeze until mushy-firm, about 1 hour.

Put mushy purée into a cold mixer bowl with unbeaten egg white. Beat until fluffy, light in color, and purée increases in volume greatly. Pour into 2-quart charlotte or melon mold rinsed in cold water. Cover with lid or foil and freeze overnight. An hour before dinner, dip mold to its depth quickly in warm water and unmold on glass serving plate. Wipe plate and decorate base of mold with whipped cream forced through a pastry tube. Cream may be lightly sweetened and flavored with apricot brandy if you like. Return mold to freezer. At serving time, decorate with a few bright berries. Cut in slices to serve.

Peach or Nectarine Velvet: Substitute orange juice for the pineapple juice. Flavor with kirsch or Grand Marnier.

CHRISTMAS DINNER
(For Eight to Ten)

CHAMPAGNE   PARMESAN PUFFS
SHRIMP RÉMOULADE   PUMPERNICKEL TOASTS
SPENCER BEEF ROAST
(EYE-OF-THE-RIB)
HORSERADISH SAUCE
BUTTER BROWN POTATOES   BROCCOLI IN CREAM
CELERY HEARTS   OLIVES   ASSORTED PICKLES
HOLIDAY BOMBE
COFFEE

Christmas is a family day and every household seems to have its own pattern and traditions for the celebration. In our family, the menu dares not vary too much or I will hear, "Aren't we having creamed onions?" or "What about the chestnuts?" My answer is turkey with chestnut stuffing and creamed onions for Thanksgiving. For the busier, Christmas Day feast, a splendid roast beef. This gives me a chance to be freer and visit with friends and relatives who often drop in for a Christmas drink and to exchange gifts. I buy the boneless Spencer roast, which is the heart or eye of the standing rib with all the bones and fat removed. It has marvelous flavor and carves easily and beautifully.

Our menus seem to get simpler each year. With the roast I serve either Yorkshire pudding or browned potatoes, but not both. As a first course, either a fish appetizer or cup of clear soup, but not both. The shrimp rémoulade makes an ideal starter that can be served in the living room with crisp pumpernickel toasts. We've eliminated salads from our Christmas dinner and serve a big platter of raw relishes instead. When we have an extra number of guests, I make celeriac rémoulade* or a molded avocado aspic. There's always fruitcake and cookies in the house, but they're usually served with eggnog or coffee and seldom with meals. Instead, after a reasonable breather we serve the gay holiday *bombe*. Sometimes, with a plate of Almond Macaroons.*

Our house is an old-fashioned red and green fantasyland at Christmas, with an occasional nod to our favorite blue. If our pyracantha berries have turned a luscious red, we use them with pine sprays and holly leaves and lots of white candles with a few fat red ones. Otherwise we use red roses or carnations with the greenery. And red satin ribbon everywhere. The buffet is set up on our dining table and smaller tables placed in the living room with the same colorful decorations, napkins, crystal, and silver.

Since this is a special day, we start with champagne—orange juice splashed with champagne for the youngsters—and enjoy a red wine with the beef, either a good red Burgundy (Beaune is nice) or a California Pinot Noir. Crisp little cheese puffs are passed with the champagne. As a first course, the shrimp rémoulade is brought into the living room on trays. My husband carves the roast beef in a few seconds and I assist everyone with potatoes and broccoli. Otherwise, everyone helps himself. It's truly a "no-sweat-no-strain" holiday meal. Expensive yes, but worth it for this special day.

Do Ahead: Make dough for cheese puffs a week or more ahead and freeze it. Bake puffs day or so before. The day before Christmas marinate fruits for the bombe and make the bombe so it can freeze overnight. Cook shrimp and make rémoulade sauce. Clean celery for relish platter and chill in plastic bag. Next day is simple. Prepare the potatoes and broccoli and make the toasts. Remove the roast from the refrigerator several hours before time to cook it. Make the horseradish sauce about an hour before dinner. It's also wise to unmold the bombe at least an hour before dinner, then return it to the freezer on its plate to firm up again. Quick-cook broccoli to be heated at the last moment.

PARMESAN PUFFS

Adapted from an appetizer served at one of my favorite three-star French restaurants, Le Taillevent, in Paris.

2 cups freshly grated Parmesan
    cheese
Freshly ground black pepper
Cayenne pepper
2 cups all-purpose flour
1 cup butter or margarine (or
    part of each)

4 ounces cream cheese (½ of
    large package)
1 egg
Paprika or poppy seeds

Stir Parmesan, a few grindings of pepper, and a dash of cayenne into flour (no salt, please). Mix well. Beat butter and cream cheese on mixer until smooth and creamy. With fingers, work in flour mixture until you can round up dough in a ball. Wrap in foil, flatten slightly, and chill overnight before baking, or freeze. Remove frozen dough from freezer 15 to 20 minutes before shaping. Divide in half (keep unused part in refrigerator). On lightly floured pastry cloth or between sheets of waxed paper, roll into oblong a generous ¼ inch thick. Keep edges even as possible. Cut into strips 1 inch wide and 3 inches long. Use a scalloped pastry wheel if you have it—puffs look prettier. Place on ungreased cooky sheets and brush with slightly beaten egg. Sprinkle with paprika or poppy seeds. Stack and reroll pastry trimmings, cut in strips until all is used. Refrigerate for 30 minutes. Bake at 375° F. until golden and slightly puffed, about 15 minutes. Shape and bake rest of dough. Cool on wire racks. Wrap in foil or stack in tightly covered tin. Makes 5 to 6 dozen.

SHRIMP RÉMOULADE

The Tabasco and green onions in this recipe I've borrowed from the Creole rémoulade, a hotter version than the original French.

2 hard-cooked eggs	2 teaspoons anchovy paste
1½ cups mayonnaise	Several drops Tabasco sauce
1 tablespoon Dijon mustard	2 pounds medium shrimp
½ teaspoon dry mustard	Salt
1 clove garlic, minced	Finely shredded iceberg lettuce
1 teaspoon dried leaf tarragon, crumbled	2 tablespoons finely chopped green onion
1 tablespoon drained capers	2 tablespoons minced parsley

Mash eggs and combine with next 8 ingredients. Let stand for several hours. Cook shrimp in boiling salted water for 3 to 5 minutes. Drain immediately, cool slightly, and remove shell and dark vein. Moisten with part of the sauce, cover and chill. Line 8 (or 10) scallop shells or small plates with a bed of lacy crisp shredded lettuce. Add green onion and dressing as needed to shrimp. Mix gently. Use just enough dressing to moisten shrimp—but not mask them completely. Heap onto lettuce and sprinkle each dish with a little minced parsley.

PUMPERNICKEL TOASTS

The toast curls served at Alexander Perino's elegant restaurant in Los Angeles are almost chiffon sheer and crisp as a cracker.

To approximate Perino's, buy a small unsliced loaf of cocktail pumpernickel bread and chill (but do not freeze it) in freezer. With a sharp, serrated bread knife, slice bread wafer thin. Spread on both sides with unsalted butter and spread on cooky sheet. Sprinkle with a little grated Parmesan if you like, but I don't always. Toast in a very slow oven (250° F.) until thoroughly dry and crisp and the slices curl slightly. Make these ahead so the oven will be free later for the roast.

SPENCER BEEF ROAST

This roast may have a different name in your area. Ask your meat man for the eye-of-the-standing rib. He will remove the bones and nearly all the fat, leaving the beautiful heart of the roast. A Spencer is not rolled or tied, but left natural. Shapes vary, but the roast is usually about 3½ inches thick in the center section. Ask that a thin layer of fat be left over the top, if possible, to keep meat moist and give roast a rich, crusty look when served.

> 6- to 8-pound Spencer roast   Freshly milled coarse pepper
>   (eye-of-the-standing rib)   Flour
> Salt

Remove roast from refrigerator about 2 hours before you cook it. Season well with salt, plenty of pepper, and rub lightly with flour. Place on rack in shallow roasting pan, fat side up. Cover with a loose open-end foil tent to prevent spatters. Preheat oven to 450° F. Roast meat for 20 minutes to sear surfaces and help give fat a rich crust. Reduce heat to 350° F. and remove foil. Insert meat thermometer and cook for 12 to 15 minutes per pound or until thermometer registers 125° F.—for rare —much below the 140° F. marked rare on the thermometer. Internal temperature of meat rises another 10° after you remove it from oven. This is a very expensive cut of meat and it's sinful to overcook it. Since timing varies with thickness and shape as well as weight of meat, a meat thermometer is the only safe way to be sure of the internal temperature. So many minutes per pound does not really work very well with this tender meat. It's cooked more like a sirloin strip roast or a boned and butterflied leg of lamb. Check the thermometer after 1 hour and 15 minutes. It probably won't take more than 1½ hours' total time. Remove from oven and remove meat thermometer. If fat is not crisp enough, put meat under broiler for a few seconds. Let roast rest in warm place for 20 to 30 minutes while you finish rest of dinner.

With this, we serve horseradish sauce only. If you wish *au jus* or a drippings sauce, skim all fat from drippings and set pan over heat. Add about 1 cup hot meat stock or bouillon and ½ cup dry red dinner wine. Stir up brown glaze from bottom of pan and boil sauce for several minutes. Season to taste with salt and pepper. Serve hot in warm gravy boat. We cut the meat into slices about ⅓ inch thick—others may prefer thicker slices.

HORSERADISH SAUCE

Drain ½ cup bottled horseradish sauce into a fine strainer and press out as much liquid as possible. Or grate fresh horseradish. Blend with a little salt, a pinch of sugar, and ¼ teaspoon dry mustard (for prepared kind only). Stir into 1 cup dairy sour cream. Let stand to develop flavors. At serving time, whip ½ cup chilled heavy cream until stiff and gently fold into horseradish sauce. Serve in sauceboat with roast beef.

BUTTER BROWN POTATOES

Thickly sliced, bathed in butter, and quickly baked, these are akin to elegant Potatoes Anna, but much easier to make.

> *6 large baking potatoes (Russets)*   *Butter (about ½ cup melted)*
> *Salt and freshly ground pepper*   *1 cup grated Swiss cheese*

Peel potatoes, and cut into halves lengthwise if they're quite portly around the middle. Cut crosswise into thickish slices, about ⅓ inch. Generously butter a large shallow baking dish (2-quart size). Lay slices slightly overlapping each other in neat rows to fill dish one layer deep. Season with salt and pepper. Melt butter and spoon evenly over potatoes to coat each slice completely. You may need to melt a little more—it depends on how you slice and overlap the potatoes. Cover whole thing with a thin layer of Swiss cheese. Cover with foil and set aside until 30 minutes before you serve. If you have 2 ovens, bake these, uncovered, in preheated oven (400° F.) for 30 minutes, until tender and lightly browned. If tender but not brown enough, put under broiler for a few seconds just before serving. Do not overcook. With one oven only, add potatoes to the 350° F. oven during the last 15 minutes the roast cooks. Raise heat to 400° F. when meat is removed. Cook potatoes for 20 to 25 minutes longer, or until tender and lightly browned.

BROCCOLI IN CREAM

Julia Child and Simone Beck recommend this superior way to cook broccoli in their Volume Two, *Mastering the Art of French Cooking*. Tough stems are peeled and broccoli cooked briefly in plenty of boiling water. It stays green and has a marvelous, delicate flavor. I've adjusted their method slightly to fit my own menu and needs.

2 bunches broccoli (3 to 4 pounds)	*1 cup heavy cream*
Water	*Freshly ground pepper*
1 tablespoon salt	*Pinch of nutmeg*
4 tablespoons butter or margarine	

Wash broccoli and trim away heavy, tough leaves. Cut off flower buds and separate into small flowerets. Cut stalks lengthwise into halves or quarters and peel off the skin. Cut stalks into 1-inch pieces. In large kettle, heat to boiling enough water to cover broccoli (2 to 3 quarts). Add salt and drop in stalks. Cook for about 3 minutes after the water boils again. Drop in flowerets, boil for 1 to 2 minutes. Stalks should be crisp-tender. Drain and spread to cool quickly on several thicknesses of paper towels. Put stalks on board and chop coarsely. Combine with flowerets and chill in plastic bag until time to serve. Melt butter in a large saucepan and add broccoli. Mix and toss gently over low heat until broccoli is heated and coated with butter. Pour in cream and season with freshly ground pepper and pinch of nutmeg. Simmer for 2 or 3 minutes, stirring gently now and then until cream thickens slightly and absorbs into the broccoli. Serve in hot vegetable dish.

HOLIDAY BOMBE

A pistachio ice cream shell surrounds a vanilla-ice-cream center wickedly laced with liquor-soaked candied fruits and chestnuts.

¼ cup mixed red and green candied cherries	*2 tablespoons Bourbon, divided*
1 bottle (10 ounces) candied chestnuts in syrup (marrons glacés)	*3 tablespoons brandy, divided*
	1 quart pistachio ice cream
	1 quart vanilla ice cream
	1 dozen whole candied cherries

Slice mixed cherries into rings and mix with ¼ cup of chopped chestnuts, 1 tablespoon Bourbon, and 2 tablespoons brandy. Cover and marinate for several hours. Chill a 2-quart melon or *bombe* mold. Put pistachio ice cream in bowl and soften slightly with wooden spoon. Spread in even layer around sides of mold. Set in freezer until very firm, about 1 hour. Put vanilla ice cream in bowl. Quickly swirl in marinated fruit-liquor mixture. Spoon into center of mold. Cover with foil or lid and freeze overnight. Chop remaining chestnuts, return to syrup, and add balance of Bourbon and brandy. Set aside. At least an hour before serving, dip frozen mold in warm water. Remove quickly, shake gently to loosen from sides. Invert wet serving plate on top of mold, then, holding onto mold, flip plate over. Shake mold gently and lift off. Return bombe to freezer to become firm again. Decorate with the whole cherries and a sprig of holly. Cut into wedges or slices and drizzle a little chestnut sauce over each serving.

FRENCH BRASSERIE DINNER
(For Eight)

MUSHROOMS ESCARGOT STYLE
POT-AU-FEU
(BOILED BEEF AND VEGETABLES)
PICKLES   COARSE SALT   MUSTARD
CHEF'S MAYONNAISE
FRENCH BREAD OR HOMEMADE BREAD
APPLE TART, NORMANDY
COFFEE

Boiled beef with vegetables is considered a family dinner in France and not company fare. I've enjoyed it in provencial restaurants and brasseries all over France, however, and I always think "What a nice idea for a buffet" when I see it so beautifully presented. I recall especially the *boeuf grand sel* (beef with coarse salt) at the Brasserie Lipp on the left bank's Boulevard St. Germain in Paris. A huge white platter was set before us laden with a succulent beef brisket which the waiter carved deftly into neat pink slices. Along with it were bouquets of tiny fresh carrots, onions, leeks, and turnips, all shapely and tender, sprinkled with parsley. Simple and delicious. A dish of coarse salt, Dijon mustard, and sour pickles were served with the beef after we drank the wonderful cooking bouillon. Crusty French bread and sweet butter and a good red wine were enjoyed with the beef. Afterwards a creamy Brie was all we wanted and a little cup of midnight black *café filtre*. For this buffet, however, I've suggested a French apple tart, made with cream in the Normandy style. With predinner drinks the mushrooms stuffed with garlic butter are just right and very easy and quick to make. Place the beef and vegetable platter on your buffet table and pour the bouillon into a tureen for guests to ladle into cups they can place on their plates.

Do Ahead: Make the pastry for the tarts (make 2 for this party) several days in advance and prebake the shell the day before. Start the bread early, if you decide to bake it, so it can rise while the beef is simmering. Or, I often bake the bread the day before, then reheat briefly in foil just before dinner for a fresh-out-of-the-oven taste. Bake the tarts and prepare the vegetables after beef is started and the bread is well on its way. I carry out the country French theme when I make this dinner with our old and treasured heavy white platter that can go in the oven, white dishes, blue and white checkered damask cloth, huge white dinner napkins, and red, white, and blue bouquets in my copper cooking pots. With this menu serve a Beaujolais Fleurie or a California Zinfandel.

MUSHROOMS, ESCARGOT STYLE

Cream together ½ cup soft butter, 2 cloves garlic, puréed, 2 shallots or green onions, grated, ½ cup minced parsley, few drops lemon juice, and a little salt and pepper. Wipe 2 dozen large fresh mushrooms (1½-inch size) with damp paper towels and pull out stems. Rub each mushroom with melted butter mixed with a little lemon juice to coat evenly. Fill with garlic butter and set in shallow baking pan. Bake in hot oven (400° F.) for 10 to 12 minutes. Slice small French rolls or cut sliced French bread into rounds a little larger than mushrooms. Set hot mushrooms on bread and spoon any buttery juices left in pan over each. Spear to bread with picks. Serve hot. Provide small cocktail plates and plenty of paper napkins.

POT-AU-FEU

This hearty one-pot dinner is a beautiful dish of marvelous flavor when properly cooked and presented. The broth must be skimmed constantly when the cooking starts and occasionally thereafter to keep the bouillon clear. After the vegetables are cooked, it must be skimmed of all fat—and neither the vegetables nor the meats should be boiled to death. Total cooking time is 4 to 5 hours, but little attention is needed except to add or remove something from the pot.

2 to 3 pounds cracked beef bones and knuckles
2 large onions stuck with 2 cloves
2 carrots, sliced
1 leek, cleaned and split
Herb Bouquet: 1 bay leaf, few celery tops, 4 sprigs parsley, 1 teaspoon thyme, 1 clove garlic, 1 teaspoon cracked peppercorns
4 to 5 pounds boneless beef brisket
2 teaspoons salt

1 (4-pound) stewing or roasting chicken
16 small carrots
8 leeks
8 small celery hearts or 8 medium zucchini
2 dozen small onions
4 turnips, sliced
Minced parsley
Coarse salt, Dijon mustard, pickles
Chef's Mayonnaise*

Put beef bones, onions stuck with cloves, and 2 sliced carrots in shallow roasting pan. Set in 400° F. oven and brown lightly, about 30 minutes. Put into a large pot or soup kettle—a 10- to 12-quart size—with one leek, the herb bouquet tied in a cheesecloth square, and the beef. Add water to about 1½ inches over top of meat. Heat to boiling and skim off scum and foam as they rise to the top. Keep boiling and skimming for 5 to 10 minutes until foaming stops. Add salt, cover pot, and simmer with hardly a bubble on the surface for 1½ to 2 hours. Tie chicken wings and legs close to its body and add it to pot. Bring liquid back to boiling, skim again until foaming stops, cover, and simmer gently until meat and chicken are tender, about 1½ hours (a roasting chicken will take less time than a stewer, so add it about 1 hour or so before beef is done). Check and skim stock occasionally. Remove beef to a bowl, spoon some broth over it. Cover with foil and keep warm in 250° F. oven. Put chicken in a bowl, spoon broth over it, cover and keep warm in oven.

Skim fat from broth (all of it) and add scraped carrots and leeks cut into 6-inch lengths. Cook for about 30 minutes. Add split celery hearts, or zucchini, cut in halves crosswise, and the small onions, and turnip slices tied in a cheesecloth square. Simmer gently for about 15 to 20 minutes longer until just tender. While the last vegetables are cooking, cut the beef into slices against the grain and place on a large deepish platter. Cut chicken into serving pieces with knife or poultry shears and arrange on platter. I cut the breast into 4 pieces and set aside the backs for snacks. Arrange vegetables in separate clumps around meats. Cover with foil and keep warm in 250° F. oven. Strain broth through several layers of cheesecloth (discard bones, seasoning vegetables, and herbs). Taste and add salt and pepper if needed and heat to boiling. Spoon a little over meat, chicken, and vegetables, pour rest into warm tureen. Sprinkle vegetables and chicken with minced parsley. Serve the hot soup in cups. Serve a bowl of coarse salt, pickles, Dijon mustard, and Chef's mayonnaise with the meat and vegetables.

APPLE TART, NORMANDY

Flan Pastry (below)
3 to 4 tart cooking apples (3 cups
*   when sliced)*
1 tablespoon lemon juice
½ teaspoon cinnamon
¼ teaspoon nutmeg
¾ cup sugar

¼ cup flour
2 eggs
1 cup heavy cream
2 tablespoons thinly sliced
*   almonds*
2 tablespoons sugar for top

Roll pastry about ¼ inch thick and fit into 10- or 11-inch flan ring or 9-inch glass pie plate. Turn ½ inch under in pie plate and pinch into a fluted rim. Turn edge forward in flan ring, press into a thick rounded edge, and mark with back of knife to make decorative trim. Line shell with foil and half fill with dry beans or rice. Bake at 375° F. until dough is set, 10 to 12 minutes. Remove foil and bake for 5 to 6 minutes longer. Cool. Peel, core, and slice apples rather thinly. Mix with lemon juice, spices, and half the ¾ cup sugar and half the flour. Pack neatly and evenly in prebaked shell. Bake at 375° F. for about 25 minutes. Beat eggs until thick and beat in rest of sugar, flour, and cream. Pour over apples and bake at 350° F. just until custard is set on top, about 15 minutes. Sprinkle with almonds and 2 tablespoons sugar mixed. Bake until custard is puffed and top is lightly browned. Cool. Cut into 8 wedges.

FLAN PASTRY

Follow method for Pâté Brisée* using 4 tablespoons butter, 4 tablespoons cold vegetable shortening, ¼ teaspoon salt, 1 teaspoon grated lemon peel, 1½ cups flour, and 4 tablespoons ice water. Add 1 tablespoon sugar if you like.

COUPLES COOK ON SATURDAY NIGHT
(Informal Buffet for Twenty-four)

CARAFES OF CHIANTI, BEAUJOLAIS, OR
CALIFORNIA MOUNTAIN RED WINE
HUMUS TAHINI   EGGPLANT MEDITERRANEAN   DRY SALAMI
MIDDLE EAST BREAD OR FRENCH ROLLS
PASTITSIO
MAKE-YOUR-OWN SALADS
ANCHOVY DRESSING
WATERMELON GRAPE BOWL
SPICED COFFEE

The kind of buffet that's easy to put together for an informal party where several persons do the cooking. It might be a fund-raising affair for a neighborhood or church organization, old college friends who meet for dinner several times a year, or a club of couples who cook and eat together frequently. The mood and food are slightly Middle East and Greek, gay and hearty. Cocktails can be served if desired, but carafes of lightly chilled wine are perfect with this informal meal. And the wine doubles as apéritif also. Set the carafes in an iced tub or deep tray along with all-purpose wineglasses for guests to help themselves. Arrange the appetizers on the same table—separate from the main course—the salami or a similar dry sausage on a board with a sharp knife for paper-thin slices, the others in bowls and baskets. Anything goes for the make-your-own salads, and they're extremely effective. A big glass punch bowl might hold the greens with all the other addables in smaller glass bowls around it. Ideally, this buffet would be served in the patio or around the pool. But it will taste just as great inside with colorful tablecloths and napkins, bright dishes and baskets of fruit or flowers for decoration.

Do Ahead: Divide the food jobs more or less evenly and ask several couples to prepare and bring the appetizers, others the *pastitsio*, salad makings, and so on. Refrigerated pastitsios can be brought to the party and baked while appetizers are being enjoyed with a glass of wine. None of the preparation is demanding or requires great skill. Just be sure each group makes plenty.

HUMUS TAHINI
(Garbanzo Sesame Spread)

The flavor of this rather exotic Middle East paste grows on you, so don't give up if it doesn't send you at first taste. Serve with chunks of Middle East bread for dunking. The *tahini* (sesame seed paste), available in cans, as well as suitable breads, can be found in Middle East food shops.

2 cans (1 pound each) garbanzo
  beans
2 large cloves garlic, chopped
½ cup water

½ cup fresh lemon juice
1 teaspoon salt
1 cup tahini (sesame seed paste)
Minced parsley

Drain garbanzos and place half of them in blender with half of each of the remaining ingredients except minced parsley. Blend until smooth. Repeat with rest of materials. Combine mixtures, cover, and chill. Mound in shallow bowl and top with minced parsley. Serve with a Middle East bread (Armenian bread* is good).

EGGPLANT MEDITERRANEAN

Pine nuts add a delightful crunch to this old-timer. It's always popular and lighter than most cocktail dunks.

Prick 2 eggplants in several places with fork. Broil about 4 inches from heat until skin is wrinkled and charred-looking and inside feels soft, about 20 minutes. Turn eggplant frequently after 5 minutes. Cool in paper bag and peel off skin under cold running water. With wooden spoon, mash 2 or 3 large garlic cloves with 2 teaspoons salt in bowl. Drain moisture from eggplant, press out seeds and add eggplant to garlic. Mash until smooth (use blender if you want) and gradually blend in ⅓ cup red wine vinegar, about ¼ teaspoon each dried basil and oregano or chopped fresh herbs, a few grindings of pepper, and ⅓ cup olive oil. Taste and add more vinegar and oil if needed, but keep mixture light. Refrigerate in airtight jar for several days. Just before serving add a peeled chopped tomato and ⅓ cup lightly toasted pine nuts. Adjust seasonings. Place in bowl and top with minced parsley. Serve with sesame crackers or cracker bread.

PASTITSIO
(Greek Macaroni Pie)

Several recipes are around for this good Greek pasta dish, but most of them use too much macaroni, not enough sauce. A thrifty Greek idea, I suppose. This recipe is better, and wonderful for a big buffet, not expensive, and easy to make. Each pie serves 8 to 10, so make 3 for this party.

1 large onion, finely chopped	*½ pound small elbow macaroni*
2 tablespoons butter or olive oil	*Creamy Topping:*
1½ pounds ground round steak	*3 tablespoons butter or margarine*
¾ teaspoon salt	*3 tablespoons flour*
Freshly ground black pepper	*3½ cups milk*
¼ teaspoon cinnamon	*3 egg yolks*
½ teaspoon oregano	*⅛ teaspoon nutmeg*
2 cups tomato purée	*½ cup freshly grated Parmesan*
2 tablespoons minced parsley	*cheese*

Cook onion in butter in large heavy pan or skillet until soft. Crumble in steak and cook, stirring it until it's lightly browned and all red is gone. Season with salt, pepper, cinnamon, and oregano. Stir in tomato purée and parsley. Cover and simmer gently for 15 to 20 minutes. Add a little more salt if needed. Cook macaroni in large kettle of well-salted boiling water, until tender but still slightly firm (*al dente*). Drain in a colander, shake out moisture, then rinse in lukewarm water. Mix through with your fingers a spoonful of olive oil to keep macaroni from sticking together.

Make creamy topping: Melt butter and blend in flour. Stir in milk and cook, stirring continuously, until sauce is smooth and thickened, about 5 minutes. (It will be a thin sauce.) Beat egg yolks lightly and gradually stir into them 1 cup of the hot sauce. Stir back into the sauce and stir over low heat for a few seconds. Do not allow it to boil. Season with nutmeg—no salt and pepper are needed. Butter a large shallow glass baking dish (12×8×2 inches). Put in a thin layer of macaroni, a layer of meat sauce, then a second thin layer of macaroni, a layer of meat sauce. Pour creamy topping over all and sort of jiggle dish so some of sauce runs through layers. Sprinkle Parmesan over the top. Bake at 350° F. for about 45 minutes, or until sauce is puffed and golden. Remove from oven and let stand for 15 to 20 minutes. Cut into large squares and serve directly from the dish.

MAKE-YOUR-OWN SALADS

A fun kind of salad and spectacular for a buffet. Guests choose whatever makings they like and dress them or not as they please. A number of the items suggested below can be purchased at the deli.

BOWL OF GREENS

Allow about 3 heads of romaine and 4 of Bibb or Boston lettuce. Separate leaves, wash, and blot dry on paper towels. Wrap in clean towel and chill. Pick stems from large bunch of watercress, wash leaves, dry gently, and wrap separately in towel. Chill. At serving time, tear larger leaves of romaine into pieces, leave rest whole. Pile all into a large glass salad bowl or punch bowl with a bouquet of watercress in the center.

PARSLEY TOMATOES

Impale about 6 large firm-ripe tomatoes on long kitchen fork. Hold and turn over flame for a few seconds until skin pops and wrinkles (or drop each into boiling hot water for 30 seconds to 1 minute). Hold tomatoes under cold running water and pull off skin with paring knife. Chill. At serving time, cut into thick slices, each slice in halves. Arrange in shallow bowl or on platter. Crumble a little sweet basil over the top and season well with salt and pepper. Drizzle with about 2 tablespoons olive oil and a few drops tarragon wine vinegar, if you wish, and sprinkle with minced fresh parsley.

GARLIC OLIVES

Drain 3 cans (6- to 7-ounce size) ripe olives and put olives in glass jar with tight-fitting lid. Add 4 cloves garlic, minced, 1 dried red chili pepper, 1 tablespoon wine vinegar, and ¼ cup olive oil. Cover and allow to stand in cool spot, not refrigerator, overnight. Shake jar occasionally.

MARINATED SHRIMP

Mix ½ cup Classic French Dressing* with 2 tablespoons minced onion, 1 crumbled bay leaf, 5 or 6 drops Tabasco sauce. Pour over 2 pounds cooked and cleaned medium, salad-size shrimp. Mix gently, cover, and refrigerate overnight.

ARTICHOKES À LA GRECQUE

Button mushrooms, tiny carrots or chunks, green pepper or celery strips, any or all may be simmered in this popular Greek marinade, but artichoke hearts seem especially appropriate for this party.

Tie in small square of cheesecloth: 1 bay leaf, crumbled, ½ teaspoon dried thyme, ½ teaspoon coriander seeds, 6 peppercorns, 1 teaspoon fennel seeds, 1 clove garlic, split. Add herbs to 2 cups water, ½ cup olive oil, 6 tablespoons lemon juice, ¾ teaspoon salt in large saucepan. Heat to boiling. Pour boiling water over 3 packages (12 ounces each) frozen artichoke hearts, drain and add to boiling marinade. Simmer until just crisp-tender, 5 to 8 minutes. Let cool in marinade. Cover and refrigerate. Flavor is superior if these are removed from refrigerator about 1 hour before they are served. Drain and serve in shallow bowl.

ICED ONION RINGS

Peel 2 sweet white Spanish or red onions. Slice very, very thin, separate into rings and drop into ice water. Salt lightly. Chill for an hour or two and drain just before serving.

ANCHOVY DRESSING

Make 3 cups Golden Vinaigrette,* replacing part of the vinegar with fresh lemon juice. Stir in ¼ cup drained capers and 1 tablespoon anchovy paste. Serve in separate bowl for guests to spoon over salad makings ad lib.

WATERMELON GRAPE BOWL

Cut 2 medium-size watermelons in thick crosswise rounds. Sprinkle slices with finely chopped fresh mint. Reassemble melon. Cover with foil and refrigerate. To serve, cut each round into 4 wedges. Arrange in a sunburst in a large glass bowl or on a tray. Center with a mound of 2 pounds chilled grapes washed and cut into clusters. Seedless green or Black Emperors are nice here. If fresh figs are in season, add a couple of pounds of these. Wash and cut in halves lengthwise and tuck around the mound of grapes.

SPICED COFFEE

If your group is adventurous, offer some of these with the coffee. Arrange on a tray: bowls of crushed, peeled cardamom seeds; small cinnamon sticks; strips of orange and lemon peel and a bottle of *ouzo* (anise-flavored liqueur) or more available anisette liqueur. Coffee should be the dark roast variety usually available in Italian or Middle East shops. Make coffee strong and serve blazing hot. (See Black Coffee.*)

V   Late Suppers

A late supper can be anything and anytime. I think of it as a lighthearted meal after the regular dinner hour—perhaps at ten o'clock, maybe at midnight or later. It's much more informal than a dinner—more like a brunch—and the foods and drinks are usually lighter and less in quantity than that served earlier.

Visions of late suppers abound in our literature. Beautiful ladies, perhaps of the theater or some distant nobility, and handsome gentlemen sipping champagne in damask-hung rooms lighted with crystal and candlelight and dining on caviar, oysters, lobster, and such. That image remains to a lesser degree in our utilitarian age. If it's a supper, it's bound to be exciting and fun. The supper menus I've planned for this book reflect some of that theatrical color and conviviality.

A supper of cold cracked crab with champagne seems perfect for a late celebration. Full-flavored vegetable soup *au pistou* is enticing and light, yet filling after an evening at the theater. And breakfast at midnight! What could it be but scrambled eggs, in a new guise to be sure, baked in a delicious oven omelet with artichoke hearts and *prosciutto*. They're all fun and easy to do.

AFTER-THEATER SUPPER FOR EIGHT

SOUPE AU PISTOU
MAKE-YOUR-OWN-SANDWICH PLATTER
(CRAB, CRISP BACON, HARD-COOKED EGGS)
CRACKED WHEAT BREAD* OR FRENCH BREAD
SWEET BUTTER   LEMON MUSTARD MAYONNAISE
CHÂTEAU NEUF-DU-PAPE BLANC
BLAZER PEACHES WITH NUTMEG CREAM
COFFEE

After a heady evening of music or the theater, nothing's more appealing than good soup and bread or sandwiches. This richly perfumed soup makes a meal with freshly baked bread or chunks of French bread and cheese. Depending on the evening's activities and the hour, we sometimes offer the making of sandwiches with the soup. A choice of delicatessen meats and cheeses or a platter of crisp bacon and hard-cooked eggs are good. For special occasions we add elegant chilled crab. Serve fresh pears and a nice creamy Brie for dessert in place of the flamed peaches if you prefer.

Do Ahead: Make the soup early in the day and stir in the fragrant *pistou* just before serving. Broil bacon and cook and peel eggs before you leave for the theater. Also make the orange peel and Bourbon sauce for the peaches. Last of all, peel peaches, halve, and arrange in a shallow dish. Drizzle over with melted butter and cover tightly with foil.

SOUPE AU PISTOU
(Provençal Vegetable Soup)

Though originally from Genoa, this distinctive vegetable soup is a favorite in Southern France also. The fragrant paste of garlic, basil, Parmesan cheese, and olive oil—called *pistou* by the French and *pesto* in Italy—is the unique ingredient. Use fresh vegetables and herbs when at all possible, otherwise a fragrant dried basil and quality frozen vegetables. This is my own personal adaptation of the classic. It's lighter with less beans.

1 onion, peeled and diced	Freshly ground black pepper
1 leek, trimmed, split, and diced	3 large cloves garlic, diced
2 cups diced, scraped carrots	¼ cup chopped fresh basil or 1
2 cups diced, peeled potatoes	tablespoon dried basil
2 cups diced, peeled tomatoes	2 tablespoons chopped parsley
2½ quarts boiling water	2 tablespoons tomato paste
2 zucchini, diced	¼ cup freshly grated Parmesan
2 cups cut green beens or 1	cheese
package frozen cut green beans	⅓ cup olive oil
1 tablespoon salt	

Prepare vegetables. Be careful to split leek carefully and wash thoroughly to get out all sand between layers. In deep soup kettle, cook vegetables in boiling salted water until tender but still shapely and colorful, 45 minutes to 1 hour. Add zucchini last half hour, frozen vegetables last 15 minutes. Season with more salt if needed and plenty of pepper. Meanwhile, make garlic paste. With wooden spoon or mortar and pestle, crush garlic, basil, parsley, and few grains of salt to a paste. Gradually work in tomato paste, cheese, and olive oil. Add a few spoonfuls of hot soup to paste, then stir all back into soup. Blend well and heat for about 5 minutes. Taste and adjust seasonings if necessary. Pour into a hot soup tureen. Ladle into warm bowls and top with more Parmesan if you like. Makes 8 servings.

MAKE-YOUR-OWN-SANDWICH PLATTER

This is strictly ad lib. You can prepare a lot or a little, and whatever assortment you like. Some of our guests make regular sandwiches with two slices of bread. Others pile the goodies open-sandwich style and some simply put whatever they like on their plate and eat it with bread and soup. For this party, cook 1 dozen eggs by directions for Hard-cooked Eggs.* Cool and peel. Arrange a pound of bacon on broiler rack (you'll need to do it in two batches) and broil-bake in hot oven (400° F.) until

Poolside buffet with glazed ribs, black beans and rice, gazpacho salad, and watermelon. (*Photo courtesy Heublein, Inc.*)

New Year's Eve champagne supper. Bubbly champagne with elegant seafood, pâté, and cheese puffs with coulibiac of salmon at midnight. (*Photo courtesy Moët champagnes.*)

crisp, 15 to 20 minutes. Drain on paper towels. Buy about 1½ pounds fresh crab meat, including some chunky legs for show (or thaw frozen king crab meat and legs by package directions). Keep very cold and loosely wrapped. At serving time, mound crab on small lettuce leaves on large platter and sprinkle with fresh lemon juice. Surround with bacon and sliced eggs. Garnish with lettuce leaves and plenty of juicy lemon wedges.

SWEET BUTTER AND LEMON MUSTARD MAYONNAISE

Soften the butter and whip to make spreadable. Pile into one tub for the buffet table or smaller ones for each small table. Zest up 1 cup homemade mayonnaise with Dijon mustard to taste and freshly grated lemon peel. Serve in sauceboat near sandwich makings.

BLAZER PEACHES

2 thick-skinned oranges
½ cup Bourbon, divided
⅓ cup sugar, divided
2 teaspoons fresh lemon juice

8 large, ripe, but firm peaches or
2 cans (29 ounces each) cling
peach halves
1 to 2 tablespoons melted butter
Nutmeg Cream (below)

Remove thin peel only from oranges in pin-size slivers with a lemon zester, or cut off peel and sliver with a sharp heavy knife. Soak in ¼ cup Bourbon for 1 hour. Squeeze the oranges and add more juice if needed to make 1 cup orange juice. Combine in small saucepan with ¼ cup sugar, the Bourbon, and orange peel. Boil until syrup is slightly thickened, 5 to 10 minutes. Add lemon juice. Blanch fresh peaches in boiling water for 30 seconds to one minute, then slip off skin under running water. Halve and remove stones, or drain canned peaches. Arrange peaches in shallow pan and drizzle over with melted butter. This much of recipe can be done ahead. A few minutes before dessert time, reheat orange syrup, sprinkle peaches with rest of the sugar, and run under the broiler a few minutes to caramelize sugar and tinge edges of fruit with brown. Place in blazer pan of chafing dish over heat (an alcohol burner or Sterno). Warm ¼ cup Bourbon and pour over peaches and flame it. As soon as flames die, add hot orange syrup. Heat and baste peaches with syrup. Serve with nutmeg cream.

NUTMEG CREAM

Whip 1 cup (½ pint) heavy cream until thick and fluffy. Flavor with 1 teaspoon vanilla and generous flicks of freshly grated nutmeg.

CAREER GIRL SUPPER FOR EIGHT

AVOCADO ENDIVE SALAD
JULIENNE OF VEAL MADEIRA
ITALIAN RICE AND PEAS   HERB BAKED TOMATOES
SAVARIN CHANTILLY
DEMITASSE

A rather elegant supper that gals who work away from home all day—
or those at home—can serve easily without too much last-minute fuss.
Veal strips can be browned early in the morning, or the night before, and
quickly reheated in the Madeira sauce while the rice and tomatoes cook.
The endive salad is extremely simple and beautiful and takes only minutes to make. While the rice cooks, I arrange the salad on chilled plates
and serve it as a first course at the table. Later, guests help themselves to
warm plates, veal in a chafing dish, the rice and peas and baked tomatoes
on a warming tray, all laid out on our dining-room buffet. You could
arrange them attractively on a kitchen counter—or your dining table—
and set up small tables in the living room. The richly glazed savarin
might be filled with strawberries, sweet cherries, peaches, pineapple, or
any seasonal fruit. But I usually serve it plain—it's a pretty sight with
no further adornment—with a bowl of softly whipped cream on the side.

Do Ahead: Make the savarin several days ahead and freeze it. Warm up
and soak with rum syrup the day (or night) before. Brown sauce for the
veal can be made anytime ahead and frozen or kept in the refrigerator.
You can brown veal strips the evening before, but they're better, I think,
if you can do them after you come home, or get up early and do them
before you leave. Fix herb crumbs for the tomatoes, wash and chill salad
materials the evening before.

AVOCADO ENDIVE SALAD

The elegant, slender white leaves of Belgian endive make a distinctive
salad that shouldn't be too gussied up, in my opinion. Here, the slightly
bitter endive is contrasted with creamy avocado and peppery watercress.

4 to 6 heads Belgian endive	*Salt and freshly ground pepper*
1 bunch watercress	*Classic French Dressing**
2 soft-ripe avocados	*(Vinaigrette)*

Separate endive leaves, wash, and put in a plastic bag to crisp and chill. Cut leafy watercress sprigs from stems, wash gently, and dry on a clean towel. Put in plastic bag to chill. To serve, arrange a fan of endive leaves on each of 8 chilled salad plates. Put a mound of watercress at the base. Halve avocados, twist slightly to separate halves and lift out seeds. Strip off skin and cut avocado into small cubes. Place on watercress. Sprinkle each salad with salt and pepper and about a tablespoon of dressing. Serve at once.

JULIENNE OF VEAL MADEIRA

This can be done entirely in a chafing dish at the table for a dinner for four. For this buffet, sauté veal strips and mushrooms ahead, then heat in the sauce.

2 recipes Brown Sauce*
3 pounds thinly sliced veal round, cut into ½-inch strips
2 chicken livers, quartered
½ pound fresh mushrooms
6 tablespoons butter or margarine
2 tablespoons light salad oil
Salt and freshly ground pepper
½ cup chopped shallots (or green onions)
2 teaspoons lemon juice
1 cup Madeira wine
2 tablespoons minced parsley

Make brown sauce ahead. Blot veal strips and livers on paper towels. Wipe mushrooms with damp paper towels and slice thickly. In large, heavy skillet, heat half the butter and oil. Brown veal strips a few at a time, then remove to a warm bowl. Continue until all veal is browned. Add livers to pan and stir until browned. Add to veal. Season well with salt and pepper. Heat rest of butter and oil. Add shallots and cook for about 2 minutes. Add mushrooms, stir until they are shiny. Sprinkle with lemon juice and cook for 2 or 3 minutes. Stir in warm brown sauce. Mash or finely chop livers and add to pan. Stir in veal. This much can be done ahead. Refrigerate, tightly covered, if you make this several hours in advance, or the night before.

To serve, heat veal until bubbly hot—in large stove-to-table dish, or in saucepan. Transfer from saucepan to chafing dish. Stir in Madeira and heat for at least 5 to 10 minutes, for flavors to blend. Sprinkle with parsley.

ITALIAN RICE AND PEAS

For superior flavor and texture, add the hot broth in 2 batches, cook until it is absorbed each time as you do with a *risotto*. Start this 30 minutes before you plan to serve. Italians don't use a long grain rice, but this delightful dish turns out better with it unless you're accustomed to cooking with Italian rice.

6 tablespoons butter or margarine *Salt if necessary*
½ cup chopped green onion *Butter*
2 cups long grain raw white rice *⅓ cup freshly grated Parmesan*
6 cups boiling hot chicken broth *cheese*
 or stock (approximately)
3 cups shelled fresh peas (about
 3 pounds) or 2 packages tiny
 frozen peas

In large, heavy saucepan, melt butter and cook onion until soft and golden. Add rice and stir until it is shiny and coated with butter. Pour in 3 cups hot broth and cook covered over low heat until liquid is absorbed, about 15 minutes. Add fresh peas and 3 more cups hot broth. Stir, cover, and cook for 10 to 15 minutes longer (add frozen peas last 5 minutes). Taste a grain of rice and you can tell if it will absorb more broth. It should be moist and tender when finished, but not mushy and soupy. Lift and stir rice gently with a fork and add a little salt if needed (depends on broth), another tablespoon of butter, and the Parmesan cheese. Mix lightly and serve in hot dish.

HERB BAKED TOMATOES

Put in blender: 3 slices firm white bread, broken into pieces, and 8 crisp sesame seed crackers. Whiz into medium-fine crumbs. Add to 3 tablespoons melted butter in small skillet. Stir over low heat until crumbs are lightly browned. Season with ½ teaspoon each of dried tarragon, basil, and marjoram, ¼ teaspoon rosemary, 1 tablespoon chopped chives, and 2 tablespoons minced parsley. Cut 4 large firm-ripe tomatoes into halves crosswise, set in shallow baking pan, and season with salt and pepper. Pack crumb mixture in mound on top to cover tomatoes completely. Bake in hot oven (400° F.) for about 20 minutes, until hot through and crumbs are browned.

SAVARIN CHANTILLY

Made of the same light brioche dough as individual rum babas and
baked in a ring, the savarin is more impressive for a buffet party. Traditionally, it's soaked with kirsch, but I prefer the orange-rum syrup,
which I use on babas also.

½ cup milk	½ cup clear apricot preserves or
1 package or cake of yeast	jam
¼ cup sugar	1 tablespoon sugar
3 eggs	Slivered, blanched almonds,
2 cups all-purpose flour	toasted
½ teaspoon salt	1 cup heavy cream
⅓ cup soft, almost melted butter	2 tablespoons powdered sugar
Orange Rum Syrup (below)	

Heat milk to lukewarm and sprinkle or crumble yeast into it. Let stand
for 5 minutes, then stir until it is dissolved. Stir in sugar. Beat eggs until
light and blend into yeast mixture. Sift flour with salt into mixing bowl,
gradually beat in egg-yeast mixture. Beat hard with wooden spoon for
4 or 5 minutes. You may find it easier to pull and lift dough with your
hands, then slap it back down on itself in the bowl and pull up and stretch
again, until dough is smooth and bouncy. Turn into a buttered clean
bowl. Cover with a damp towel and let rise in warm place until doubled
in bulk, 45 minutes to 1 hour. Stir dough down with fingertips and work
in the very soft butter by tablespoons until dough is shiny and smooth
and springy. Spread in well-buttered 9-inch ring or savarin mold. Dough
must not fill mold more than half full or it will rise out of the top and
drop all over your oven. Cover mold with towel and let rise in warm
place until dough rises to top of mold, 30 to 45 minutes. Bake in preheated oven (375° F.) for 30 to 35 minutes. If top browns too quickly,
cover loosely with a sheet of foil. Make orange rum syrup while savarin
bakes. Remove from oven and let stand in mold for 10 minutes. Loosen
sides of cake with small, narrow spatula, then turn onto wire rack. Let
cool for a few minutes. (To freeze ahead, cool completely, wrap in foil,
and freeze. Defrost for several hours, heat for 10 minutes at 375° F.)
Prick all over with a metal skewer or cake tester. Turn over carefully, using another rack, and prick crust side also. Handle carefully—cake is
delicate and soft. Transfer to a deep plate crust side down. Slowly spoon
syrup over cake, waiting until it is absorbed before adding more. Save
out a spoonful of syrup for glaze. Let soaked cake stand for 2 hours.
Carefully spoon up excess syrup in bottom of plate, wipe plate with clean

damp cloth (you may soak cake on wire rack placed in a shallow pan—
but it's soft and tricky to move then). Strain preserves or jam, add 1
tablespoon sugar, and 1 tablespoon of the rum syrup. Heat for 2 or 3
minutes and spoon over cake to glaze it completely. Sprinkle top with
almond slivers. Chill cream and powdered sugar together for at least ½
hour. Whip until thick and fluffy. Serve in separate bowl. Fill or circle
savarin with fresh, seasonal fruits if you wish. Cut into wedges.

ORANGE RUM SYRUP

Combine coarsely grated peel of 1 large orange, juice of the orange, and
enough water to make 1 cup with 1¼ cups sugar. Heat to boiling, then
simmer for about 3 minutes. Remove from heat and add ½ cup dark
Jamaica rum. Cool.

STAG BUFFET FOR EIGHT
(Recipes can be doubled for a party of Sixteen)

CHILE CON CARNE
WITH
PINTO BEANS
SALSA FRÍA   TOASTED FRENCH ROLLS
BEER
CHEDDAR AND APPLES   BROWNIES
COFFEE

Meat with chile seasonings is a favorite dish with many men (and women
too). Chile con carne is actually a Texan-Mexican border dish and no
doubt evolved from the original Mexican *carne con chile colorado* or meat
in red chile sauce. Mexicans use a myriad of chiles, each contributing its
own characteristic flavor and degree of *picante*. Commercial chili powder,
which most of us use, is made of several dried chiles ground along with
the herbs. It varies in flavor and hotness, so use accordingly.

Ladies would certainly enjoy this supper also. But I had in mind a
spread for men after a ball game, the fights, or an evening of poker. It
would be equally good for a cool Saturday evening get-together. With the
chile, serve pinto beans to be added by each guest ad lib. The *salsa fría,*
a cold sauce or relish of chopped vegetables, makes a cooling accompaniment for the hot foods. If you prefer, serve a crisp coleslaw dressed
simply with oil and vinegar, salt and pepper. And good cold beer to
round out the feast. To end it all, some crumbly sharp Cheddar cheese

and crisp, cold apples. For those who need a bite of sweet, bake a pan of brownies. They please everyone, even the most blasé.

This could easily be a kitchen buffet. Arrange plates, bowls, relish or salad, and bread on a counter near the stove. Guests help themselves to chile and beans from the cooking pots.

Do Ahead: Everything almost! Beans and chile can be done a week or so ahead and frozen, if you like. Or you can cook them a day or two before, refrigerate, and reheat for the party. Flavors of both improve with standing. Make the brownies in the morning and chop the vegetables for the salsa fría so it can chill.

CHILE CON CARNE

For best flavor, select a piece of boneless chuck beef (not round steak, which is too lean). Ask your meat man to put it through the grinder, using the coarse plate or blade which chops the meat into ½-inch dice. Otherwise, take the meat home and cut it into ½-inch dice. Include some of the fat. Or use regular ground chuck.

3 pounds boneless beef chuck (or ground chuck)
2 dried, hot red chiles (available in the spice section)
½ cup warm water
3 cloves garlic, chopped
3 tablespoons chili powder
1 teaspoon oregano leaves, crumbled
1 teaspoon cuminseeds

¼ cup cooking oil
½ pound ground pork or fresh sausage meat
2 onions, chopped
1 tablespoon salt
3 tablespoons flour
3 to 4 cups hot water or beef stock
1 can (8 ounces) tomato sauce

Cut beef into strips ½ inch thick. Then dice it. Slit chiles, scrape out seeds, and soak chiles in warm water for ½ hour. Cut into pieces. In small bowl with wooden spoon or with mortar and pestle mash to a paste the garlic, chiles with a little of their soaking water, chili powder, oregano, and cuminseeds. Set aside.

Heat 3 tablespoons oil in large heavy pot or Dutch oven until very hot. Add beef, a few pieces at a time. Stir until meat browns lightly or loses red color. Push to side of pan and add more beef. Scoop out some of the first pieces if too much liquid forms in skillet. Crumble in ground pork and stir until it is gray-looking. Meats won't brown much because of the liquid in pan by now. Push all to side of skillet and add last spoonful of oil. Stir in onions and cook until soft. This whole procedure takes

10 to 15 minutes and is important to the flavor of the chile. Lower heat, add any meat that was removed, and sprinkle all over with salt and flour. Mix well, then stir in chili paste, the water in which chiles were soaked, 3 cups hot water or stock, and tomato sauce. Stir well, turn heat very low, and simmer chile for 1½ to 2 hours. Stir occasionally and add hot water and additional salt if needed. To serve, spoon pinto beans —a lot or a little—into warm bowls and ladle hot chile over the beans.

PINTO BEANS

These richly flavored beans of the Southwest are tan and brown speckled like the pretty little pinto ponies of the area. They cook up into a soft, pinky brown. Ask for them in your markets. They're being packed in cans now, also.

Pick over 1½ pounds pinto (or red or California pink) beans (see note below on soaking beans), wash thoroughly, and put in large, heavy kettle with about 3 quarts water. Heat slowly to boiling and skim off foam that rises to the top. Reduce heat to very low and add 2 cloves crushed garlic. Cook gently, with barely a bubble on the liquid's surface until beans are nearly tender, 1½ to 2 hours. Stir occasionally and add hot water, if needed, to keep beans soupy. Season with about 1 table-spoon salt, 4 to 6 tablespoons bacon drippings, and 1 teaspoon crumbled oregano. Simmer gently until beans are very tender, another 30 minutes to 1 hour.

To Soak Beans: Soak overnight in water to cover if you wish. However, Mexicans, who've been cooking beans superbly since Aztec days, usually don't. Drain soaking water, add fresh water, and cook as suggested. Or use the modern, quick-soak method, which many cooks like. Heat beans and the water to boiling and boil for 2 minutes. Remove from heat, cover tightly, and soak for 1 hour before cooking.

SALSA FRÍA

Vary the proportions in this crispy-cold relish to suit your own tastes.

4 large tomatoes, peeled and chopped	*1 clove garlic, minced*
	2 tablespoons wine vinegar
1 large onion, peeled and chopped	*1 to 2 tablespoons salad oil*
1 can (4 ounces) green chiles, seeded and chopped	*Salt and freshly ground black pepper*

Combine all ingredients. Season well and chill. Top with chopped cilantro* (fresh coriander) if you wish.

TOASTED FRENCH ROLLS

Split 8 French rolls and spread with soft butter or margarine. Place on cooky sheet and run under the broiler for a few minutes to heat and toast lightly. Serve hot in a napkin-lined basket.

CHEDDAR AND APPLES

Look for a good, sharp, well-aged Cheddar. Tillamook, Vermont Cheddar, Canadian black rind, a nippy New York, or Kraft's Coon brand all are good with apples. Remove cheese from refrigerator an hour before you serve it. It will have a creamier, more crumbly texture and maximum flavor. Serve on a cheese board with cheese knives. Pile chilled apples in a bowl or basket.

BROWNIES

My sister's recipe—and one of the best. She says shortening makes a superior brownie. Butter or margarine makes good brownies too.

2 squares unsweetened chocolate
½ cup vegetable shortening (or butter or margarine)
½ cup flour
½ teaspoon baking powder
½ teaspoon salt
2 eggs
1 cup sugar
1 teaspoon vanilla
1 cup coarsely chopped walnuts

Combine chocolate, cut in pieces, and shortening in small saucepan and melt over low heat. Cool slightly. Sift together flour, baking powder, and salt. Beat eggs and beat in sugar. Stir in flour, slightly cooled chocolate mixture, vanilla, and nuts. Spread in greased 8-inch square pan. Bake at 350° F. for about 25 to 30 minutes. Do not overbake—brownies should look slightly moist on top. Cool in pan and cut into squares.

CRAB FEAST FOR EIGHT

CHAMPAGNE

CHEESE EMPANADITAS   COCKTAIL ALMONDS

COLD CRACKED CRAB   LEMON MAYONNAISE

HOT FRENCH BREAD   SWEET BUTTER

ROMAINE SALAD, AVOCADO DRESSING

PINOT CHARDONNAY

PAPAYA SHERBET ON THE HALF SHELL

COFFEE

On the West Coast Dungeness crab[1] is so highly regarded we like to celebrate its arrival with a festive champagne supper. The menu is little work, you'll find—all you need is money. Both crab and champagne are expensive, so plan such a party for special friends and occasions. The chilled Chardonnay or a similar quality dry white wine can replace the more costly champagne. And at less cost still, cold beer and crab make a delicious combination.

Serve the little cheese pastries and crisp almonds—not too much of either—with the champagne. Then steer your guests into the dining room, where a buffet is laid with a huge platter of glistening pink and white cracked crab, fresh lemony mayonnaise, tons of hot French bread, and a crisp salad of romaine. The mayonnaise can go directly onto the cold dinner plates, but separate plates for the salad should be provided. And also small tables where your guests can sit in comfort and dig out each sweet morsel of crab from its shell. Digging for crab is a messy experience, but the rewards are delectable. We usually set up two tables with checkered cloths and huge napkins and, for each table, wineglasses and silver, a nutcracker, tubs of sweet butter, and Worcestershire, Dijon mustard, and Tabasco for those who wish to doctor up their mayonnaise. Bowls are needed for the crab shells. They pile up incredibly fast! If you're wondering why we don't pick the crab meat from the shells and serve it neatly or merely buy shelled crab meat, it simply does not taste the same.

When the last crab shell has been picked clean, I pass a tray of finger

[1] Dungeness crab live only in West Coast waters and, regrettably, are not the same when frozen and transported. Similar parties could be planned around local specialties in other areas—steamed clams and boiled lobster in the East, a peel-and-dunk-shrimp party in the Gulf states, a crayfish feast in Wisconsin or Minnesota.

towels that have been dipped in lemon-freshened hot water, wrung out, and rolled tightly. Cool papaya sherbet, frozen and served in its own half shell, makes a fitting climax for this blissful meal.

Do Ahead: Make cream cheese pastry for *empanaditas* several weeks (or days) in advance. Shape pastries and freeze. Bake just before serving. Make papaya sherbet day before and freeze overnight in the papaya shells. Next morning, wash romaine, chill in plastic bags. Pick up crab, clean, and crack it if you did not have fish dealer do it. Wrap loosely to chill. Incidentally, all shellfish should be wrapped loosely, with room for air circulation, when it is refrigerated. Make avocado dressing and slice French bread the last thing. Chill champagne, of course.

CHEESE EMPANADITAS

A spicy Cheddar filling in flaky cream cheese pastry.[1]

Cream Cheese Pastry*
2 cups shredded sharp Cheddar
*   cheese*
1 tablespoon dairy sour cream

¼ cup chopped canned green
*   chiles, seeded, blotted dry*
1 egg yolk
2 teaspoons milk

Make pastry and chill overnight. Combine and blend cheese, sour cream, and chiles. Divide pastry in half (return half to refrigerator until you're ready to roll it). Roll each half to about ⅛-inch thickness and cut into 2½-inch rounds. Stack trimmings and reroll until all are used. You can't overwork this pastry. Put small spoonful of cheese filling on each round, moisten edges, and fold over in half-moon shapes. Pinch edges to seal or press with tines of fork. (At this point you may wrap them in foil and freeze.) Otherwise put pastries on ungreased cooky sheet and chill for one hour. Brush with egg yolk lightly beaten with milk. Bake at 350° F. for about 20 minutes, or until a rich gold in color, but not brown. (Overbaking changes the delicate quality of cream cheese pastries.) Brush prefrozen pastries with egg yolk mixture and bake unthawed. Add 5 to 10 minutes' extra baking time. Makes 2½ dozen.

[1] Seasoned ground cooked meats, chicken, chicken livers, cooked and canned fish also make exciting and delicious *empanaditas* (miniature turnovers).

COLD CRACKED CRAB

The famous Dungeness crab of the West Coast is one of the great taste treats of the world. It is usually sold whole, freshly boiled, and chilled rather than as picked crab meat, though that is available at some fish dealers. As is true with all fish, the flavor and texture of this delicacy are best preserved if you can pick out your crab live at the pier when the fishing boats bring them in. Have it cooked, cleaned, and cracked for you. Otherwise, buy it freshly chilled (not frozen) from a reliable fish dealer who knows the best source for these delicious crustaceans and also which commercial fishermen take proper care of the perishable crab en route to the pier. Dungeness crab is shipped frozen to the East and other areas, but unfortunately it suffers in the process.

For this supper, allow ½ to 1 whole crab per person. They range in weight from 1½ to 3 pounds. The larger are more succulent and meaty, of course. Ask your fish dealer to clean and crack the crabs for you. Or if you want to do it at home, remove the apron portion of the shell and the back and spongy parts under the shell. Rinse all under cold water then cut the snowy white body section into 4 holdable parts. Crack the brilliant pink claws or legs lightly with a mallet so the meat can be removed fairly easily at the table. Keep all very cold—loosely wrapped. At serving time pile the crab on a huge platter—the body sections at one end, the claws at the other, with plenty of juicy fat lemon wedges. Have fresh lemony mayonnaise nearby and let the feast begin. Bibs are often provided with cracked crab at restaurants. The huge soft napkins mentioned earlier serve as napkins, lapkins, and bibs all in one. I make them from soft old damask or colorful terry cloth.

LEMON MAYONNAISE

Add fresh lemon juice to taste and 1 teaspoon Worcestershire sauce (to Chef's Mayonnaise).

ROMAINE SALAD, AVOCADO DRESSING

This fantastic avocado dressing is good on any simple green salad. The extra dressing will keep for several days in the refrigerator if tightly covered. It discolors slightly but the flavor is not impaired. I stir in 2 or 3 drops green food coloring to bring back its delicate avocado color.

2 to 3 heads romaine	*¼ cup dairy sour cream*
1 soft-ripe avocado	*2 tablespoons wine vinegar*
1 tablespoon grated onion	*1 to 2 teaspoons anchovy paste*
1 tomato, peeled, seeded, finely	*¼ cup light salad oil*
diced (½ cup)	*Salt, freshly ground pepper*

Separate romaine leaves, wash, drain, and dry on clean towel. Chill in plastic bag. Halve and seed avocado, strip off peel, and mash fruit with fork. Leave it sort of lumpy. Add and blend in onion, tomato, sour cream, vinegar, and anchovy paste. Slowly blend in oil. Season to taste with salt and pepper. Cover tightly and chill. Break greens into glass salad bowl. Add dressing, a few spoonfuls at a time, and toss until all leaves are coated. Do not add too much dressing—greens should remain crisp. Season salad with salt and pepper. Top with halved cherry tomatoes if you wish.

HOT FRENCH BREAD

Allow 2 large fat loaves or 3 of the thinner type. Slice into thick chunks and press slices together again in loaf shape. Wrap in foil and heat for about 10 minutes at 400° F. Open foil loosely to recrisp top. Heat for 2 or 3 minutes longer. Serve in a napkin-lined basket with sweet butter. You may spread bread with the butter, chopped chives, garlic, or other herbs before heating. I prefer warm bread with cold butter.

PAPAYA SHERBET ON THE HALF SHELL

Papaya sherbet frozen in its own half shell makes a spectacular dessert. Serve the frosty shells on a glass plate decorated with shiny green leaves and a tiny blossom or two. If fresh papayas from Hawaii aren't flown into your area, serve fresh Lemon Sherbet[1] in the shell.

1½ cups sugar
4 teaspoons unflavored gelatin
2½ cups milk
1 cup heavy cream
4 fresh Hawaiian papayas

2 teaspoons freshly grated lemon peel
1½ tablespoons fresh lemon juice
½ cup light rum
2 egg whites

Combine sugar and gelatin in saucepan, stir in the milk, and heat slowly, stirring continuously, until gelatin is melted. Blend in cream and cool in bowl of ice or in freezer for 15 to 20 minutes. Halve papayas lengthwise, scrape out black seeds and membrane. Scoop out papaya meat with spoon, leaving a substantial shell. Press papaya meat through sieve. (You will need 2½ cups purée.) When gelatin mixture is completely cool, slowly blend in lemon peel and juice, rum, and papaya. Pour into freezing tray and freeze until firm around edges but mushy in the center. Turn into chilled bowl with unbeaten egg whites and beat until light and fluffy. Heap into papaya shells, cover tops with plastic wrap, and freeze overnight. Remove from freezer about 15 minutes before serving. Makes 8 frozen half shells.

SUPPER FOR TWELVE AFTER A MUSICALE

CHILLED WHITE WINE
WINE CHEESE POT   QUICK STICKS
CURRY GLAZE CHICKEN
BROWN RICE WITH PINE NUTS
GARLIC DILL BEANS   HEARTS OF ROMAINE
LEMON RUM MOUSSE/FRESH PINEAPPLE
COFFEE

One of my sisters has a circle of musical friends including a concert pianist. She frequently asks guests in for a two-hour home concert and supper afterwards. Glasses of chilled white wine such as a California

[1] See Lemon Sherbet, Kahlúa.

Mountain White or Swiss Neuchâtel (or champagne, on occasions) are served arriving guests along with the cheese pot and freshly made bread sticks. Everything is ready for the buffet which follows. After an hour, during the intermission stretch, she puts the chicken in the oven and gets the rice started. When the musicale is over, while friends clear out the small chairs or rearrange them near tables and trays in the living room, she arranges the food on her dining-room table. It makes a gala evening and one you could duplicate—perhaps with a talk by a celebrity lecturer, a special book review, a showing of some new travel films.

With the richly glazed chicken my sister serves brown rice with raisins. I add exotic pine nuts. Toasted almonds would be delicious if you can't find the more unusual pine nuts.

Do Ahead: Make the lemon mousse the day before and freeze it in a mold. Both the cheese pot and dilled beans improve in flavor if they're made several days ahead. The day of the party, get the chicken ready and make the honey mustard sauce. Wash greens and wash and slice radishes. Chill in plastic bags. Prepare fresh pineapple and chill it. Bake the biscuit sticks an hour or two before guests arrive.

WINE CHEESE POT

Our family has made this with various cheeses and wines or brandies for years. It's always popular with our guests. Mash together 1 (8-ounce) package of cream cheese, ½ pound Roquefort cheese and ½ pound sharp Cheddar cheese, grated. Blend in ¼ cup soft butter and ¼ cup port wine, or a few drops more—depends on moisture of the cheese. Season to taste with a generous dash of Worcestershire sauce and several drops of Tabasco sauce. Pack into small pots or tubs, cover with foil, and let ripen for several days in refrigerator. Remove from refrigerator an hour or two before serving. Serve with biscuit sticks or unsalted crackers and chunks of celery.

QUICK STICKS

Make these just a few hours before serving. Recrisp for a few minutes in a 350° F. oven. Open 3 packages refrigerated biscuits and separate biscuits. Roll each into a pencil-slim rope 15 inches long. Cut into 2 sticks and brush with beaten egg yolk. Sprinkle with caraway, fennel or sesame seeds. Place on cooky sheets and bake at 450° F. for 10 to 12 minutes, or until golden and crisp. Turn off heat and leave in oven for a few minutes. Cool on wire racks then recrisp later.

CURRY GLAZE CHICKEN

Easy and exotic! Simply pour honey-mustard mixture over raw chicken pieces and bake. I've tried doctoring this recipe—with less honey, less butter. It sounded too rich, too sweet. But the amounts are perfectly balanced with the mustard and curry, I've found after many trials. It's pungently sweet like a number of Chinese dishes and beautifully glazed.

6 whole chicken breasts, split	2½ tablespoons curry powder
6 chicken thighs	¾ cup prepared mustard (I use
6 chicken legs	Dijon, but any good mustard
Clove of garlic, cut	can be used)
Salt and freshly ground pepper	1 cup natural honey
½ lemon	1 teaspoon soy sauce
½ cup (1 stick) butter	6 or 8 small green onions

Wipe chicken with paper towels and rub all over with cut clove of garlic. Season with salt and plenty of freshly milled pepper. Squeeze lemon juice over it. Lay pieces, skin side up and one layer deep, in large stove-to-table baking dish (or 2 dishes). Melt butter slowly and stir in curry powder. When heated through, blend in mustard, honey, and soy sauce and pour sauce over chicken. Cover with foil and refrigerate. Warm to room temperature before cooking. Cook in 350° F. oven for 1 hour, until chicken is tender and richly glazed. Do not overcook. Baste chicken occasionally with sauce. Decorate edge of dish with green onion plumes (below) when you're ready to serve.

Green Onion Plumes: Earlier, cut green onions into 1½-inch pieces. Fringe each by making several cuts about ½ inch long all around each end. Dip in cold water, shake, and chill in plastic bag.

BROWN RICE WITH PINE NUTS

I use the new quick brown rice for this. It cooks up flaky with a rich, nutty flavor. Pine nuts can be purchased in Italian and Middle East stores as well as most health food shops.

½ cup pine nuts (or slivered,	½ cup butter or margarine
blanched almonds)	3 cups quick brown rice, or
⅓ cup dark seedless raisins,	regular brown rice
rinsed	½ teaspoon mace

Toss pine nuts and raisins in melted butter over low heat until nuts are lightly toasted and raisins are puffed and shiny. Set aside. Cook brown rice by directions on package. Or use my favorite method described in Fluffy Dry Rice.* Add mace to cooking water. Quick brown rice cooks in about 15 minutes; regular brown rice requires about 45 minutes on top of the stove or 1½ hours in a covered dish in 350° F. oven. To serve, combine rice and pine nut mixture. Toss gently together with fork and pile into a warm serving dish.

GARLIC DILL BEANS

Another family favorite for buffet parties.

4 pounds fresh green beans (or 2 quarts canned green beans)
Boiling salted water
3 cloves garlic, chopped
2 bay leaves
1 tablespoon dill seeds
1 teaspoon dried tarragon leaves
½ teaspoon basil
Seeds of 2 cardamom pods, crushed lightly
2 cups red wine vinegar
½ cup brown sugar
2 white onions

Trim fresh beans and cut into 2-inch pieces. Cook briskly in boiling salted water to cover until crisp-tender, no more than 10 minutes. With slotted spoon, remove beans to refrigerator dish. Measure 3½ cups of cooking liquid and add rest of ingredients except onions. Heat to boiling and simmer for 8 to 10 minutes. Slice onions paper thin over beans. Cover with boiling liquid. Cover and refrigerate for several days. Serve as relish or salad in glass bowl, rimmed with cherry tomato halves if you wish.

HEARTS OF ROMAINE

An easy, effective salad for a buffet. Wash 3 heads romaine, trim off tough outer leaves and leave head of romaine intact. Drain and dry. Chill in plastic bags. Wash and trim one bunch crisp red radishes. Cut into beautiful lacy thin slices. A 4-sided grater does it speedily. Or use a French knife on a board. Rinse slices in slightly salted cold water, drain and chill, tightly wrapped in plastic bag. To serve, split each romaine head into quarters lengthwise and arrange symmetrically on a large salad platter. Scatter sliced radishes on top. Set salt and pepper mill, a decanter of Classic French Dressing* (Sauce Vinaigrette) alongside.

LEMON RUM MOUSSE/FRESH PINEAPPLE

This is light and cool refreshment after the spicy chicken.

4 egg whites
Dash of salt
¾ cup sugar, divided
2 cups heavy cream
¼ cup light rum
¼ cup fresh lemon juice

2 teaspoons freshly grated lemon
  peel
1 fresh pineapple
Powdered sugar
Additional rum for pineapple

Beat egg whites with salt until softly peaked. Gradually beat in ½ cup sugar until whites are stiff and shiny. With same beater, whip cream until stiff and beat in the remaining ¼ cup sugar. Gently blend rum, lemon juice and peel into cream, then fold in egg whites. Turn mixture into a 2-quart mold. Cover with foil and freeze overnight. One hour before dinner unmold onto a wet dessert platter and return to freezer to firm up again. Remove from freezer a few minutes before serving. Ahead of time cut fresh pineapple lengthwise into halves through the leafy crown. Tear off rough outer leaves but leave a tuft of small green leaves on each half. With a sharp knife cut out pineapple meat from each half into bite-size pieces. Sprinkle with a little powdered sugar and rum. Cover and chill. Pile back into pineapple shells. Serve with lemon mousse.

BREAKFAST AT MIDNIGHT
(For Eight)

TORTINO OF ARTICHOKES
(BAKED ARTICHOKE OMELET)
SALADE NIÇOISE   SALT CRESCENTS
APPLE PECAN TORTE
COFFEE

Breakfast at midnight often means scrambled eggs in the kitchen and endless cups of coffee. There's nothing better after an evening out. The *tortino* is a sort of omelet, Italian style, baked in the oven with strips of artichoke hearts and *prosciutto*. With it I serve a *salade niçoise,* a delightful combination I first enjoyed years ago in Rome. I can see and taste them now—the vivid salad and creamy baked omelet as they were served in the Hotel Hassler's roof-top restaurant at the top of the Spanish Steps.

Frequently no dessert is necessary with this menu—just more coffee and brandy or a liqueur. At other times some fruit and a wedge of Bel Paese seem appropriate. However, the easy apple pecan torte—it takes 15 minutes to put together—is a delicious bit of crunch that makes a pleasant ending. If you have a big table in the kitchen, put all your food on it and bid your guests welcome. My table is too small for this, so I set the silver, napkins, coffee cups, and such on the dining table. Then line up the plates, salad, and bread on the wooden counter in the kitchen so I can add the hot omelets the minute they come from the oven. It's one of the easiest and happiest suppers imaginable.

Do Ahead: The morning of the party, make dressing and cook potatoes and green beans for the salad. Sprinkle warm potatoes and beans with a little dressing and chill. Prepare and chill rest of salad materials. Bake the apple torte. Later, defrost artichoke hearts and sauté briefly. Set aside until time to beat eggs and bake omelets. To serve, arrange salad on a big platter and bake salt crescents. Keep them warm while you bake the omelets.

TORTINO OF ARTICHOKES

This is easier to serve and has better texture if the eggs are prepared separately for each omelet. Tortino is firmer, more like an Italian *frittata* than a soft French omelet.

1 package (9 ounces) frozen *artichoke hearts*	*12 eggs* *1 cup heavy cream*
Flour	*Salt and freshly ground pepper*

6 to 8 wafer-thin slices prosciutto
    (about 4 ounces)
	1 teaspoon marjoram leaves,
	    crumbled

2 tablespoons light salad oil	*½ cup freshly grated Parmesan*
4 tablespoons butter or margarine	*cheese*
½ cup chopped green onion	

Defrost artichoke hearts just enough to separate and slice lengthwise into slivers (this is easier while they're still partly frozen). Roll in flour to coat evenly. Cut *prosciutto* into thin strips. Have ready 2 (9-inch) stove-to-table skillets or round baking dishes. Butter each generously and set in 350° F. oven to warm. In a heavy skillet, heat half the oil and butter.

Add onion and cook until soft. Remove onion to a small bowl. Heat rest of oil and butter and add artichoke strips. Cook until light brown, stirring frequently. Add prosciutto and onion and stir until mixture is heated and well mixed. Divide mixture evenly between the two skillets or baking dishes. (You can do this ahead and heat in the oven while you beat eggs.) Beat 6 eggs lightly with ½ cup cream. Season with salt and pepper and ½ teaspoon marjoram. Pour over artichokes in one dish and mix lightly. Repeat with 6 more eggs and seasonings. Pour into second dish. Sprinkle each with grated Parmesan. Bake at 350° F. until set and puffed (don't overbake), 20 to 25 minutes. Cut in wedges and serve from baking dish.

SALT CRESCENTS

Use 3 packages (8 ounces each) refrigerated crescent rolls. Unroll dough and shape into crescents as label directs. Place on cooky sheets and brush with lightly beaten egg. Sprinkle with coarse kosher or sea salt (or use poppy seeds or caraway if you prefer). Bake at 375° F. until golden brown, about 12 minutes. Bake these before you put omelets in oven. Keep warm, then stick back in oven for a few seconds just before you serve them.

SALADE NIÇOISE

This has been made and made and made—in dozens of variations, all colorful and good. Perhaps a test of its durability and appeal.

1 cup Classic French Dressing*
    (Sauce Vinaigrette)
4 to 6 new potatoes (at least 2
    cups when cooked and sliced)
Salt and freshly ground black
    pepper
1½ pounds green beans
1 large, sweet red onion
2 red or green sweet peppers

2 tablespoons capers, drained
1 can flat anchovies, chopped
Romaine, Boston, or butter
    lettuce
2 cans (6½ to 7 ounces each)
    solid white meat tuna (chilled)
16 cherry tomatoes, halved
1 jar or can ripe or black olives

Make salad dressing ahead of time. Cook potatoes in jackets, peel, and slice. While warm, sprinkle with about a tablespoon of the dressing and season with salt and pepper. Cook green beans, whole or cut, in boiling salted water until just crisp-tender. Drain and sprinkle with a tablespoon or two of the dressing. Peel onion and slice paper thin. Chop 2 slices and add to beans. Chill rest in plastic bag. Slice peppers into thin rings. Chop 2 rings and add to beans. Chill rest in plastic bag. Sprinkle bean mixture with a little more dressing, capers, and half the anchovies. Mix lightly, cover, and chill. To serve, outline big platter with crisp spears of romaine or small leaves Boston or butter lettuce. Mix potatoes gently with more dressing to moisten, and spread in a flat mound on platter. Add more dressing to beans if needed, mound on top of potatoes. Break tuna into big chunks and arrange neatly on each side of bean mixture. Circle the whole business with groups of onion and pepper rings, cherry tomatoes, and olives. Top with rest of the anchovies. Pour enough dressing over all to moisten everything but not to soak it. I've made this caution several times in describing a salad. To me, there's nothing so dismal as beautiful crisp vegetables, soaked, and sogged beyond recognition in dressing.

APPLE PECAN TORTE

This easy fresh apple torte can be topped with whipped cream or ice cream. I prefer it spread with thick sour cream and lightly dusted with cinnamon.

¾ cup chopped, peeled tart apples	¼ teaspoon nutmeg
1 cup chopped pecans	2 eggs
½ cup all-purpose flour	1 cup sugar
1½ teaspoons baking powder	1 teaspoon vanilla
Dash salt	Sour cream, whipped cream, or
½ teaspoon cinnamon	ice cream

Prepare apples and pecans before you start dessert. Grease and flour a 9-inch square cake pan. Sift together the flour, baking powder, salt, and spices. Beat eggs and sugar together in mixer until very light and creamy and pale in color. Stir in flour mixture, apples, pecans, and vanilla. Spread in prepared pan. Bake at 325° F. for about 30 minutes, until the meringue-like top puffs up and is light brown. It falls slightly when removed from the oven, which is characteristic of this type dessert. Cool and loosen around edges with narrow spatula. Spread with sour cream and dust lightly with additional cinnamon. Cut into squares and remove from pan.

MIX-AND-SWITCH MENUS

CANNELLONI SUPPER FOR EIGHT

BAGNA CAUDA*
GRISSINI   RAW VEGETABLES
CRÊPES CANNELLONI
ZUCCHINI CARROT VINAIGRETTE
BOMBE ROMA   RUM CHOCOLATE SAUCE*
COFFEE

Everything for this impressive supper can be done ahead. Make the easy ice-cream bombe 2 days in advance. The day before, the crêpes and filling as well as zucchini vinaigrette can be prepared. The day of the party make Parmesan sauce and assemble cannelloni dish. Prepare *bagna cauda*, vegetables for it, and the chocolate sauce. Purchase good crisp *grissini* (the very thin Italian bread sticks) from an Italian store or bakery to serve with bagna cauda. Serve a lightly chilled Valpolicella with this supper.

CRÊPES CANNELLONI

French crêpes wrapped around a velvety Italian filling of chicken and spinach and topped with a creamy sauce.

Make 24 Crêpes,* cool, and refrigerate as suggested. Make filling: Put 3 chicken breast halves (½ to ¾ pound each) in shallow baking pan with 2 cloves, 1 slice each lemon and onion, sprig of parsley, and ½ cup dry white wine. Season with salt and pepper and cover tightly with foil. Oven-poach at 350° F. until tender, 30 to 40 minutes. Cool, remove skin and bones, and chop meat coarsely. (Save broth.) Cook 1 package (10 ounces) frozen chopped spinach and drain thoroughly. Add to chicken. Cook 6 sliced green onions and 1 cup sliced mushrooms in 4 tablespoons butter until soft. Add to chicken. Add 4 quartered chicken livers to pan and brown lightly. Season with salt and freshly milled pepper. Combine with chicken. Put in blender 2 cups at a time with 2 eggs. Whiz until smooth. Add ½ cup Parmesan Sauce,* ¼ cup grated Parmesan cheese, and season well with salt, pepper, and a generous dash of nutmeg.

To assemble dish: Spread each crêpe with about 2 tablespoons filling, fold in sides slightly, then roll up. Place seam down one layer deep in 2 shallow baking dishes. Spread each dish with Parmesan sauce and sprinkle with 2 tablespoons Parmesan cheese, dot with butter. Cover dish with foil and refrigerate. Bake at 375° F. for 10 to 15 minutes, or until bubbly hot and brown flecked. Run under broiler for a few seconds for additional glaze if you wish.

PARMESAN SAUCE

Make Sauce Béchamel* using 6 tablespoons butter or margarine, ¼ cup flour, 3½ cups milk, and ½ cup chicken-wine broth (previously reserved). After sauce boils, add ½ cup heavy cream and season with ¼ cup freshly grated Parmesan cheese, 1 teaspoon salt, a little freshly milled pepper, and ¼ teaspoon nutmeg. Heat gently but do not boil.

ZUCCHINI CARROT VINAIGRETTE

Make Zucchini Vinaigrette* adding 3 or 4 carrots, sliced lengthwise and crisp-cooked. Omit pimiento from vinaigrette.

BOMBE ROMA

Make Ribbon Bombe* using 1 pint coffee ice cream, 1 pint raspberry sherbet, and 1 pint vanilla ice cream in that order. Serve with Rum Chocolate Sauce.*

CURRY BUFFET FOR EIGHT

BANANA BACON WRAP-UPS
SEAFOOD COCONUT CURRY   SAFFRON RICE
FRENCH-FRIED ONIONS   FRUIT CHUTNEY   SALTED PEANUTS
BEAN SALAD MIMOSA*
FRUITS EXOTIQUE   HOT TEA

A glamorous supper menu that offers infinite variations in the accompaniments, the decorations, and serving pieces. Brass trays and candlesticks, lacquer bowls, masses of green leaves, and fruits all contribute to the exotic atmosphere. You can make the sauce ahead for this delicious curry, then add the seafood and coconut milk when you reheat it. Make the bean salad in the morning, chill it, and ring the platter with thickly sliced tomatoes when you serve it. Fix fruits and curry accompaniments in the afternoon. Accompany the curry with chilled beer or hot tea.

BANANA BACON WRAP-UPS

Cut 6 to 8 firm-ripe bananas into 4 chunks each and dip in soy sauce. Sprinkle lightly with ginger and wrap in bacon. Secure with picks and broil until crisp and brown.

SEAFOOD COCONUT CURRY

Chop and cook 3 large onions and 2 cloves garlic in ½ cup butter until soft. Sprinkle with 2 tablespoons curry powder, crushed seeds of 2 cardamom pods, and ½ cup flour. Stir over low heat for 2 minutes. Blend in 1½ quarts chicken broth (half of it may be milk or bottled clam juice), 2 teaspoons grated, peeled fresh gingerroot or a dash cayenne pepper. Stir over low heat until sauce boils and is smooth. Season to taste with about 1½ teaspoons salt, pinch of mace, and 2 teaspoons grated lemon peel. Cook gently for 10 minutes. Add 1 pound cooked lobster meat in chunks, ½ pound each cooked, cleaned shrimp and crab meat, 1 tablespoon lemon juice, and 1 cup Coconut Cream (below). Heat gently, preferably in a chafing dish, for 5 to 10 minutes, but do not boil. Serve with Saffron Rice,* a good mango or date chutney, salted peanuts, and crisp French-fried onions. (Use canned or frozen, heated until crisp.)

Coconut Cream: Put 2 cups coarsely chopped, peeled fresh coconut in blender with 1 cup hot milk or cream. Blend until mushy, then strain through several layers cheesecloth. Press out all creamy substance possible. Discard rather tasteless coconut pulp.

SAFFRON RICE

Cook 2 cups long grain white rice by directions for Fluffy Dry Rice,* adding ¼ teaspoon (or to taste) powdered saffron. Toss with ½ cup plumped raisins and a tablespoon grated lime or lemon peel.

FRUITS EXOTIQUE

Mound colorful fruits on a bed of ice on a deep lacquer tray. Fresh pineapple sticks, strawberries with stems, clusters of grapes, fresh figs, mandarin oranges, kumquats all are good. Serve with sauce for Star of the Sea Strawberries.*

SUNDAY EVENING SUPPER FOR EIGHT

SHRIMPS TARECO   OVEN-FRIED DRUMSTICKS*
ITALIAN RICE AND PEAS*   SLICED TOMATOES
FRESH FRUIT BASKET   CHEESE BOARD
COFFEE

Not a late supper, but an easy Sunday buffet planned for around five or six in the afternoon after a late breakfast. Clean and prepare shrimp early and refrigerate. Allow one or two drumsticks per person and serve warm or cold. Sauté shrimp quickly while the rice cooks. Use only 1 pound or package of peas in the rice dish and add a little extra cheese. No dressing is needed for the tomatoes, but they're colorful and tasty topped with diced green pepper and doused with a light olive oil and few drops of tarragon vinegar. Serve whatever fruits are in season—peaches, pears, and figs are good for late summer and early fall; crisp apples, pears, and grapes for later. Bel Paese, elegant green-veined Gorgonzola, Camembert, and simply good sharp Cheddar all are good with the menu. Drink a well-chilled Soave, or a California Dry Semillon.

SHRIMPS TARECO

Clean and prepare 2 pounds large shrimp by directions for Lemon Shrimp.* Cook as directed, using 3 to 4 tablespoons oil (no bay leaf and garlic). Remove shrimp from pan and keep warm. Wipe pan with paper towel and add 3 tablespoons butter, 1 minced garlic clove, ¼ cup minced shallots or green onions. Cook for a few minutes, until soft. Stir in 1 cup dry white wine or vermouth, cook for a few minutes to reduce slightly. Add a handful minced parsley and pour over shrimp.

VI Cocktail Parties

Many food writers pooh-pooh cocktail parties as a poor way to entertain. But guests still love them and hostesses do also. However, cocktail parties have changed in recent years, and the drinking party per se seems almost passé except for big come-and-go receptions. Rather, a cocktail party has become an opportunity to get together a goodly number of friends for convivial drinks and snacks before a meeting, dinners, or other sociable affairs. Or it's a party for the evening with drinks and good foods to follow. These are the kinds of cocktail parties that interest me and the type you'll find in this book. Drinks and food are forever interwoven in my thinking.

With the drinks we serve at our house there's always several very good appetizers. A great favorite welcomed by everyone are big platters of crisp fresh vegetables with a variety of piquant dips or dunks. You'll find several throughout the book. Usually there's a hot appetizer, too, made ahead in most cases and frozen. And always, plenty of substantial food at the end of the party. It may be the makings for sandwiches with good bread and a salad, a hearty casserole, or, as in the elegant New Year's Eve Champagne Supper, a beautiful hot Russian pastry filled with salmon and hard-cooked eggs. Finally, we like to send our guests home with a cup of good hot coffee under their belts and a bit of dessert.

A few pointers I've found helpful. Keep the drinks simple and make them good. Check with your local supplier for some of the reliable bar guides put out by various companies. Have on hand Bourbon and scotch for highballs and the occasional old-fashioned, gin and vodka for martinis and tonic drinks. The lovely, exotic rum drinks—daiquiris, mai tais, fizzes—and the tequila Margarita are better for brunches or luncheons or special small parties. Nonalcoholic drinks should always be provided

—fruit juices, tomato or V8 juice as well as dry sherry, chilled white wine, and an apéritif or two (vermouth, Dubonnet, Lillet).

How much liquor to buy? It will vary with your guest list, but allow three to four drinks each. Some guests drink one, or two at the most; others drink nonstop all evening. If you have more than twenty or so guests, hire a bartender and a gal to help with glasses and ashtrays, to keep hot foods cooked and served, and to assist later with the buffet food. Make the appetizers interesting and plentiful, such as a big, spectacular platter of vegetables with a dunk, a tray of both familiar and unusual cheeses, or perhaps one great *pâté*. Personally, I don't go in for lots of little canapés. They're time-consuming, get dried out, and unless you're very professional with them, they look a little sad. However, hot little pastries with spicy fillings, which can be made ahead, go well with drinks, and I've included a number of them in various menus in the book. A cocktail party can be a gay, fun affair or a sort of dutiful, once-a-year drag. I hope you'll find the suggestions here are all fun and worth while.

HOLIDAY OPEN HOUSE
(For Forty to Fifty guests)

COCKTAILS OR HIGHBALLS   OPEN HOUSE PUNCH
BRANDADE DE MORUE   LION'S HEAD PASTRIES   SALTED NUTS
CHEESE BOARD   PARMESAN PUFFS*
CRISP VEGETABLES WITH SHRIMP CURRY DIP
PERFECT ROAST BEEF   COLD BAKED HAM
CRACKED WHEAT BREAD*   FRENCH BREAD   HOMEMADE BREAD*
WHIPPED MUSTARD BUTTER, MUSTARDS, PICKLES, OLIVES
HOLIDAY POTATO SALAD
FRUITCAKE*   EGGNOG   COOKIES*   COFFEE

The guest list for a holiday open house usually grows. I start with thirty or so names and end up with fifty or more persons we'd love to have come to our house for a holiday drink and food. This is an expandable menu—an assortment of hot and cold appetizers to go with drinks, and rare roast beef and ham for do-your-own sandwiches later. The amounts of foods can be increased according to your guest list and your cooking, refrigerator, and freezer facilities.

For the cheeses, if your party grows, buy another variety or two to add to your basic selection of Swiss Emmenthaler, Edam, and Roquefort. Make another recipe of the exotic little Lion's Head Pastries and freeze them, to be baked as the party progresses. Parmesan puffs may be baked ahead and reheated. Or they're equally good cold.

Lowly salt codfish makes the unctuous *brandade de morue,* which can be served either warm or cold. With a huge platter of crisp raw vegetables and the curry-flavored dip for them you have ample ballast for whatever drinks your guests may wish. A spirited, nonsweet punch is festive and easy to serve, and I sometimes make one. But my husband prefers to serve highballs and simple mixed drinks.

For a party of sixteen to twenty, George likes to make the drinks himself. For more than twenty he asks several friends to spell him at thirty-minute intervals so he can visit with our guests. Or we hire a professional bartender. I do all the cooking—even for an open house for seventy-five to one hundred—but for that number I have help come in the day before to assist with dips, sauces, dishes, table arrangements, and the more substantial food part of the buffet. During the party, she keeps the pastries baked, replenishes bowls with sauces and dips, crackers, breads, and so forth and empties and cleans ashtrays and glasses.

The cheese board, with appropriate knives, breads, and crackers, is arranged on the buffet table with the salt cod spread and raw vegetable platter. A friend passes the hot pastries and Parmesan puffs as they come from the oven. Later, or sometimes on a separate table, I add platters of thinly sliced ham and beef, baskets of bread, and the potato salad. Eggnog, fruitcake, cookies, and coffee I usually place on a separate table in the living room so guests may serve themselves before they leave.

BRANDADE DE MORUE

A specialty of Provence—salt cod beaten to a smooth, creamy purée with garlic, olive oil, and milk. This makes about 4 cups rich yet subtle spread. Double the amounts for this party.

1 pound boneless salt cod fillets	*Few grains cayenne or several*
1 onion slice	*dashes Tabasco*
¾ cup olive oil	*2 tablespoons heavy cream*
1 garlic clove, puréed	*Toast strips*
¾ cup warm milk	*Minced parsley*
Salt	
White pepper or freshly ground	
black pepper	

Rinse salt cod, place in bowl, and cover with cold water. Soak for at least 12 hours. Change water 3 or 4 times. Drain and place in saucepan with onion slice and fresh water. Heat to boiling, lower heat, and push pan so that it's more than half off the heat. Leave for 10 minutes, turning pan several times. Drain fish and remove any skin and bones. Flake fish. In small saucepan heat olive oil and garlic over low heat until almost boiling hot. In another saucepan, heat milk until hot. Put half the fish in blender, pour in half the oil, and start motor on low speed. Add half the warm milk and blend until mixture is smooth, stopping motor often to push mixture under blades. Add rest of fish, hot oil, and milk. Blend until creamy white and smooth. Pour into a bowl and season with salt to taste, about ½ teaspoon, plenty of white pepper (or freshly ground black pepper), and a dash of cayenne or Tabasco. Add the cream and beat again with wooden spoon or mixer until very white and creamy, about the texture of fluffy mashed potatoes. You may need to add another spoonful of oil. Serve in a warm fondue pot or other small pot over a warmer with crisp toast strips. Or heap in mound on plate, sprinkle with minced parsley, and surround with toast strips.

LION'S HEAD PASTRIES

The filling's my adaptation of the unusual Chinese mixture of crab, fresh pork, and water chestnuts. The pastry is fabulous, flaky and easy cream cheese pastry. This makes 8 rolls of about 12 slices each or 8 dozen appetizers.

Cream Cheese Pastry*
1 pound ground lean pork
½ cup flaked crab meat (or finely
   minced shrimp)
1 teaspoon salt
2 green onions, minced
½ cup minced water chestnuts
2 teaspoons grated peeled fresh
   gingerroot (or ½ teaspoon
   ground ginger)

2 tablespoons soy sauce
1 small clove garlic, crushed
1 egg
¼ cup fine dry bread crumbs
Egg yolk plus 1 teaspoon milk

Make pastry ahead and chill overnight. In a heavy skillet, cook and stir pork for a few minutes, only until it is whitish looking, not dry and crumbly. Add remaining ingredients except egg yolk, mix well, and cool. Remove pastry from refrigerator and cut in 4 equal pieces. Roll as directed in basic recipe into rectangle 9×12 inches, and cut in half lengthwise to make 2 rectangles, each 4½×12 inches. Spread the 2 rectangles with ¼ of the filling and press it lightly onto dough. From long side, roll up tightly like a jelly roll. Moisten edges and press to seal. With wide blade spatula, lift carefully and place seam side down on ungreased cooky sheet. Chill for 1 hour. Repeat with rest of dough and filling. Four rolls may be placed on one cooky sheet to chill, then baked together or each roll baked as needed. Brush each roll with egg yolk beaten with milk. Bake in moderately hot oven (375° F.) for 30 to 35 minutes, or until light golden brown. Cool slightly and cut into one-inch slices. Good warm or cold.

CHEESE BOARD

Anything goes here. You know your guests—serve what you think they will enjoy. A big piece of Roquefort or blue is imposing and delicious with holiday drinks, though we think of it more often with wines and fruits. Edam is colorful and mild—a good contrast for the Roquefort—and appealing for the holidays. Add a big three- or four-pound chunk of good sharp Cheddar or Swiss Emmenthaler, or some of each. And if you want something more unusual, creamy French Gourmandise is delicious. Serve on an attractive cheese board with knives and plain crackers or, the French way, with sliced French bread. I like the thin, thin flutes. Remove all cheeses from refrigerator several hours before serving.

CRISP VEGETABLES WITH SHRIMP CURRY DIP

1 tablespoon salad oil
1 to 1½ tablespoons curry powder
Dash chili powder
1 package (8 ounces) cream
  cheese
2 cans (4½ ounces each) tiny
  cleaned shrimp, drained
1 cup dairy sour cream
1 cup cooked green peas (frozen
  are fine)

½ cup finely chopped onion
½ clove garlic, chopped
1½ teaspoons salt
1 teaspoon Escoffier Sauce Diable
Vegetables: Celery hearts, fennel
  hearts, Belgian endive,
  radishes, carrots, cauliflowerets,
  broccoli flowerets

Heat oil in small saucepan and add curry powder and chili powder. Stir and cook over low heat for a few seconds. Stir into cream cheese. Put half the cheese in blender and gradually add half the shrimp, sour cream, peas, and onions, running the motor on low speed. Stop motor frequently to push mixture under blades. Blend until smooth. Empty into bowl and gradually put remainder into blender. Add garlic, salt, and sauce Diable. Blend as before. Combine with first mixture, taste, and adjust seasoning if needed. It should be spicy and piquant. Cover and refrigerate overnight. Wash and separate 2 celery hearts. Cut on a slant into 3-inch pieces. Wash and trim 2 heads fennel and cut the white bulby heart into neat sticks. Separate 3 or 4 heads Belgian endive and drop leaves into cool water. Blot dry on paper towels. Wash and trim 2 bunches radishes, leave a curl of leaves on each for a handle. Wash and scrape 2 bunches carrots. Cut into flat, lengthwise slices. Wash cauliflower and broccoli and separate into small flowerets. Slice thickly. Chill everything, each in a separate plastic bag. Arrange attractively in pretty groups on large deep platter lined with crushed ice. Place bowl of dip in the center.

PERFECT ROAST BEEF

For do-your-own buffet sandwiches, boneless roasts, not too thick, are best. Serve them cold, or cooled, sliced very, very thin. For fifty guests you will need, besides the ham, two beef roasts, which may be roasted in the oven at the same time. This recipe is patterned after a recipe in the cookbook published by the Docent Council of Gamble House (see Gamble House Luncheon). They serve this delicious, pink juicy beef frequently at their popular buffet luncheons.

> 1 (3- to 4-pound) watermelon-cut　　　Salt
> (wedge shape) boneless beef　　　　　Coarsely ground black pepper
> rump roast or a 3- to 4-pound　　　　Flour
> boneless sirloin tip, no thicker　　　　1 can (10¾ ounces) consommé,
> than 3 inches　　　　　　　　　　　　heated to boiling
> Clove of garlic, cut

Remove meat from refrigerator at least 1 hour before cooking and rub all over with cut clove of garlic. Preheat oven to 500° F. Place meat in shallow roasting pan, fat side up, and season well with salt and coarsely ground pepper. Rub all over with flour and place an open-end foil tent loosely over the top. Roast at 500° F. for 20 minutes. Add 8 to 10 minutes if roast is thicker than 3 inches. Slide oven rack out and pour hot consommé over it. Replace foil tent, close oven door, and after 2 minutes turn heat off. Leave either roast in oven with door closed for 40 minutes to 1 hour. Remove from oven and let stand for at least 15 minutes before slicing. Or cool completely and slice very thin for sandwiches. Serve with a choice of mustards, hot and mild.

Note: Roast may be cooked by the conventional method at 400° F. for 20 minutes then at 350° F. for 30 to 40 minutes, or to an internal temperature (use meat thermometer) of 130° F.

COLD BAKED HAM

Cook an 8- to 12-pound (bone-in) ham or 8- to 10-pound boneless ham by directions for either Braised Ham, Madeira* or Spicy Glazed Ham.* Glaze and cool as directed in specified recipes. Slice paper thin for sandwiches. The Whipped Mustard Butter (below) is good with either the ham or roast beef sandwiches.

BREADS FOR BUFFET SANDWICHES

Bake 2 loaves Cracked Wheat Bread* and 2 loaves Homemade Bread*
a couple of weeks ahead and freeze (or buy 4 loaves good firm bread).
Buy 2 large, long loaves French bread. Slice some of each kind thinly and
arrange on buffet in napkin-lined baskets.

WHIPPED MUSTARD BUTTER

Soften ½ pound sweet butter and whip into it on mixer 2 tablespoons
Dijon or Düsseldorf mustard and a few drops lemon juice.

HOLIDAY POTATO SALAD

Some delicious and rather glamorous additions to favorite potato salad.
This makes about twenty servings or more. Double or make half again
if you think no one will be able to pass it by.

3 small celeriac (celery root)	2 cups chopped boiled, peeled
Salt	chestnuts[1]
Lemon juice	Freshly ground pepper
5 pounds small boiling potatoes	2 cups mayonnaise
(I use the small red potatoes)	⅓ cup hot prepared mustard
½ cup chopped chives	Lemon juice or wine vinegar
½ cup chopped parsley	½ dozen hard-cooked eggs

Peel celeriac and cut into ½-inch dice. Cook in boiling salted water
with a few drops lemon juice, 6 to 8 minutes, or until just crisp-tender.
Drain and cool. Cook potatoes in boiling salted water until just tender,
drain, cool slightly, peel, and cut into ½-inch dice. Combine the two with
chives, parsley, and chestnuts in large bowl. Sprinkle with salt and
pepper, mix lightly. Combine mayonnaise and mustard and thin slightly
with a tablespoon or two of lemon juice or wine vinegar. Pour over
salad and mix gently. Season with salt and freshly ground pepper. Cover
and chill. To serve, heap ⅓ to ½ of the salad in a large glass bowl.
Peel and chop eggs. Sprinkle salad with part of the eggs. Save rest for the
back-up salad.

[1] You may use boiled or roasted fresh chestnuts, canned chestnuts, or dried
chestnuts, soaked overnight in water, then boiled until tender, about 1 hour.

OPEN HOUSE PUNCH

A lively punch we frequently serve. Double or triple these amounts if you are not serving other drinks (see Index for nonalcoholic Spicy Punch* and others).

Put into a mixing bowl 4 tablespoons pin-size slivers of fresh lemon peel and ¼ cup brown sugar. Dash generously with Angostura bitters and add 1 can (6 ounces) frozen lemonade concentrate and 1 can (6 ounces) frozen orange juice concentrate. Mix and let stand for 1 hour. Add 1 pint dark Jamaica rum, 1 pint brandy, and ¼ cup curaçao. Mix well and pour over block of ice. Add club soda (1 pint, 12 ounce bottle). Add cold water or more soda if ice does not dilute punch enough. Serve in small punch cups. Makes 20 to 24 servings.

EGGNOG

Serve in lieu of dessert or with fruitcake and cookies. For 40 punch cup servings, beat the yolks of 12 eggs with 1 cup sugar until thick and light. Slowly beat in 1 pint Bourbon, 1 cup dark Jamaica rum, 1 cup brandy, and 1 cup milk. Cover and refrigerate for 2 or 3 hours. Beat the 12 egg whites with pinch of salt until stiff and softly peaked. Whip 1½ quarts heavy cream until stiff. Fold cream into egg yolk mixture, then fold in egg whites. Pour into punch bowl and refrigerate for 1 hour. Grate nutmeg over the top and dash lightly with cinnamon.

FRUITCAKE AND COOKIES

Serve thin slices of the Fabulous Fruitcake* with holiday cookies. These are our favorites—Almond Macaroons,* Anise Wafers,* and the snowy Vanilla Crescents.*

NEW YEAR'S EVE CHAMPAGNE SUPPER
(Planned for Sixteen)

CHAMPAGNE
PÂTÉ MAISON   SALTED ALMONDS
LA GOUGÈRE
LOBSTER AND CRAB CHUNKS
CAVIAR SAUCE
AT MIDNIGHT
MORE CHAMPAGNE
COULIBIAC OF SALMON   SALAD MUSETTA   FRESH FRUIT
FRUITCAKE*   CHOCOLATE MOUSSE CHARLOTTE   VANILLA CRESCENTS*
COFFEE

An elegant menu for special friends for the gala New Year's Eve
festivities. It could start at nine-thirty or ten with the most festive of all
drinks, a bubbly cold champagne with crisp salted almonds and a creamy
rich *pâté*. For something hot, serve la gougère, made of cream puff
paste seasoned with Swiss cheese. For this party the paste is baked in
miniature puffs. On the cool side, a platter of chilled lobster and crab
chunks to be dunked in a lively sour cream sauce laced with caviar. All
beautiful, tasty food, fitting accompaniment for the champagne, and
appropriate for the occasion. Provide cocktail plates and forks for the
pâté and lobster. For the midnight supper, bring out the hot salmon
coulibiac and salad Musetta of cooked potatoes, artichoke hearts, and
mushrooms, among other good things. Fruitcake and cookies seem to be
a necessity for holiday parties, and I always have a plate of those. The
frozen chocolate mousse charlotte, however, makes a smashing finale
for this special party.

Do Ahead: Make the pâté and frozen charlotte about a week in advance. Freeze charlotte and refrigerate pâté. Fruitcake and cookies have
been made ages ago, we hope. Make brioche dough or easy sour cream
puff paste for the coulibiac several days ahead and refrigerate. Make
cream puff paste for la gougère one or two days ahead and refrigerate.
The day before or morning of the party, cook and chill lobster tails
(crab is usually purchased cooked), and make sauce for them. Add
caviar just before serving. Make coulibiac and refrigerate on cooky
sheet. Bake it about 45 minutes before midnight. In late afternoon, shape
miniature cream puffs on cooky sheets and refrigerate. Bake after the

guests arrive, or bake in the afternoon and heat before serving. Make the salad and chill it.

Chill the champagne well (it should be either a brut or extra dry) and serve it in tall, tulip-shaped glasses. The wide, saucer-type glasses popular several years ago lose too many bubbles and are not suggested at all by people who know about champagne. One bottle will make about 5 glasses, so buy accordingly. You know your guests and how much they are likely to drink, but allow at least 3 glasses for each person. Probably more will be needed for a party such as this.

PÂTÉ MAISON

A delicious, simple pâté even without the colorful strips of ham and chicken breast. However, they add flavor and an interesting pattern and texture when the loaf is sliced.

6 ounces ham, cut into strips ¼ inch thick
6 ounces raw breast of chicken, cut into strips ¼ inch thick
¼ cup cognac
1 onion, finely chopped
2 tablespoons butter
½ cup fresh bread crumbs (2 slices firm white bread)
¼ cup dry white wine
1 clove garlic, chopped
½ pound lean fresh pork
½ pound pork, chicken, or beef liver

½ pound raw chicken meat (light or dark or mixed)
½ pound fresh pork fat
1 egg, well beaten
2½ teaspoons salt
¼ teaspoon each nutmeg, thyme, allspice, tarragon
½ teaspoon freshly ground black pepper
Thin slices fresh pork fat or blanched salt pork (about 6 ounces)
1 bay leaf

Put ham, chicken breast strips, and cognac in small bowl to marinate. Cook onion in butter until very soft but not brown. Combine bread crumbs and wine and mix to a paste. Put garlic, pork, liver, chicken meat, the ½ pound pork fat, onion, and crumbs through meat grinder twice, using finest blade.

Stir in egg and seasonings and beat with a wooden spoon until all are well blended in. Fry a small patty of the mixture, taste it, and adjust seasonings if necessary. Line a 1½-quart loaf pan or terrine with thin slices (⅛ inch thick) of fresh pork fat or salt pork (simmer salt pork in water to cover for 10 minutes, drain, rinse, and dry). Pack about ⅓ of the forcemeat in bottom of dish on fat layer and press down evenly. Lay half the ham and chicken breast strips on top lengthwise in alternate strips. Cover with another ⅓ of forcemeat, the strips, and the last of the forcemeat. Press it down evenly all around, then cover with pork slices and a bay leaf. Cover tightly with foil and set in a roasting pan containing hot water to ½ the depth of the meat. Bake at 350° F. for about 2 hours, or until pâté has shrunk slightly from sides of dish. The bubbling juices around it should look clear and yellow, no longer pink and cloudy. Remove dish from roasting pan and pour out water. Set dish back in pan and put a smaller loaf pan on top of the foil to fit snugly inside the top of dish. Fill it with a heavy can or two to compress the pâté and give it a firm texture when cooled. Cool completely, then refrigerate still weighted down. Flavor improves if it is allowed to ripen in refrigerator 2 or 3 days. Unmold onto a board or platter. Provide a knife so guests may cut pâté into slices about ⅓ inch thick. Serve with French bread or crisp thin toast. Provide cocktail plates and forks. Makes 24 servings. This will keep in refrigerator for a week to 10 days. Flavor and texture are impaired if pâté is frozen.

PATÉ EN GELÉE

Encase cooked pâté in a sparkling aspic for a holiday look. Make Madeira Aspic: Simmer together 3 cups clear, fat-free chicken broth, ½ cup Madeira, port, or dry white wine, 1 crumbled bay leaf, and 1 teaspoon dried tarragon leaves until liquid is reduced to 3 cups. Cool and strain. Sprinkle over the cooled broth 2 tablespoons unflavored gelatin, and stir over low heat until gelatin is clear and melted. Chill until syrupy-thick. Remove cooked, cooled Pâté Maison (above) from terrine or baking dish and scrape off fat layer. Wash and dry dish and pour into it a thin layer of the thickened aspic. Decorate in a rather formal pattern with neat, small cutouts of truffle or black olives, pimiento, green pepper, or fresh tarragon leaves. Cover with a thin film of aspic and chill until set. Carefully place pâté in dish and pour rest of thickened aspic around it and on top to completely enclose pâté. Chill until set. Unmold onto serving platter or tray. Serve as suggested above.

LA GOUGÈRE

A specialty of Burgundy usually baked in a big, fat puffy loaf and served with wine. The batter is cream puff paste made with milk, and for this party it's baked in miniature puffs. The dough may be made ahead and refrigerated for several days. If more convenient, the puffs may be shaped several hours in advance and chilled, then baked at party time, or they can be baked ahead and reheated.

Make Cream Puff Paste* (*pâté à choux*), replacing the water with 1 cup milk. Season with a little freshly ground pepper and a pinch of nutmeg. Add to the warm paste after the eggs are beaten in 1 cup coarsely grated Swiss cheese. Drop by teaspoonfuls onto cooky sheets in mounds about 1 inch across and spaced about 2 inches apart. Use a pastry bag with ½-inch plain tube if you prefer. Top each puff with a few pieces cheese cut in fine dice (about ½ cup in all). Place in hot oven (425° F.) and bake until puffed, golden brown, and crisp-looking, about 15 minutes. Reduce heat to 350° F. Pierce each puff with point of knife near bottom to let out steam. Turn off heat and leave in oven until puffs are completely dry, 15 minutes or more. Makes 3 to 3½ dozen 1½-inch puffs.

Make Ahead Note: If paste is chilled, warm up slightly over very low heat, just to lukewarm, before shaping. If puffs are shaped on cooky sheets and refrigerated, let stand outside refrigerator for 10 to 15 minutes before baking. To reheat baked puffs, lay on sheet of foil, pull it up around puffs loosely, but don't cover completely, and heat for about 10 minutes in 350° F. oven.

LOBSTER AND CRAB CHUNKS

Cook 3 to 4 lobster tails (about 6 ounces each) in boiling water seasoned with 1 tablespoon salt, 1 slice onion, 1 slice lemon, and 2 tablespoons white wine tarragon vinegar. Simmer for about 6 minutes after water comes back to boiling. Drain and cool. Cut out soft under-shell and pull out lobster meat in one piece. Cut each tail into 6 to 8 chunks. Wrap loosely and chill. Purchase about 1 pound fresh lump crab meat or the frozen Alaska king crab, which comes in legs or chunks. Defrost frozen crab overnight in refrigerator. Arrange lobster and crab in deep platter around a bowl of Caviar Sauce.* Garnish with lemon wedges. Cocktail plates and forks and plenty of napkins are suggested for this.

CAVIAR SAUCE

Combine 1 cup each Chef's Mayonnaise* and dairy sour cream, 2 teaspoons grated lemon peel, 3 tablespoons lemon juice, 1 tablespoon grated onion, 1 tablespoon chili sauce with a little salt, white pepper, and Tabasco. Chill. Place in a small bowl and swirl in lightly ½ cup caviar—don't mix too much. Use black or red caviar, or some of each.

COULIBIAC OF SALMON

All sorts of pastries and meat pies are popular in Russia. The plump meat-filled *pirog*, the individual *piroshki*, often served with borsch, and this rather long and narrow *coulibiac*, the most elegant of all. Fillings vary with fish of all kinds, vegetables, meats, and eggs, and the pastry may be a yeast-raised dough such as the brioche used here or puff paste. This *coulibiac* serves eight to ten, so make two for this party.

Brioche Dough* (½ recipe for
  each coulibiac) or 1 recipe
  Quick Puff Paste* for each
1 cup uncooked bulgar or cracked
  wheat
2 cups chicken broth
Salt
3 tablespoons butter or margarine
1½ pounds boneless fresh salmon,
  poached in dry white wine, or 1
  can (1 pound) red salmon
1 onion, finely chopped

1 cup sliced fresh mushrooms
2 tablespoons minced parsley
2 tablespoons chopped fresh dill,
  or 2 teaspoons dried dill weed
Generous pinch of nutmeg
Lemon juice
Freshly ground black pepper
3 hard-cooked eggs, sliced
1 egg, beaten
1 pint sour cream
Chopped fresh dill to taste

Make brioche dough or puff paste several days ahead and refrigerate. Combine cracked wheat, broth, ½ teaspoon salt, and 1 tablespoon butter in saucepan. Cook rapidly, stirring, for 3 or 4 minutes. Turn heat to lowest, cover pan tightly, and cook for about 25 minutes longer, or until liquid is absorbed and wheat grains are separate and flaky. Drain cooled poached salmon or canned salmon and save ¼ cup of the liquid. Flake into bite-size pieces. Cook onion in 2 tablespoons butter until soft. Add mushrooms and cook for 2 or 3 minutes, until mushroom moisture has cooked out. Add to salmon and lightly stir in cooled wheat, parsley, dill, nutmeg, the ¼ cup liquid, and several drops lemon juice. Season with pepper and more salt and lemon juice if needed. Punch cold brioche dough to deflate it and roll on lightly floured pastry canvas (or sheet of foil) into a rectangle about 11×15 inches. Place half the salmon mixture on it in a compact mound, leaving a 4-inch margin on the sides, 2 inches on the ends. Cover with sliced eggs, then rest of the salmon. Mound should have a neat sort of meat loaf shape. Moisten edges of pastry. Round ends off slightly and fold over filling. Fold long sides up over filling envelope style and pinch edges together to seal completely. A perfect seal is very important. Grease and flour a jelly roll pan, place alongside *coulibiac*. Lift pastry cloth or foil and gently roll pie over on its back onto the pan so seam side is down. Make 3 or 4 diagonal slits on top for steam vents (or cut round holes if you prefer). Brush top with beaten egg. Cut pastry trimmings into diamonds or leaves and arrange in pattern on top of pie. Brush with egg. Cover with foil or plastic wrap and keep in refrigerator until 10 or 15 minutes before time to bake. Bake in preheated 400° F. oven for 15 minutes. Reduce heat to 350° F. and bake for 20 minutes longer, or until pastry is a rich brown. Slide onto a large tray or platter. Serve warm cut in slices about 1½ inches thick. Season sour cream lightly with fresh or dried dill to taste, serve in a sauceboat with *coulibiac*.

SALAD MUSETTA

A luxurious Continental salad ideal for a buffet. Substitute a teaspoon crushed fennel seeds for the fresh fennel if that's not available in your market, and add 1 cup lentil or bean sprouts instead.

5 cups diced cooked potatoes
2 cups diced celery hearts
1 cup diced fennel heart (this vegetable may be called finocchio or sweet anise in your market)
1 cup diced Swiss cheese
2 cups (1-inch pieces) heart of chicory
1 dozen marinated artichoke hearts (in oil), halved

1 dozen marinated mushrooms (in oil), sliced
4 hard-cooked eggs, chopped
3 tablespoons drained capers
Salt
Freshly ground black pepper
5 tablespoons wine vinegar
¼ cup mayonnaise
1 cup olive or other salad oil
Romaine leaves

Combine everything in large bowl except salt and pepper, dressing ingredients, and romaine. Season lightly with 1 to 1½ teaspoons salt, plenty of pepper. Blend vinegar into mayonnaise, then slowly blend in olive oil. Pour over salad and mix gently. Chill. Mound in a glass bowl rimmed with romaine spears.

CHOCOLATE MOUSSE CHARLOTTE

Creamy chocolate mousse and macaroons frozen in a ring of lady-fingers.

1 cup Almond Macaroon* crumbs	¼ cup boiling water
4 tablespoons dark Jamaica rum	6 eggs, separated
12 ounces semisweet chocolate	2 teaspoons vanilla
squares	2 cups heavy cream
¼ cup orange curaçao	2 packages ladyfingers (16 to 18)
10 tablespoons sugar, divided	Candied violets (optional)

Crumble macaroons and soak in rum. Combine chocolate, cut in pieces, and curaçao in top of double boiler. Melt over simmering, *not boiling,* water. Stir until smooth and beat in 6 tablespoons sugar and the boiling water. Turn into a large mixing bowl and beat in egg yolks, one by one. Beat well after each is added. Flavor with vanilla. Beat egg whites until soft peaks form. Gradually beat in remaining ¼ cup sugar and beat until whites are stiff but not dry. Stir a big scoop of egg whites into chocolate mixture to lighten it, then gently fold in rest of egg whites. Rinse beaters, rinse and dry bowl, and whip cream until thick and fluffy. Set aside about 1 cup for piped rosette decorations. Fold rest of cream into mousse. Separate ladyfingers into halves but keep rows of halves hinged together. Sprinkle ladyfingers with a little rum, if you like, and line sides of an 8-inch spring form, rounded sides against pan. Line bottom, cutting ladyfingers into pieces to fit snugly. Spread ⅓ of mousse evenly over ladyfingers, sprinkle with half the macaroon crumbs. Spread with another ⅓ of the mousse, the crumbs, and the last of the mousse. Cover with plastic film or foil and freeze until top is firm. Place rest of whipped cream in pastry bag with star tube. Pipe rosettes over top of charlotte. Cover and freeze overnight. Remove from freezer at least 20 minutes before serving so mousse will become creamy. Release sides of spring form and set charlotte on dessert plate. Decorate top with a few candied violets if you wish. Cut into 16 wedges.

COCKTAIL PICNIC IN THE GARDEN
(Planned for Twenty-four)

HARVEY WALLBANGER PUNCH   SANGRÍA*

NUTS AND SEEDS   SHERRY GREEN OLIVES

CLAM SAUSAGE BALLS   JACK CHEESE PUFFS

RAW VEGETABLES, TAPENADE

CEVAPCICI IN PITA ROLLS   HEROES OR SUBMARINES

TOMATOES, ONIONS, AND ROASTED PEPPERS

QUICK RUM CAKE   FRESH FRUIT BASKET

COFFEE

This is half picnic-half cocktail party and ideal for warm weather in your garden or patio. To make it easy on hosts and guests alike, two lively punches are served instead of cocktails. Harvey Wallbanger is fashioned after the newly popular vodka, orange juice, and Galliano drink. And cool, easy *sangría* made with citrus juices and red wine has just about become a staple for summer parties. With the punches, all sorts of goodies go well—salted nuts and olives, and lots of crisp vegetables with the assertive *tapenade* dip. The two hot appetizers, cheese puffs and clam balls, are easy make-aheads. For more solid food, two kinds of make-your-own sandwiches are offered. Submarines or heroes of delicatessen meats and cheeses, and hot little beef sausages grilled over the hibachi and popped into warmed *pita* rolls. End the party with coffee and the quick rum cake and fruit.

To serve, arrange the punch bowls and cups with the cold appetizers on the buffet or patio table so everyone, with a little help from the host and hostess, can serve himself. When you feel the punch party should come to an end, bring out the sandwich makings, the salad platter, and beef sausages to be grilled. Most of these foods can be eaten out of hand, but provide plates anyway—strong paper ones if you like—and plenty of big paper napkins. Separate small plates are needed for the cake—mugs are fine for the coffee.

Do Ahead: Make the quick rum cake from poundcake mix (or your own) a week or so ahead and freeze it. Several days in advance prepare the green peppers, sherried green olives, and nuts and seeds. The day before, mix and shape the clam balls to be baked the next day. Chill the makings for both punches. The cheese puffs may be made ahead and frozen. The morning of the party, make the tapenade* and prepare the vegetables for it. Chill everything.

HARVEY WALLBANGER PUNCH

This makes about thirty-two (four-ounce) punch cup servings. You will probably want to double or triple the amounts for this size party. (Consult Index for other punch recipes.)

2 quarts orange juice (fresh or
   frozen)
½ cup fresh lemon juice
1 bottle (⅘ quart) vodka
1½ cups Galliano liqueur, or to
   taste

1 bottle (1 pint, 12 ounces) club
   soda
Block of ice
Strips of lemon peel or halved,
   thin orange slices

Chill juices, vodka, and Galliano. Mix and pour over block of ice. Add club soda and taste. Add more lemon juice and/or Galliano if needed, but don't make it sweet. Decorate with lemon strips or orange slices if you like.

SANGRÍA

Make a triple recipe of sangría and serve over ice in punch bowl or large pitcher. This is dry enough to be drunk along with the sandwiches.

NUTS AND SEEDS

Spread in 2 jelly roll pans 1 pound each salted Virginia peanuts and cashews, ½ pound each *pepitos* (salted pumpkin seeds) and toasted sunflower seeds. Heat in 350° F. oven for about 5 to 8 minutes. Sprinkle while warm with chili powder and a little cayenne. Mix well.

SHERRY GREEN OLIVES

Drain 2 or 3 large bottles green Spanish olives. Heat 1 cup dry sherry, 2 dried red chile peppers, cut in pieces, for 2 or 3 minutes. Pour over olives, leaving enough room in each bottle for a tablespoon olive oil. Add oil and olive juice if needed to keep olives covered with liquid. Cover bottles and marinate olives for several days. Shake occasionally.

CLAM SAUSAGE BALLS

If you have help in the kitchen, bake these just before the party starts. If not, bake them about an hour ahead and place on a sheet of foil. Wrap loosely. To serve, sprinkle with a little of the clam juice and heat in a 400° F. oven for about 10 minutes. Transfer to fondue pot or warmer.

3 cans (8 ounces each) minced
   clams
1½ pounds pork sausage meat
1½ teaspoons grated lemon peel
2 tablespoons grated onion
2 tablespoons minced parsley

1 large egg
½ cup fine dry bread crumbs
Tabasco sauce
Cornstarch
Melted butter

Drain clams and reserve 3 or 4 tablespoons juice (use rest in soup or a sauce). Combine clams with sausage meat, seasonings, 2 tablespoons of the juice, egg, crumbs, and about 8 to 10 drops of Tabasco. Mix well with your hands and shape into 6 dozen small walnut-size balls. Roll lightly in sifted cornstarch and lay on wire rack in jelly roll pan, 1½ inches apart (you'll need 2 pans). Drizzle lightly with a little melted butter. Bake in hot oven, 500° F., for about 5 minutes. Turn and bake for 4 to 5 minutes longer. Remove to chafing dish or fondue pot and keep warm. Serve with picks. No sauce is needed.

JACK CHEESE PUFFS

This makes 6 dozen bubbly hot appetizers. Shape ahead and refrigerate or freeze. Bake and serve as needed.

6 long sourdough French rolls
Butter
1 pound Monterey jack cheese
   (or Muenster), coarsely grated
1 pound sharp Cheddar cheese,
   coarsely grated

2 canned green chiles, drained,
   seeded, chopped
2 tablespoons grated onion
2 tablespoons minced parsley
6 egg whites
Big pinch of salt
8 slices lean bacon, finely diced

Slice each roll crosswise into 12 round slices. Place on cooky sheets and toast lightly on one side under broiler. Remove, turn, and spread untoasted side with a little soft butter. Combine cheeses, chiles, onion, and parsley. Beat egg whites with pinch of salt until stiff. Gently fold in cheese mixture. Mound on roll slices, covering edges of toast completely. Sprinkle each with a few pieces bacon. Broil at least 6 inches from heat until puffed and bacon is crisp, about 3 minutes.

Freezer or Refrigerator Note: Cover prepared puffs with plastic film or foil and refrigerate or freeze. Let stand in room for a few minutes before broiling. Boil one half to a minute longer.

RAW VEGETABLES, TAPENADE

Use your favorite assortment of crisp raw vegetables. Include some cherry tomatoes and radishes, both with leaves or stems on if possible, celery and carrots cut into manageable lengths, raw cauliflowerets, crisp turnip slices, small romaine leaves, fennel hearts cut into pieces, unpeeled cucumber sticks, and thickly sliced mushrooms. Drop mushrooms into salt water as you slice them, drain, put in a plastic bag and sprinkle with fresh lemon juice. Chill everything in plastic bags. Serve in a deep tray or platter lined with chipped ice with the Tapenade (below) imbedded in the middle.

TAPENADE

Put in blender (in two batches if necessary): ¼ cup lemon juice, 1 can (6½ to 7 ounces) white meat tuna, 1 bottle (about 3 ounces) capers, drained (save juice), 2 crushed cloves garlic, 2 tablespoons Dijon or other mild mustard, 1 tin flat anchovy fillets, cut in pieces. Whiz until smooth and gradually blend in ½ cup olive oil. Stop motor frequently and push mixture under blades and scrape down sides of jar. When mixture is smooth, combine with 1 cup mayonnaise. Mix well and add freshly milled black pepper, a little of the caper juice, and more lemon juice if needed. Cover and chill for several hours.

CEVAPCICI IN PITA ROLLS

These little Croatian beef sausages are fun and easy to make. Some recipes, as this one, use part lamb; others all beef. They're juicier and have more interesting flavor made with part lamb, I've found. Tear off pieces of the warm *pita*[1] rolls, wrap around the sausage, and eat with peppers, onion, and tomatoes. Or, slit a whole pita, fill it with a couple of sausages, onions, tomatoes, and so on, ad lib. This makes 4 dozen. They cook so quickly guests could almost grill their own as they want them.

3 pounds ground lean chuck beef	2 cloves garlic, crushed
1½ pounds ground lean lamb	1½ teaspoons salt
Warm water	½ teaspoon freshly ground black
¼ cup minced parsley	pepper

Combine meats, ⅓ to ½ cup warm water, or enough to moisten well, and seasonings. Mix well with your hands. Wet your palms and roll meat between them into fat cigar-shaped sausages about 2½ inches long and 1 inch thick. You should end up with about 4 dozen sausages. Grill a dozen at a time on hibachi or other grill, turning frequently until browned. Takes 4 or 5 minutes only. A hinged wire grill with long handles for easy turning is excellent for these little sausages. Serve hot with warm pita rolls.

HEROES OR SUBMARINES

Use whatever meats and cheeses you like on good crisp submarine rolls, French or Italian. You can buy everything at the deli—1 pound each of sliced provolone and Swiss cheese, about 2 pounds sliced Genoa salami, 1½ to 2 pounds mortadella, a pound or two of sliced ham (or bake a boneless ham by one of the recipes for ham described elsewhere in the book). Thin slices of the Perfect Roast Beef* would be good here too. Arrange meats and cheeses on large platters, 2 dozen rolls in a basket nearby with a pot of softened butter, and a bowl of Italian pickled peppers.

TOMATOES, ONIONS AND ROASTED PEPPERS

Roast, peel, and marinate 8 to 12 firm red or green sweet bell peppers as described in Sliced Tomatoes and Roasted Peppers.* Arrange on large platter (or two), with a dozen large tomatoes, sliced, and 4 large

[1] *Pita*—This flat Middle East bread-with-a-pocket has become so popular many supermarkets now stock it. Otherwise look in Armenian and other Middle East bakeries and markets for it. To heat, wrap pita rolls in foil, several stacked together. Heat at 375° F. about 15 minutes. Serve in napkin-lined basket.

sweet onions thinly sliced and soaked briefly in ice water. Season tomatoes lightly with salt and pepper, a few drops olive oil. Sprinkle onions with a little salt.

QUICK RUM CAKE

Bake Poundcake* in two loaf pans or bake 2 packages poundcake mix
in loaf pans. Cool and cut off rounded tops so you have flat, even cakes.
Slice each horizontally into 4 layers. Sprinkle layers with dark Jamaica
rum, using in all ⅓ to ½ cup. Let stand for 30 minutes. Reassemble cakes
with Chocolate Butter Cream (below) between layers, on sides and top.
Chill overnight before serving. Or chill until frosting is set, wrap in foil,
and freeze. Thaw before serving. Cut cake into thin slices.

CHOCOLATE BUTTER CREAM

Melt 8 squares unsweetened chocolate over low heat. Beat 1½ sticks (¾
cup) soft butter in mixer and gradually beat in 2 cups powdered sugar
until mixture is fluffy. You may need a little more sugar to make frosting
proper texture and sweetness—but don't add too much. Gradually beat
in melted chocolate, 3 tablespoons boiling water, and 1 tablespoon dark
rum. One by one, beat in 3 egg yolks. Chill in refrigerator until cream is
firm but still soft enough to spread.

FRESH FRUIT BASKET

Since this is obviously a summer affair, how about a basket or tray of
beautiful peaches, nectarines, black and green grapes, pears, and luscious
sweet figs. Line several small baskets with green leaves, if you like, and
heap with an assortment of fruits as a centerpiece for the buffet table.

AFTER THE GAME BUFFET
(Planned for Twelve)

COCKTAILS   HIGHBALLS   MOUNTAIN RED WINE OR BEER
BAGNA CAUDA
(HOT ANCHOVY DIP)
GRISSINI   CUCUMBER AND GREEN PEPPER STRIPS   CAULIFLOWERETS
SLICED FENNEL AND CELERY   SLICED TURNIPS AND CARROTS
SPICY EGG MOLD   PUMPERNICKEL BREAD
CASSOULET
CHEESE TRAY   FRUITS   COFFEE

After a cold afternoon at the ball game, you can ask everyone to come to your house for drinks and supper if you've planned ahead. The menu above is a good example—and it will look as if you'd been home all afternoon at work in the kitchen.

In most areas except Southern California, football weather is cool weather, and the earthy hot anchovy appetizer will be welcome with a drink. Less highly seasoned is the spicy hard-cooked egg mold. With these two appetizers serve whatever drinks your group enjoys—cocktails or highballs, jugs or carafes of wine or beer. Later, everyone will be ready for the cassoulet heating in the oven. This is an ideal dish for a hungry crowd on a cool day. After all the vegetables with the *bagna cauda* you may not want a salad with the cassoulet. However, you might have a big platter of sliced tomatoes or crisp onions.

Usually we have no dessert after this affair—just black coffee and perhaps a tray of cheese and fruit. Grapes and pears are especially good in the fall and would be nice after the hearty bean dish.

Do Ahead: Make the cassoulet a day or two in advance and reheat during the cocktail hour. Make egg mold the day before. Wash and prepare vegetables for the *bagna cauda*. Or wash them, chill in plastic bags, and slice or prepare next morning before you leave for the ball game. Chill. Combine the makings for the anchovy dip in the morning. Finish it later in your fondue pot or other suitable pot set over a warmer. If you plan to serve a cheese tray, set the cheeses out of the refrigerator when you come home so they'll be creamy and in full flavor and aroma when you serve them. Buy the thin, thin *grissini*, or bread sticks, at a good Italian bakery if possible. Or beforehand, make the Quick Sticks* and bake them extra crisp.

BAGNA CAUDA

Bagna cauda means hot bath in Italian, and this heady blend of olive oil, butter, garlic, and anchovies is, literally, a hot bath for cold raw vegetables. Don't try to cut down too much on the garlic or the whole thing will lose its impact.

Iced vegetables: 2-inch chunks of celery and fennel, diagonal slices carrot, half-moon slices turnip, strips of cucumber and green or red pepper, thickly sliced cauliflowerets
¾ cup butter

¾ cup olive oil
5 cloves garlic, crushed or puréed
2 cans (2 ounces each) flat anchovies, minced
Salt and freshly ground pepper
Grissini (thin bread sticks)

Prepare vegetables as described and chill in plastic bags. Combine butter, oil, and garlic in double boiler top or fondue pot. Heat gently for 10 to 15 minutes, to infuse fat with garlic flavor, but do not brown garlic. Add minced anchovies and stir over low heat with wooden spoon until anchovies are completely integrated and blended into sauce. Season lightly with salt and a little freshly ground pepper. To serve, place fondue pot on tray over warmer and keep sauce warm. Stir it frequently. Place basket of bread sticks and bowls of iced vegetables on tray. Supply plenty of paper cocktail napkins (and I like to have a stack of small plates or cocktail trays handy, also).

SPICY EGG MOLD

12 hard-cooked eggs
⅓ cup soft butter or margarine
Sweet Hungarian paprika
2 tablespoons minced green onion
2 tablespoons minced radish
2 tablespoons mayonnaise

Salt to taste
1 tablespoon Dijon mustard
1 teaspoon curry powder
4 slices crisp-cooked bacon, finely crumbled
Pumpernickel bread

Cook and peel eggs. While warm chop fine and mix in butter, 1 teaspoon paprika, and the remaining ingredients except bacon and bread. Taste and add salt, more curry and paprika if needed. Press mixture into a small bowl, cover with foil, and chill overnight. Unmold onto a plate and sprinkle with paprika and bacon. Serve with thinly sliced pumpernickel bread or rounds of cocktail rye.

CASSOULET

There's a great deal of romance and lore connected with this historic French dish of pork and beans. My recipe is lighter than the classic and uses ground beef to replace some of the rich pork, enough fresh and smoked sausage for good flavor, and the traditional seasonings. On occasions, I make it with the meat of a roasted duckling, in which case, I cut down on the amounts of sausage and fresh pork. This dish will feed this party of twelve bountifully with leftovers for another day.

2 pounds small white beans
2 onions, each stuck with 2 whole
cloves
Herb bouquet: 1 bay leaf, 2 sprigs
parsley, ½ teaspoon dried
thyme leaves, few celery tops
¼ pound slab bacon or salt pork,
diced
Salt
½ pound fresh pork sausage
2 large onions, sliced
2 cloves garlic, chopped

½ pound Polish or other smoked
garlic sausage
1½ pounds fresh lean pork, cut in
cubes
1½ pounds ground chuck beef
Freshly ground pepper
1 cup tomato sauce
2 cups dry white wine
1 cup coarse dry bread crumbs
2 tablespoons melted butter
2 tablespoons minced fresh
parsley

Soak beans overnight in cool water to cover. Drain, cover with water (3 to 4 quarts) in large kettle. Heat to boiling and skim off all the foam that rises to the top. Add onions, herb bouquet tied in a cheesecloth, and diced bacon or salt pork. Cover pot and simmer beans until tender, about 1½ hours. Add 1 tablespoon salt last half hour. Crumble fresh sausage into large, heavy skillet or Dutch oven and cook until fat begins to cook out. Add onions and garlic and stir until they are soft. Add sliced smoked sausage and cook until lightly browned. Remove to a bowl. Drain off all but 2 tablespoons fat, add pork cubes and brown lightly. Crumble in beef and stir until it is lightly browned or loses red color. Add to sausages. Season meats with about 2 teaspoons salt and plenty of freshly milled pepper. To frying pan add tomato sauce, white wine, and about 1½ cups bean liquid. Heat for about 5 minutes, stirring up all brown glaze from bottom of pan. In large casserole (5- to 6-quart size, or 2 smaller casseroles) put half the beans and top with a layer of half the meats. Repeat with beans and meat. Pour hot liquid over beans and meat and stir gently so liquid can run through. Add more bean liquid if needed. Cover and bake at 350° F. for 1 to 1½ hours, adding more bean liquid if needed. Toss crumbs with frothy hot butter, add parsley, and spread over casserole. Bake, uncovered, for about 30 minutes longer. Serve with more of the bread sticks or French bread and any vegetables left from the *bagna cauda* or the platter of sliced tomatoes. In France, red wine is served with a cassoulet.

FRUIT AND CHEESE

Have the pears and grapes chilled. Arrange in a pretty glass bowl or compote. A husky big wedge of Roquefort or Gorgonzola would be perfect with the fruit. To contrast with the blue cheese, Bel Paese or a creamy Brie would be nice. Serve these at room temperature, on a cheese tile or board with knives for cutting, and French bread or crackers if you wish. If you feel you must have something sweet to finish the party, a plate of Brownies* would be welcome. Or, how about a dish of those creamy, chocolate-covered mints?

VII Dessert and Coffee Parties

You don't need a menu for a dessert or coffee party. Simply make two or three of your greatest desserts or coffee breads with a contrast of flavors, textures, and appearance. Serve pridefully to a dozen or so friends with a choice of drinks. It's an inexpensive, fun way to entertain and appropriate for many occasions, particularly during the holidays.

Coffeecakes and pastries are more welcome in the morning, cakes and fancy desserts in the afternoon and evening. But coffee and Danish or coffee and doughnuts make a favorite treat anytime. In this chapter, I've suggested several combinations of sweets that are good for a dessert or coffee buffet. Mix and match to your own taste but use some of the guidelines given. For instance, the elegant *dacquoise* of crisp meringue layers contrasts beautifully with the cream puff ring, Paris-Brest. The delicious and easy yeast Danish *kringle* I've paired with a quickie date coffeecake. Other combinations vary in a similar way.

You can buy a number of these desserts and pastries at fancy bakeries. But nothing flatters a guest more than a special homemade dessert or fancy coffee pastry.

WORLD'S GREAT DESSERTS AT 10 P.M.
(Planned for Sixteen to Twenty)

GÂTEAU DACQUOISE   PARIS-BREST   GLAZED FRUIT TARTS
BLACK COFFEE   HOT TEA*
TINY BOTTLES ASSORTED LIQUEURS

Do Ahead: Make pastry for tarts several days ahead. Shape and bake the cream puff ring. Next day make pastry cream for tarts and Paris-Brest. Assemble tarts in afternoon, Paris-Brest just before serving.

GÂTEAU DACQUOISE

The French pâtissier makes almond meringue layers a little different from this. This method works best for me and makes a delicious crisp meringue.

6 ounces shelled, blanched
   almonds
2 tablespoons cornstarch
1½ cups superfine sugar, divided
¼ teaspoon salt

6 large egg whites, at room
   temperature
Mocha Butter Cream (below)
Chocolate curls

On heavy brown paper, mark 3 (8-inch) circles with round cake pan. Butter well and flour lightly. Put 2 of them diagonally on one large cooky sheet, one on another cooky sheet. Whiz almonds in blender until finely ground and powdery-looking (you should have about 1½ cups). Mix with cornstarch and ½ cup sugar. Add salt to egg whites and beat on electric mixer until soft peaks form. Gradually beat in 1 cup sugar until whites stand in stiff, sharp peaks. Gently and quickly fold in almond-cornstarch mixture. Spread meringue within circles on paper and smooth tops. Bake at 250° F. for 1 hour. Turn heat off and leave in oven until cool and crisp, 1 to 2 hours. Carefully peel off paper. To assemble, spread mocha butter cream between layers and on top. If you wish, frost sides also and pipe some of the cream around top in rosettes. Sprinkle center with chocolate curls. Chill overnight. Cut carefully into 12 to 16 wedges.

MOCHA BUTTER CREAM

Put in mixer and beat until creamy 4 egg yolks. Gradually beat in 2 cups sifted powdered sugar, then alternately ¼ cup hot, double strength coffee and 1 cup (2 sticks) slightly softened butter, bit by bit. Beat in another ½ cup sifted powdered sugar, 1 teaspoon vanilla, and 2 tablespoons crème de cacao. Beat until smooth and fluffy. It may curdle when coffee is added, but smooths out as butter is added. Chill until firm enough to spread.

GLAZED FRUIT TARTS

For 1 dozen tarts, make Cream Cheese Pastry* or Pâte Brisée,* adding 1 tablespoon sugar and 1 teaspoon grated lemon peel to latter. Chill overnight and roll as directed slightly thicker than ⅛ inch. Cut into rounds and fit into 3-inch tart pans. Brush with beaten egg yolk, prick with fork, and chill 5 to 10 minutes. Bake cream cheese shells at 350° F. (pâte brisée at 400° F.) for 15 to 20 minutes, until golden (after 5 minutes, prick shells again if they puff up). Cool shells. Make Pastry Cream* (Crème Pâtissière) and, when cool, fold in ½ cup sour cream, 1 teaspoon grated orange peel. Spread a layer of the pastry cream in each shell. Top with whole raspberries, blueberries, or strawberries or halved strawberries. Melt 1 cup red currant jelly or apricot jam, sieved, with a tablespoon orange juice or Grand Marnier. Spoon over fruits to glaze. Chill.

PARIS-BREST

If you can make cream puffs and a soft custard cream, you can make this famous French pastry specialty.

2 tablespoons slivered red glacé cherries	Egg yolk
2 tablespoons kirsch	1 cup heavy cream
Pastry Cream (Crème Pâtissière)*	Apricot glaze
Cream Puff Paste (Pâte à Choux)*	2 tablespoons chopped pistachios

Marinate cherries in kirsch. Make pastry cream as directed and cool. Make cream puff paste. Preheat oven to 400° F. Draw a 9-inch circle on sheet of heavy brown paper. Butter it and flour lightly. Place on a cooky sheet and drop cream puff paste by tablespoons in big mounds on line of the circle. Brush paste lightly with beaten egg yolk. Bake for about 50 minutes. With small sharp knife, make 5 or 6 slits around bottom of ring. Bake ring for about 10 minutes longer, until crisp and golden brown. Turn off heat, leave door ajar, and let ring stand in oven to dry, about 15 minutes. Remove from paper and cool on wire rack. To assemble dessert, split ring in half with long sharp knife. Lift off top and scoop out and discard any soft dough inside. Whip cream and fold into cool pastry cream with cherries and kirsch. Spoon into bottom of ring. Replace top. Brush lightly with sieved apricot jam and sprinkle with pistachios. Makes 10 to 12 servings.

SWEETS IN THE AFTERNOON
(Planned for Twelve to Sixteen)

GÂTEAU AUX MARRONS   SHORTBREAD FANS
COFFEE PROFITEROLES/RUM CHOCOLATE SAUCE
VIENNESE COFFEE*   HOT TEA* OR CHAMPAGNE PUNCH*

Do Ahead: Make shortbread a week or more ahead. Day before make sponge layers for *gâteau* and make *profiteroles.* When puffs are cool, fill with ice cream and freeze overnight. Assemble cake next day and make chocolate sauce and drinks.

GÂTEAU AUX MARRONS

Light sponge layers sprinkled with rum, filled and frosted with pastry cream and preserved chestnuts. Delectable and easy.

*Quick Spongecake**	*2 teaspoons grated lemon peel*
Pastry Cream (Crème	*⅓ cup dark rum*
*Pâtissière)**	*1½ cups heavy cream*
1 bottle marrons glacés	*Glacé cherries*
(preserved chestnuts)	*Pistachios*

Bake and cool spongecake layers. Make and cool pastry cream. Carefully split layers with serrated knife. Mix syrup from marrons, 1 teaspoon lemon peel and rum. Sprinkle evenly over cut surfaces of layers. Whip cream until stiff and fold 1 cup of it and rest of lemon peel into cool pastry cream. Spread between layers. Chop drained marrons. Save a few pieces for top and gently fold rest into whipped cream. Frost top and sides of cake. Chill for several hours. Decorate top with marron pieces, glacé cherries, and pistachios if you wish. Cut into small wedges. Makes 16 rich servings.

SHORTBREAD FANS

Combine 2½ cups sifted all-purpose flour with ½ cup rice flour (from health food store), ½ cup superfine granulated sugar, and a pinch of salt. With fingertips work in ½ pound (2 sticks) butter and 1 teaspoon vanilla until dough can be formed into a ball. Knead until smooth and chill for 1 hour. Roll ¼ inch thick on floured surface and cut into 3-inch rounds. Cut each in quarters and with back of table knife mark in ridges to resemble a fan. (For the holidays, if you like, use a star cutter if you have one, and press a quartered glacé cherry in center of each.) Sprinkle fans lightly with sugar and place on cooky sheets. Bake at 350° F. for 15 to 20 minutes, until pale gold only. Cool on wire racks. Makes about 5 dozen.

COFFEE PROFITEROLES

Miniature cream puffs filled with coffee ice cream and topped with a marvelous chocolate sauce.

Cream Puff Paste (Pâte à Choux)*   *1 pint coffee ice cream*
1 tablespoon sugar   *Rum Chocolate Sauce (below)*
1 egg yolk, beaten

Preheat oven to 425° F. Make cream puff paste as directed and add the sugar. Drop by teaspoons onto baking sheets in 1-inch mounds spaced 2 inches apart. Brush lightly with egg yolk, using your fingertip. Bake until puffed and crisp 15 to 20 minutes (touch them). Reduce heat to 350° F. and bake for 5 to 10 minutes longer. Pierce each with point of knife at base. Turn off heat and leave in oven for 10 minutes to dry out completely. Cool on wire racks. Split each in half and fill with rounded spoonful ice cream. Lightly press top in place—let the ice cream show a bit around the sides. Freeze several hours or overnight. Make rum chocolate sauce. To serve, set puffs in a shallow bowl and serve chocolate sauce in separate bowl alongside. Dessert forks and plates are needed. Makes 36 to 40 *profiteroles*.

RUM CHOCOLATE SAUCE

Melt 6 ounces (1½ packages) sweet chocolate over hot water with ⅓ cup water, 2 tablespoons double strength liquid coffee and 2 tablespoons dark rum. Stir until blended and cool slightly. Cut 3 tablespoons cold butter into pieces and beat into lukewarm chocolate, bit by bit. Beat well after each addition. Makes about 1½ cups.

HOLIDAY SWEETMEATS TABLE
(Planned for Twenty)

FABULOUS FRUITCAKE*   BUNDT CAKE, GRAND MARNIER

VANILLA CRESCENTS   SALT GLAZED NUTS   ALMOND MACAROONS*

ANISE WAFERS   SHERRIED DATES   TOFFEE BARS

EGGNOG*   COFFEE   SPICY PUNCH*

These are all pick-up treats and are made ahead, so it could easily be a come-and-go affair—in the late afternoon or in the evening.

Everything can be made ahead except the coffee. Bake the fruitcake weeks ahead, the macaroons and dates a couple of weeks before the party. Do the anise wafers and salted nuts two or three days in advance; the bundt cake, toffee bars, and eggnog the day before.

BUNDT CAKE, GRAND MARNIER

Prepare Poundcake* batter or 2 packages poundcake mix and bake in bundt cake pan by poundcake direction or those on the label. Cool in pan for 10 to 15 minutes. Remove and cool on wire racks. Combine 1 tablespoon grated orange peel, 2 tablespoons finely slivered candied orange peel, ½ cup orange juice, ½ cup sugar and heat to boiling. Add ¼ cup Grand Marnier and 1 teaspoon lemon juice. Spoon evenly and slowly over poundcake to glaze it. Spoon up dribbles from plate until all syrup is used.

VANILLA CRESCENTS

Old World flavor of vanilla bean and almonds in a rich butter crescent.

2 cups powdered sugar
2-inch piece whole vanilla bean,
   split
½ pound blanched almonds

1 cup soft butter
1 egg yolk
2½ cups sifted all-purpose flour
½ teaspoon vanilla extract

About a week ahead, sift powdered sugar and remove 1 tablespoon. Mix it with the vanilla bean and pound bean to extract the vanilla flavor. Return to rest of sugar, cover tightly, and store. Spread almonds on cooky sheet and toast in 300° F. oven until pale gold only, 8 to 10 minutes. Cool on paper towels. Whiz in blender for a few seconds until ground but still light and powdery-looking (you should have about 2 cups). Beat butter and ½ cup of the vanilla sugar until light and beat in egg yolk. Stir in flour, almonds, and vanilla extract until dough is smooth. Mound on sheet of foil, wrap tightly, and chill for at least 1 hour. Break off small pieces. Shape on cold, ungreased cooky sheet into crescents about ½ inch thick and 2 inches long. Bake at 350° F. only until pale gold, 12 to 14 minutes. Spread vanilla sugar in mound on foil. Carefully lay warm crescents, tops down, in sugar and roll gently to coat evenly. Cool on wire racks. Makes about 6 dozen.

ANISE WAFERS

Reduce the nutmeg in Cream Cheese Wafers* to ½ teaspoon and add 1 tablespoon anise seeds, crushed lightly with rolling pin. For this holiday party, sprinkle tops with red and green sugar if you like. Bake as directed.

SHERRIED DATES

Rinse 2 pounds fresh dates with boiling water and pack into jars, adding a half dozen cloves to each jar. Heat cream sherry to boiling, pour over dates to cover them. Cover and soak for at least 2 weeks before serving.

SALT GLAZED NUTS

Use all one kind or a combination of blanched almonds, walnut halves, pecan halves, blanched Virginia peanuts. For each 2 cups, lightly beat one egg white. Add nuts and stir until completely coated. Sprinkle with coarse salt (kosher or sea salt). Spread evenly in jelly roll pan and heat in 350° F. oven until heated through and glazed, 5 to 8 minutes. Stir often.

TOFFEE BARS

Almost as rich as the candy for which they're named.

2 cups sifted all-purpose flour
½ teaspoon baking powder
½ teaspoon salt
1 cup butter or margarine
1 cup firmly packed brown sugar

1 egg
1 teaspoon vanilla
½ pound semisweet chocolate
1 cup chopped walnuts, pecans,
 or toasted almonds

Resift flour with baking powder and salt. Cream butter and beat in brown sugar until light and fluffy. Beat in egg until mixture is light. Stir in flour mixture and vanilla. Blend well. Spread smoothly in greased jelly roll pan, 10×15 inches. Bake at 350° F. for about 20 minutes. While cookies bake, melt chocolate over hot water. Remove cookies from oven and spread with chocolate while warm. Sprinkle with nuts. Cool and cut into bars (1×2½ inches). Makes 5 dozen.

INTERNATIONAL COFFEE BUFFET
(Planned for Sixteen)

AMBROSIA, GRAND MARNIER*
BRIOCHE CROWNS   LEMON SAFFRON BUNS*   CHURROS
SWEET BUTTER   CREAM CHEESE   MARMALADE   CURRANT JELLY
HOT COFFEE   MEXICAN HOT CHOCOLATE

Sensational coffee breads from France, England, and Spain. Serve them for a special holiday party with plenty of good hot coffee—make special ones if you like (see Spiced Coffee* or Viennese Coffee*)—or cups of foamy hot chocolate. The brioche dough and cream puff paste for *churros* can be made several days ahead and refrigerated. Make saffron buns the day before the party and reheat as directed in recipe. Brioche crowns may be made the day before also and reheated or served cold, but I prefer to bake them early the morning of the party. Fry churros about an hour before serving.

BRIOCHE CROWNS

Make Brioche* dough, increasing sugar to ¼ cup. Refrigerate overnight. Divide in half, return one piece to refrigerator. Quickly shape dough into a fat roll about 15 inches long. Form into a ring on a greased cooky sheet and pinch ends together to seal. Shape rest of dough into ring on separate cooky sheet. Cover with towel and let rise in warm place until doubled, at least 30 minutes. Brush with beaten egg yolk. With scissors, snip small gashes about an inch apart around rings to form peaks for the crown effect. Bake at 400° F. for about 25 minutes, or until richly browned. Serve warm or cold, in thick slices with sweet butter, cream cheese, marmalade, and currant jelly.

CHURROS

These airy little doughnut puffs are popular in both Spain and Mexico and completely irresistible. I'll never forget my first—crisp, fragile, gossamer light with a faint hint of orange—served with a cup of foamy hot chocolate across the plaza from the Palace Hotel in Madrid.

For 2 dozen churros, make Cream Puff Paste,* reducing butter to 2 tablespoons and adding 1 tablespoon sugar. The paste is a little heavier than in the regular recipe, so beat in each egg very vigorously until dough is smooth and shiny (use mixer if necessary). Heat a deep pot of oil with 3 or 4 strips of orange peel until very hot (370° F. on fat thermometer). Put dough in pastry bag with ½-inch star tube. Squeeze 4-inch pieces into hot fat, snipping off each with wet scissors or knife. Cook, turning as needed, until crisp and a rich golden brown, 4 to 5 minutes. Drain on crumpled paper towels. Cool for a few moments and roll, still warm, in mixture of granulated sugar and cinnamon. Serve with hot chocolate or coffee.

MEXICAN HOT CHOCOLATE

This is delicious made with Mexican chocolate, but its effect can be approximated with American sweet chocolate and cinnamon. For a dozen servings, coarsely grate 6 ounces (1½ packages) sweet chocolate. Combine with 2 quarts milk, a pinch of salt, and vanilla and cinnamon to taste. Heat over very low heat until hot and chocolate has melted. Beat with an egg beater or a Mexican *molinillo*, if you own one, until chocolate is foamy. Serve hot in warm mugs or tall chocolate cups. Cinnamon stick stirrers add an extra touch.

COME FOR DANISH AND COFFEE. . . .
(Planned for Twelve)

PAPAYA WEDGES WITH LIME
PRUNE BOUCHÉES   DATE COFFEECAKE
DANISH KRINGLE   HOT COFFEE

Two beautiful Danish *kringles* are the stars of this coffee party. The unusual little sausage-stuffed prune pastries and luscious date coffeecake are good and easy contrasts. Make dough for kringles 2 days in advance and bake kringles the day before. Prepare prune *bouchées* and freeze overnight. Make date coffeecake early next morning. Bake bouchées and brew coffee just before serving.

PRUNE BOUCHÉES

Drain well 2 dozen extra-large cooked prunes and slit down one side. Remove pit. Brown and drain 8 pork sausage links and cut each in 3 pieces. Stuff into prunes. Roll Pastry* thin and cut into oblongs 2½ × 3 inches. Wrap around prunes, moisten edges, and press to seal. Place seam down on cooky sheets or foil. Cover and freeze overnight. Bake at 400° F. for 12 to 15 minutes or until crisp and golden brown.

DATE COFFEECAKE

Prepare a package date bread mix by directions, adding to batter 2 tablespoons each brown sugar and melted butter, 1 tablespoon grated orange peel. Bake in greased, floured 9-inch square pan at 350° F. for 30 minutes. Cool for 5 minutes. Mix together 1 cup sour cream, ¼ cup brown sugar, 1 teaspoon cinnamon and spread over cake. Sprinkle with ⅓ cup thin-sliced almonds or walnuts. Bake for 10 minutes. Serve warm or cold. Cut into 16 to 18 squares.

DANISH KRINGLE

A flat, flaky, rich coffeecake patterned after the Danish made by Ostergaard Bakery in Racine, Wisconsin, and shipped all over the country. It's one of the easiest and best yeast pastries you'll ever bake.

1 packet active dry yeast
¼ cup warm water (see yeast
*   label)*
½ cup milk, scalded
1 egg, separated
2 cups sifted all-purpose flour
2 tablespoons sugar
½ teaspoon salt

½ cup butter or margarine (or
*   part shortening)*
Almond Paste Filling (below)
Date Pecan Filling (below)
1 egg white for topping
¾ cup sliced almonds
½ cup powdered sugar

Sprinkle yeast over warm water and let stand for 5 minutes. Cool milk to lukewarm and stir in egg yolk. Sift flour, sugar, and salt into mixing bowl. With fingertips work in butter until mixture is crumbly and well blended. Stir in milk and dissolved yeast. Mix until thoroughly blended. Scrape down sides of bowl—it's a soft dough—and butter top of dough. Cover bowl tightly and chill for at least 2 hours, but preferably overnight. Make desired filling (half of each if you want 2 kinds).

To make *kringle*, divide dough and return half to refrigerator. On well-floured pastry cloth, roll one part into a long, narrow rectangle, 6×18 inches. Beat the egg white and spread half of it in a 3-inch strip down center of dough. Spread half the filling over it. Moisten edges of dough. Fold one side over filling, then other side, overlapping by 1½ inches. Press to seal. Lift carefully onto a greased cooky sheet, seam side down. Curve into a flat horseshoe shape and pinch ends to seal dough. Roll, fill, and shape second half of dough and place on a second cooky sheet (or do it later). Cover kringles with towel and let rise for 30 to 45 minutes, until dough is light and no longer cold. Beat egg white until frothy, add almonds, and put in a strainer to drain briefly. Drop drained almonds into powdered sugar and roll until lightly coated. Scatter half of them over each cake. Bake at 375° F. for about 20 minutes or until golden brown. Cut in wedges to serve. To reheat, wrap in foil and put in 400° F. oven for about 10 minutes. Each kringle makes 8 to 12 servings.

Almond Paste Filling: For 2 kringles, cream ½ cup soft butter with 1 cup firmly packed brown sugar until smooth and fluffy. Gradually beat in 1 cup softened almond paste.

Date Pecan Filling: For 2 kringles, combine 1 cup firmly packed brown sugar with 2 tablespoons soft butter, ½ cup finely chopped fresh dates, and 1 cup chopped pecans. Blend into a paste.

VIII Recipe Repertory

BASIC SAUCES AND VARIATIONS

SAUCE BÉCHAMEL
(Basic White Sauce)

The basis for hundreds of dishes and classic white sauces such as Mornay, velouté, chaud-froid, etc.

2 tablespoons butter or margarine
2 tablespoons flour
1¼ cups milk (or chicken, fish, or
vegetable broth)

Salt and freshly ground pepper
Nutmeg

Melt butter in heavy small saucepan over low heat. Stir in flour without letting mixture brown. A wire whisk is best for this but a wooden spoon will do. Stir and cook mixture for about 2 minutes. Remove from heat and add cold milk all at once (or scalded, if you prefer, but it's not necessary. Neither is it necessary to slowly and gradually blend in milk. Just remove pan from heat and pour in milk). Return pan to heat and simmer, stirring until sauce boils and thickens. Flavor is improved if you can simmer and reduce sauce for another 5 minutes. Season with about ½ teaspoon salt, white or black pepper to taste, and a dash of nutmeg. This makes about 1 cup medium-thick sauce.

CREAM SAUCE

Blend 2 to 4 tablespoons light or heavy cream into finished Sauce Béchamel* before seasonings are added.

MORNAY SAUCE

To Sauce Béchamel* add ⅓ cup grated Parmesan cheese or 3 tablespoons each grated Parmesan and Gruyère cheese. Blend in well and return to heat until melted.

SAUCE VELOUTÉ

Make same as Sauce Béchamel,* using fish, chicken, white veal stock, or vegetable broth. Fish stock or bottled clam broth is used for fish dishes, chicken broth for chicken dishes, etc. Seasonings will vary with the finished dish. Frequently but not always this sauce is finished with the addition of ¼ to ½ cup heavy cream.

BROWN SAUCE
(Sauce Espagnole)

If you want to make classic dishes and improve your sauce cookery 100 per cent, spend the time to make this sauce from scratch and keep it on hand. It is the *sauce espagnole* of French cuisine and the basis of marvelous bordelaise, Robert, diable, sauce Madère, etc. It starts with a homemade stock but can be made with canned bouillon if you don't want to spend the time on homemade stocks. It makes a difference in your finished sauces.

¼ cup butter
1 onion, minced
1 carrot, minced
1 stalk celery, minced
¼ cup flour
1 quart homemade beef stock or canned bouillon

Herb bouquet of 1 sprig parsley, ½ bay leaf, 1 clove garlic, 2 cloves, ½ teaspoon each dried thyme and marjoram leaves
6 tablespoons tomato purée
Salt and freshly milled pepper

Heat butter in large saucepan and add onion, carrot, and celery. Cook over low heat until vegetables are soft and tender. Sprinkle with flour and cook, stirring over low heat until *roux* is a rich brown. Add beef stock or canned bouillon, the herb bouquet tied in a small cheesecloth square, and tomato purée. Mix well, lower heat, and simmer for about 2 hours. Skim when necessary. Sauce should be reduced to about 2 cups and should be thick enough to lightly coat a spoon—but not too thick. Add more hot stock if necessary. Cool sauce and season to taste with salt and freshly milled pepper if you plan to use it now. If you plan to freeze it, salt after it's defrosted. Sauce will keep in refrigerator several weeks if tightly sealed. Makes 1 pint.

ENGLISH CUSTARD CREAM
(Crème Anglaise)

A light top-stove custard sauce that's the basis for many more complicated desserts—Bavarian creams, pastry cream for fillings, trifles, and such.

2 cups milk
1 (3-inch) piece vanilla bean (or
  2 teaspoons vanilla extract)

4 egg yolks
½ cup sugar
1 teaspoon cornstarch (optional)

Heat milk and vanilla bean in double boiler until film forms on top (add extract later if used). Beat egg yolks and gradually beat in sugar and cornstarch if used (this helps prevent curdling) until they are light and creamy. With wire whip slowly blend in hot milk, beating until blended. Return to double boiler. Cook over hot, *not boiling,* water, stirring with whisk constantly until custard thickens slightly (but never boils) and will coat a clean metal spoon with a creamy, cooked-looking film. Add extract now if used. Cool custard, stirring now and then. Remove vanilla bean. If chilled for later use press sheet of foil directly on surface. May be flavored with 1 to 2 tablespoons rum, brandy, kirsch, or any of the orange liqueurs in place of vanilla. Makes 2 cups.

PASTRY CREAM
(Crème Pâtissière)

Like custard cream except it's heavier. It contains flour and must be boiled. Used in dozens of desserts—fruit tarts, cream puffs, crêpes, fancy fillings for puff pastries. Whipped cream, dissolved gelatin, pralinés, macaroon crumbs, all sorts of extras may be folded into this.

Make like English Custard Cream* except you may do it in a heavy saucepan. Beat 4 egg yolks in saucepan and gradually beat in ¾ cup sugar, 6 tablespoons flour, ¼ teaspoon salt. With wire whisk slowly blend in 2 cups boiling milk until smooth. Cook over moderate heat, stirring constantly with wire whisk until mixture boils. Turn heat to low and cook for 3 to 4 minutes longer, stirring constantly. If lumps form, keep stirring until cream is smooth. Remove from heat and beat in one tablespoon butter and 2 teaspoons vanilla or other flavorings. Cool, stirring occasionally. If chilled for later use, press foil directly on surface. Makes about 2½ cups.

BASIC DRESSING AND VARIATIONS

CHEF'S MAYONNAISE

Chef Gregoire, who operates a French cooking school and also runs a fine restaurant in the Sherman Oaks area of Los Angeles, makes mayonnaise this delicious way. He marinates egg yolks in vinegar and Dijon mustard before beating in the oil. "It cooks the yolk," he says, "and takes away the raw egg taste." At the end he beats in boiling water to further cook the yolks and ensure against separation. This is a home recipe in smaller amounts I've worked out from watching him.

2 egg yolks
1 tablespoon Dijon mustard
2 tablespoons vinegar
½ teaspoon salt (or to taste)

1 cup olive oil or other good salad oil
1 to 2 tablespoons boiling water
Freshly milled pepper
Desired herbs

Rinse small mixing bowl or small bowl of electric mixer in hot water, drain, and dry. Put in egg yolks and stir smooth with a fork. Stir in mustard and vinegar. Let stand for 30 minutes. Add salt. Beat mixture with wire whisk or on moderate speed of mixer until smooth and thickened. Start adding oil by droplets and beat after each addition until oil is absorbed, then add a few more drops until you have beaten in about ⅓ cup and a smooth emulsion has formed. Slowly beat in rest of oil by tablespoons until all is added and sauce is smooth and thick and fluffy. Add a few drops of vinegar as you beat if sauce becomes too thick. As a final insurance against separation, beat in 1 to 2 tablespoons boiling water. Taste and add salt if needed, and any desired herbs. Store in covered jar in refrigerator until ready to use. Makes 1¼ cups.

HERB MAYONNAISE

Season Chef's mayonnaise with 2 tablespoons each capers, chopped chives, parsley, and fresh tarragon leaves (or 2 teaspoons dried tarragon) and lemon juice or wine vinegar to taste.

CLASSIC FRENCH DRESSING
(Sauce Vinaigrette)

Three parts oil to one part wine vinegar, salt, and pepper. That's the true *sauce vinaigrette* of France. This is the way I make it.

Put into small bowl ¾ teaspoon salt, 1 crushed garlic clove, and 1 teaspoon Dijon mustard. With whisk blend in 4 tablespoons wine vinegar. Gradually whisk in ¾ cup salad oil (I use half olive oil, half peanut oil). Beat until slightly thickened and smooth. Season with freshly milled pepper (white pepper for some salads such as fresh mushroom salad), more salt to taste, and any desired herbs. May be stored in covered glass jar in refrigerator. Shake before using. Makes 1 cup.

GOLDEN VINAIGRETTE

Looks like hollandaise and with the addition of a little tarragon tastes like a light béarnaise—but it's so easy to make. Perfect on salads, hot or cold vegetables, or fish. The trick is to marinate egg yolk in vinegar before making sauce—an idea I borrowed from Chef Gregoire.

1 egg yolk
6 tablespoons white wine vinegar
2 teaspoons Dijon mustard
1½ cups olive oil (or part light corn oil)

1½ teaspoons salt
Freshly ground pepper
1 clove garlic, crushed (optional)

Stir egg yolk, vinegar, and mustard together and let stand for 20 to 30 minutes, until yolk is no longer cold. With wire whisk, beat until well blended. Gradually beat in oil until mixture is smooth and creamy. Season with salt, a few grindings of black pepper and the crushed garlic if used. Because of the egg yolk this dressing should be refrigerated. Makes about 2 cups.

HALF A RECIPE

To make half a recipe of Golden Vinaigrette (above), beat yolk with fork, measure ½ of it or 2 teaspoons (one yolk usually measures 3 to 4 teaspoons). Use rest of yolk for glaze on pastries, bread, etc. Reduce rest of ingredients to half the amount.

TARRAGON VINAIGRETTE

Add 1 tablespoon chopped fresh tarragon leaves (or 1 teaspoon dried tarragon) to Golden Vinaigrette.*

PASTRIES

FLAKY PIE PASTRY

Shortening makes a flakier crust, butter gives rich flavor.

2 cups all-purpose flour
½ teaspoon salt

⅔ cup cold vegetable shortening
(or part butter) cut in pieces
Ice water

Sift flour and salt into bowl. Cut in half the shortening with knives or pastry blender until mixture is like coarse meal. Work in rest of shortening into big flat flakes the size of peas. Add just enough ice water to be able to gather mixture into a ball that fairly well cleans the sides of bowl. It takes 4 to 6 tablespoons—too little and your crust will fall apart, too much and it will be tough. Round up dough in foil and chill for at least 30 minutes. Roll about ⅛ inch thick and use as directed in specific recipes. This makes pastry for 2 shells or one double-crust pie.

PÂTE BRISÉE
(Rich Butter Pastry)

For flans, quiches, and other tarts and pastries.

2 cups sifted all-purpose flour
½ teaspoon salt
½ cup (1 stick) unsalted butter

3 to 4 tablespoons cold vegetable
shortening
5 to 6 tablespoons ice water

Sift flour and salt into mixing bowl. Cut butter and shortening into pieces and quickly work into flour with fingertips until mixture is flaky-looking. Sprinkle with water and lightly mix with fork or your cupped fingers until dough holds together and you can round it up in a ball. Scoop it up in a cupped sheet of foil and press it firmly together to form a compact mass. Wrap and chill for several hours or overnight. Roll as directed in specific recipes. It may be frozen for several weeks and used as needed. For fancy tarts and *gâteaux,* add 1 to 3 tablespoons sugar, 1 teaspoon grated lemon peel.

CREAM CHEESE PASTRY

Delicate, rich, and fragile, and unbelievably easy to make. It puffs and flakes and may be used for appetizers, patty shells, tiny fruit tarts, and many other dishes that call for puff paste.

1 cup butter (2 sticks)
1 package (8 ounces) cream
cheese

2 cups all-purpose flour
½ teaspoon salt

Cream butter and cheese together in electric mixer. Sift flour with salt and work into butter with wooden spoon or your fingers until completely blended. Round up in a ball in sheet of foil. Chill overnight before rolling. Divide dough in half, or quarters, for ease in rolling, and let it stand for a few minutes, but keep it cold. Roll on a floured pastry cloth with a stockinet-covered rolling pin. These are available in housewares departments and are a great help in rolling all pastries. Otherwise roll this rich pastry between 2 sheets of foil or waxed paper. Shape as directed in specific recipes. Chill again before baking, and in most cases brush pastries with egg yolk beaten with a teaspoon milk. A moderate oven (350° F.) is usually best for this pastry. The delicate flavor and texture are impaired if it's baked too fast or too much.

SOUR CREAM PUFF PASTE

Not real French puff paste, but it's rich and buttery and flakes into airy layers similar to puff paste. You can make it in a minute.

2 cups all-purpose flour   ¾ cup dairy sour cream
1 cup cold butter or margarine,
    cut in pieces

Sift flour into bowl. With fingertips or pastry blender, work in butter until mixture is crumbly. Add sour cream and mix until dough holds together. Round up in ball in sheet of foil. Wrap and chill overnight. Roll on floured pastry cloth and use as directed in specific recipes.

QUICK PUFF PASTE

Sometimes called mock or rough puff paste, this is easier than real puff paste, though it is flaky and rich.

2 cups all-purpose flour   Ice water
¼ teaspoon salt   1 tablespoon lemon juice
1 cup butter or margarine

Sift flour and salt into bowl. Work in butter with fingertips or a pastry blender until mixture is like fine meal. Quickly mix in about 5 tablespoons ice water and the lemon juice until dough holds together and can be rounded into a ball. Press together in a sheet of foil into a compact mass, then place on floured pastry cloth. On warm days, chill for about 30 minutes before rolling. Roll into a rectangle about 10×14 inches. Fold in 3 layers and turn so open edge is to your right. Roll again, lightly, to original shape, fold, and turn again. Fold and turn a total of 3 times. Wrap in foil and chill overnight before rolling and shaping. Puff pastries are usually brushed with an egg wash of egg or egg yolk beaten with a teaspoon milk or water.

CREAM PUFF PASTE
(Pâte à Choux)

A versatile, easy-to-make pastry. For éclairs, *profiteroles,* miniature appetizer puffs, tea and luncheon entree puffs, fancy desserts like Paris-Brest and Gâteau St. Honoré.

1 cup sifted all-purpose flour
½ teaspoon salt
1 cup water

½ cup (1 stick) butter or
margarine
4 large eggs (1 cup)

Sift flour and salt together. Heat water and butter to boiling in heavy saucepan. Leave on heat only until butter melts. Remove from heat and dump in flour all at once. Beat vigorously with a wooden spoon. Return to low heat a minute or two and beat until paste leaves sides of pan and forms a ball and a light film shows on bottom of pan. Remove from heat, add one egg, and beat until paste is smooth and glossy. One by one, beat in rest of eggs, beating each time until paste is smooth and glossy. Drop onto greased cooky sheet 2 inches apart—in rounded tablespoons for regular puffs, by teaspoons for miniature puffs (or put through pastry bag, using plain tube). Bake at 425° F. for 20 minutes, until puffs have about doubled in size. Reduce heat to 350° F. Bake for about 15 minutes longer (small puffs 5 to 10 minutes) until crisp, dry, and browned. With knife tip make a slit near bottom of each puff to release steam. Leave in turned-off oven for 15 minutes or more to dry out completely. Cool on wire racks. Makes 12 large puffs, about 3½ dozen miniatures.

CRÊPES
(Thin French Pancakes)

These versatile pancakes may be rolled or folded, stuffed or topped, served as entree or dessert.

Sift 1 cup flour with pinch of salt (add 1 tablespoon sugar for dessert crêpes). Beat 4 large eggs until light and beat in 2 cups milk. Beat in flour until mixture is smooth and texture of cream (a blender is great for this). Blend in 2 tablespoons melted butter (add 1 tablespoon cognac for desserts). Refrigerate for at least 1 hour.

Heat small 5- or 6-inch skillet or crêpe pan until drops of water sizzle across it. Brush with about ¼ teaspoon butter. With one hand on handle of pan, with the other quickly ladle in 2 tablespoons batter, tilting and rotating pan so batter spreads evenly and very thinly over bottom. Cook for about 1 minute. Turn with thin spatula and cook second side until lightly browned. Crêpe should look lacy, have some holes, be soft and rollable. Spread (do not stack) on towel until all are cooked. Add a little butter to pan for each crêpe. Cover crêpes with foil until ready to reheat. To refrigerate overnight or freeze for later use, spread paper towels between crêpes, wrap in foil. Makes about 2 dozen crêpes.

BREADS AND CAKES

BRIOCHE

Rich yet light, fabulous French classic.

1 cake or package yeast
¼ cup warm water (see yeast label)
1 cup (2 sticks) soft butter
2 tablespoons sugar

1 teaspoon salt
6 eggs
¼ cup lukewarm milk
4 cups sifted all-purpose flour

Crumble or sprinkle yeast into warm water. Let stand for at least 5 minutes, then stir until yeast is completely dissolved. In mixer, cream butter, sugar, and salt until soft and pliable. Add eggs, one at a time, and beat well after each is added. On low speed, beat in yeast mixture, milk, and 2 cups flour. Stop mixer frequently to raise and scrape beaters and bowl. If your mixer is powerful enough or has a dough hook, beat in the remaining flour. Otherwise, beat in rest of flour with wooden spoon, beating hard until dough is smooth and springy, 3 or 4 minutes. Or easier, using your fingers, knead this soft, sticky dough in the bowl. Pull up dough with right hand and turn bowl with left (or vice-versa, if you're a southpaw). Continue to pull and stretch dough, slap it back down into bowl and turn bowl until dough becomes smooth and very light and will come away from sides of bowl. Scrape dough into lightly floured bowl and cover tightly with foil, then a folded towel. Let rise in warm spot until more than doubled, 2 to 3 hours. Punch dough down and beat out air bubbles with a wooden spoon. Cover with foil and a folded towel. Let rest in refrigerator for 8 hours or overnight. Shape into about 2 dozen individual topknot rolls (described below) or a large loaf or cake.

Refrigerated and Frozen Dough—Dough may be kept for several days in refrigerator and baked when needed. Punch dough down if it starts to rise before you are ready. Dough may be frozen for a week or so, either after the second rising or after the rolls are shaped before the final rise.

BRIOCHE ROLLS

Divide chilled Brioche* dough in half and return one part to refrigerator. Shape dough into a long roll about one inch thick. Cut off ¼ of it, wrap in foil, and put back in refrigerator (dough dries out easily). Cut rest into 12 equal pieces and shape into smooth balls. Place in buttered muffin tins (½-cup size) or small fluted brioche pans. Cut the smaller piece of dough into 12 equal bits and roll each into marble-size balls. Roll balls into cone shapes. With scissors, cut a deep x in tops of larger rolls and gently press the cone-shaped dough into each. Cover shaped rolls and let rise until more than doubled in bulk, about 1 hour. Brush tops with egg yolk beaten with a teaspoon water. Bake in 425° F. oven until golden brown, 18 to 20 minutes. (Shape rest of dough into 12 brioche rolls or keep refrigerated and use otherwise.)

HOMEMADE BREAD

Two perfect loaves of homemade white bread—fine of texture with a wonderful flavor. Dough is allowed to rise twice before it's shaped into loaves.

2 cakes or packages yeast	1 tablespoon sugar
½ cup warm water (see yeast packet for directions)	2 teaspoons salt
	1 cup cold water
1 cup milk	6 cups (approximately)
2 tablespoons butter or margarine	all-purpose flour

Crumble or sprinkle yeast into warm water and let stand for 5 minutes. Heat milk in small saucepan until bubbles form around edges. Stir in butter, sugar, and salt. Pour into a large warm bowl. Add cold water. When mixture is lukewarm, stir in yeast. Gradually beat in flour, saving out about ¾ cup for kneading. Dough should be medium stiff—you may have to work in last part of flour with your hands. Sprinkle part of the ¾ cup flour on a board and dump dough into it. Knead vigorously, working in the flour until dough is smooth and elastic, about 5 minutes. Wash the large bowl and oil it well. Turn dough around in oil until it is greased all over. Cover with towel and let rise in warm place until doubled in bulk, about 1 hour. Punch dough down with your fist, pulling in the edges of dough, turn it over to coat with oil. Cover and let rise again until doubled in bulk, 45 minutes to 1 hour (this second rising accounts for the marvelous texture of this bread). Knock dough down with your fist and knead lightly on floured board to work out air bubbles. Cut in half and shape in 2 loaves or freeze half of it to bake later. Place in well-greased loaf pans (3×5×9 inches). Cover and let rise until doubled in size, about 1 hour. Place in preheated 375° F. oven. Bake for 50 to 60 minutes, or until a rich brown and loaf sounds hollow when rapped with your knuckles. Remove from pan and cool on wire racks. Brush tops with butter if you like a soft crust. Cool on wire racks.

CRACKED WHEAT BREAD

Two wonderful brown loaves with a texture and appearance similar to popular "Indian bread." Great for sandwiches, with soup or salad or cheese. Buy cracked wheat at health food stores and many supermarkets.

1½ cups milk
1 cup cracked wheat
1½ cups warm water (see yeast packet)
3 packages active dry yeast
¼ cup honey
¼ cup molasses
¼ cup safflower or corn oil

3½ cups unbleached white flour (preferably bread flour)
4 cups whole-wheat flour (preferably stone-ground)
½ cup yellow corn meal (preferably stone-ground)
1 tablespoon sea salt or regular salt

Combine milk with cracked wheat in small saucepan and heat just until bubbles form around edges. Set aside to cool to lukewarm. Put warm water in large warm mixing bowl. Sprinkle in yeast and let stand for 5 minutes. Mix well and stir in honey, molasses, and oil. Beat in 2 cups white flour and 2 cups whole-wheat flour. Then beat in lukewarm milk and cracked wheat, the corn meal, salt, remaining whole-wheat flour, and all but about ¾ cup of the white flour. Sprinkle board with some of the white flour and dump dough out onto it. Sprinkle with a little of the flour and knead dough until it's smooth, springy and has sort of stretched or broken bubbles on the surface.

Place dough in clean oiled bowl, turn it over to grease top. Cover with a folded damp towel and set in a warm spot to rise until doubled in bulk, about 1½ hours. Punch dough down with heel of your hand and pull in sides so oiled top is up. Cover again and let rise until doubled, about 45 minutes. With sharp knife, cut dough in half (part may be frozen if you need only one loaf now). Shape into a plump round loaf and place on greased cooky sheet. Or shape into an oblong loaf and place in greased loaf pan (3×5×9 inches). Cover again and let rise until doubled, about 45 minutes (this makes 3 risings). Bake in preheated oven

(350° F.) for about 50 minutes, or until loaf is richly browned and sounds hollow when rapped with your knuckles. Turn out onto wire rack to cool. Makes 2 loaves.

POUNDCAKE

This freezes beautifully and is the basis for many other delicious desserts. Some purists are very picky about any flavorings other than mace added to their poundcake. Use whatever you prefer.

3 cups sifted all-purpose flour	1 pound butter
½ teaspoon salt	1 pound sugar (2 cups)
1 teaspoon mace or freshly grated	9 eggs, separated
nutmeg	1 teaspoon vanilla (optional)
Grated peel of 1 lemon (optional)	2 tablespoons cognac (optional)

Grease a large (10-inch) tube pan or 2 loaf pans and dust lightly with flour. Sift flour with salt and mace or nutmeg. Add lemon peel if you use it. Cream butter until fluffy, then beat in sugar a little at a time. Beat egg yolks until light and beat them into the creamed mixture. Stir in flour mixure, mixing lightly only until all flour is blended in. Stir in vanilla and/or cognac if used. Beat egg whites until stiffly peaked and gently fold into batter. Pour into prepared pans and bake at 325° F. for about 1 to 1¼ hours. Test doneness in center with wire cake tester —it should look dry and clean when removed from cake. Let cakes stand for about 10 minutes and invert onto wire racks to cool.

QUICK SPONGECAKE

Quickly made and usually baked in layers as the basis for other interesting and more complicated desserts such as Italian rum cake, *gâteau aux marrons*, Tipsy Squire.

1 cup sifted cake flour	⅓ cup cold water
1 teaspoon baking powder	1 teaspoon vanilla or ½ teaspoon
½ teaspoon salt	almond extract
4 eggs, separated	1 teaspoon grated lemon peel
1 cup sugar, divided	

Sift flour together again with baking powder and salt. Beat egg whites until softly peaked and gradually beat in ½ cup sugar until whites form stiff peaks. Set aside. Beat egg yolks until thick and gradually beat in remaining ½ cup sugar until mixture is very thick and light. Alternately fold flour and water into egg yolks. Stir in flavoring and lemon peel. Gently fold in egg whites. Spread in 2 buttered 9-inch round cake pans. Bake at 350° F. for 25 to 30 minutes. Cool in pans inverted over wire racks. Remove from pans.

FABULOUS FRUITCAKE

The easiest of all fruitcakes to make and, if necessary, it can be cut into paper-thin slices next day. Not a traditional fruitcake—this is all whole nuts, candied fruits and dates with barely enough batter to hold it together. It's expensive, but our favorite for holiday parties and gifts.

2 pounds fresh California dates
1 pound whole red and green candied cherries
½ pound candied pineapple, cut in large pieces
1 pound pecan halves (about 4 cups)
1 pound Brazil nuts (1½ to 2 cups shelled nuts)
1½ cups all-purpose flour

1½ teaspoons baking powder
½ teaspoon salt
4 large eggs
¾ cup sugar
1 teaspoon vanilla
2 tablespoons cream sherry or brandy
Candied cherries for top
Corn syrup for top

This makes about 6½ pounds of fruitcake and an assortment of pans may be used. I usually bake in 1 loaf pan (3×5×9 inches) or a small (9-inch) tube pan, and several small loaf pans (6- and 4-inch sizes) for gifts. Grease pans well, then line with greased heavy brown paper strips cut to fit pans. Pit dates and leave whole. Combine in large bowl with cherries, pineapple, and whole nuts. Sift flour, baking powder, and salt together. Beat eggs until frothy, gradually beat in sugar until mixture is light. Stir in flour, vanilla, and sherry or brandy. Pour over fruits and mix with your hands until all pieces are well coated and evenly distributed. Pack into prepared pans and press down tops to make mixture more compact—though it will still look open and bumpy. Decorate tops with a few halved candied cherries if you wish. Bake at 300° F. (275° F. for the tiny cakes). Bake large loaf cakes for 1¼ to 1½ hours, small tube cake about 15 minutes less. Small cakes usually require 45 minutes to 1 hour. Cakes do not brown. Test with a wire cake tester. Remove from oven, cool for a few minutes, then invert onto wire cake racks. Peel off paper. Cool completely, wrap in foil and store in airtight containers. Glaze tops with a little heated corn syrup if you wish. Let it set before slicing or wrapping cakes for gifts.

MACAROONS

The original, classic almond macaroon that goes in countless good dishes, keeps well, and is easy as pie to make. These can't be replaced with any other kind flavorwise.

½ pound almond paste   *1 cup fine granulated sugar*
2 or 3 egg whites (see note below)   *Powdered sugar*
¼ teaspoon salt

Knead almond paste with hands until soft and break into small pieces. Put egg whites with salt in bowl of electric mixer. Add granulated sugar and almond paste, a little at a time, beating until all is added and mixture is smooth and thick. Beat in powdered sugar, up to ½ cup if necessary, to make a batter thick enough to hold its shape. Cover baking sheets with 2 layers of heavy brown paper. Drop batter onto paper by teaspoons into mounds about 2 inches apart. Bake at 300° F. until lightly browned, 20 to 25 minutes. Remove from oven, slide paper off baking sheet onto a damp dish towel folded same size as baking sheet. Let stand until macaroons are cool or can be removed from paper with small metal spatula. Cool on wire racks. Store in tightly covered container. Makes 3 to 4 dozen.

Note: Eggs vary in size and moisture content. Actually 2½ egg whites make a perfect macaroon.

BEVERAGES

CHAMPAGNE PUNCH

For 40 punch cups, chill 2 bottles dry white wine—Pinot Chardonnay, Chablis, Dry Semillon, Chenin Blanc all are good—and 4 bottles champagne. To wine add sugar and lemon juice to taste (about ½ cup each) and a cup brandy or Grand Marnier. Pour over block of ice and add champagne. Decorate with spirals of lemon peel and whole strawberries.

SPICY PUNCH
(non-alcoholic)

For 32 punch cups, boil for 5 minutes 1½ cups water, ¾ cup sugar with 1 dozen *each* whole cloves and allspice, 4 cinnamon sticks, strips of peel from 2 lemons and 2 oranges. Cover and cool. Strain and combine with 1 cup lemon juice, 1 quart each orange and pineapple juice. Pour over block of ice and add 2 (12-ounce) bottles club soda or Bitter Lemon. Float quartered orange slices on top.

A GOOD CUP OF TEA

There's nothing like a cup of good hot tea, properly brewed, unless it's that first cup of coffee in the morning. And, there are those who prefer tea then. I'm fussy about tea! A tea bag dragged through a cup of so-so hot water that's been sitting on a coffee warmer for ages doth not a cup of tea make. Make it with freshly drawn cold water heated just to the boiling point. Pour immediately into a warmed (nonmetallic) teapot over loose tea leaves—1 teaspoon for each cup is standard but too much for some blends. Cover pot, keep it warm, and steep for about 5 minutes. Stir, let leaves settle a moment, and pour into cups (it tastes better in a china cup, I don't know why). Serve with sugar and lemon, or milk in the English tradition.

Iced Tea: Make it the same way as hot tea, in a pot, but use double the amount of tea leaves. Pour hot over ice cubes in glass. Serve with sugar and/or lemon.

A GOOD CUP OF COFFEE

Like tea, coffee is best made fresh and drunk as you want it. Use the method you prefer—boiled, percolated, whatever—but in my opinion, filtered or drip coffee gives the best flavor. If you're a real coffee buff like some of my friends, buy the beans and make your own blend and grind it fresh each time you make coffee. Otherwise shop around for the blend that suits you best. For filter or drip coffee, use 2 tablespoons ground coffee for each cup of freshly drawn cold water heated to a boil. Pour a couple tablespoons of the hot water through grounds and let them swell for a few moments. Then pour rest of the boiling water through, in 2 or 3 portions if possible. Let water drip through each time before you add more. Keep coffee hot over low, low heat but never boil it. Serve at once. Make another pot when you want more.

VIENNESE COFFEE

Brew extra-strength coffee or espresso (see Black Coffee*). Pour into server. Arrange on tray with small cups and a bowl of softly whipped cream, the nutmeg shaker, and sugar. Have a bowl of grated orange or lemon peel also for those who might prefer an Italian accent on their cream topper.

BLACK COFFEE FOR DEMITASSE

The demitasse, or half cup, of black coffee is served between meals and after dinner. In France it is made of a finer quality coffee than the regular breakfast brew, and each cup is generally filtered individually. French coffee for *café noir* or the demitasse, like the Italian coffee for espresso, is made from a darkly roasted bean, almost black and slightly bitter. You can't get the same effect with American roast coffee. To approximate the French café noir, for each cup put into a prewarmed filter or drip coffee maker 1 tablespoon Italian roast ground coffee and 1 tablespoon American ground coffee. Pour through the grounds 2 tablespoons freshly drawn, boiling water. Let stand for 5 minutes. Add remaining boiling hot water, a small amount at a time, after each addition has dripped through. Keep hot and serve at once in small cups.

Index